alternate roots

blind desire

red fox/second hangin'

you can't judge a book by looking at the cover: sayings from
the life and writings of junebug jabbo jones, volume ii

mr. universe

dark cowgirls and prairie queens

blood on blood

a preacher with a horse to ride

*This publication was made possible by a grant from the National
Endowment for the Arts, a federal agency in Washington, D.C.,
through its Theatre Program: Special Projects Category.*

alternate roots

plays from the southern theater

Edited by Kathie deNobriga and Valetta Anderson

HEINEMANN Portsmouth, NH

Heinemann
A division of Reed Elsevier Inc.
361 Hanover Street   Portsmouth, NH 03801-3912
Offices and agents throughout the world

This anthology copyright © 1994 by Heinemann. *Blind Desire* © 1986 by Margaret Baker, John Fitzpatrick, Emily Green, Robert H. Leonard, Christine Murdock, and Eugene Wolf. *Red Fox/Second Hangin'* © 1976 by Don Baker and Dudley Cocke. *You Can't Judge a Book by Looking at the Cover: Sayings from the Life and Writings of Junebug Jabbo Jones, Volume II* © 1986 by John O'Neal. *Mr. Universe* © 1988 by Jim Grimsley. *Dark Cowgirls and Prairie Queens* © 1983 by Linda Parris-Bailey. *Blood on Blood* © 1987 by Rebecca Ranson. *A Preacher with a Horse to Ride* © 1993 by Jo Carson.

Library of Congress Cataloging-in-Publication Data is on page 341.

Design: Wladislaw Finne
Editor: Lisa Barnett
Production: J. B. Tranchemontagne
Printed in the United States of America on acid-free paper
99 98 97 96 95 94 EB 6 5 4 3 2 1

contents

foreword

KATHIE DENOBRIGA

This collection of plays has been a long time coming. Ten years ago or so, when Dudley Cocke was the chairman of Alternate ROOTS (a coalition serving southeastern performing artists), he asked Jim Grimsley to investigate publishing possibilities for plays written by ROOTS members. There were a lot of writers in the organization then, as now, and a lot of their plays were being forgotten and lost. And so Jim started writing regional publishers and university presses to find out if any of those folks might want to help with such a project. Jim's initial report to Dudley, outlining the many fruitless leads and lines of investigation, sat silently and stubbornly in my files when I became ROOTS' Executive Director in 1988.

Then something fortuitous happened: playwrights in the region (some of them ROOTS members) revitalized another service organization called the Southeast Playwrights Project. As it happened, Jim became their administrator, and he and I began to cook up some ideas that could serve both groups. The idea of the anthology, still alive after all those years, was a natural place to start.

Jim and I figured that prospective publishers might be more interested in this anthology if we could cite specific authors, so together we chose seven plays—seven good plays previously produced but not published that, taken together, would represent the variety of themes that living southern playwrights were addressing, would reflect the cultural and aesthetic diversity of our region, and provide insights into a variety of creative processes, from the solo playwright delivering a finished script, to the collaboration of an ensemble. We chose to celebrate the first ten years of ROOTS' history by focusing on plays from 1976–1986. And finally, we decided to commission three original essays to put this body of work into a context: of ROOTS history, of southern dramatic literature in particular, and the nature of regionalism in general.

We started scattering seeds of interest among a number of funders. The most fertile soil turned out to be (as it so often is) the National Endowment for the Arts, under the Special Projects category of the Theatre Program. So, a moment's praise for the NEA and its staff, past and present.

Here we are finally, book in hand, somewhat astonished. I won't take up too much space writing about ROOTS: I'll let Ruby Lerner do that in her essay. But because ROOTS *is* about joining forces, pooling resources, collaboration and cooperation, I'd like to acknowledge the others who caused this volume to be: Valetta Anderson, director of the Southeast Playwrights Project (SEPP) and co-editor, whose steady administrative attention has made it possible to organize not just one author, but seven; Jim Grimsley, whose simultaneous leadership of ROOTS (Chair 1990–92) and SEPP provided the critical mass; and Dudley Cocke, whose constant but gentle persistence is finally rewarded. And of course the playwrights; long may they prosper.

Valetta Anderson: As Executive Director of a southeastern play and playwright development organization (SEPP) and as a southeastern playwright, the impact of this publication is more than "somewhat" astonishing. Theaters and readers worldwide now have direct access to the works of southeastern playwrights. These writers have gained prominence and audience recognition in the region about which they write, as well as in neighboring regions from coast to coast. This anthology represents who we are to ourselves, as well as what we can accomplish, when we join forces among our own regional organizations.

Jim Grimsley: Maybe it was ten years ago or maybe it was less. I hope it was less. Anyway, one day at a ROOTS meeting Dudley Cocke asked me to explore ways to get plays published here in the South. He thought it would be a good thing for the writers in ROOTS, the organization to which we both belonged. I started to write letters and talk to people. Everybody thought the anthology was a good idea. Only a certain much-maligned federal arts agency offered money to help. That money, along with the genuine enthusiasm and support of Heinemann-Methuen Books, in the person of a remarkably patient Lisa Barnett, has made this anthology possible. I am very grateful to have the anthology here at last. It is tangible evidence of something many of us have suspected as true all along: the strong work of southern artists is helping to change the face of the South. This anthology offers some pictures of that new face.

Dudley Cocke: In theater, southern roots style, the audience is part of the show. It is not necessarily rude to interrupt the actors with a pertinent fact, observation or exclamation. There is a tradition of call and response, of standing and moving when stirred. Church remains one of our most vibrant playhouses. In the next fifty years, I hope this unique style will continue to be reinvented and made new by our southern thespians.

Linguists say that there are about 6,000 cultures worldwide and that an equal number have disappeared (forever) since the turn of the century. Apparently, we lose our biology as we lose our songs. Herein are a few of those songs crafted from particular ecologies during the Carter-Reagan years—for many of us, years of resistance.

It was "Senator" Bland Simpson's fertile mind, being well irrigated one summer night on the southern highlands, that caused this anthology idea to drop from our mouths.

creative expression and regional identity

JOHN EGERTON

They don't have conferences on "The Mind of the North." There isn't a vast body of literature on the subjects of Midwestern history or cookery or music, as far as I know, and the term "Eastern religions" isn't a reference to New England Congregationalists or Manhattan's Irish Catholics and immigrant Jews. If there is a new wave of Northeastern fiction writers, I haven't heard of it, and if there is a cohesive school of creative artists of the Far West, that too has escaped my attention.

But the South—ah, the South! The whole anatomy and physiology: the mind of the South, the eyes and ears and mouth of the South, the heart and soul of the South, the stomach of the South. Southern voices in speech and song. southern history, southern politics, southern religion, southern art and culture. Southern writers reading tone poems at inauguration ceremonies for southern presidents—James Dickey for Jimmy Carter, Maya Angelou for Bill Clinton. (Okay, so it was New Englanders who started it with Robert Frost for John F. Kennedy.)

And southern theater: regionally rooted stage productions filled with the self-conscious sense of history and humor and tragedy, the sense of place, that comforts and haunts and inspires just about every breathing soul who ever tarried here. There is something profound lurking in these wisteria-scented shadows, but I'll be damned if I can put my finger on it—and neither can anyone else.

Whatever it is, it has to do with language, with what the scholars call verbal facility (that's people talking). Porch talk, hearth talk, table talk, pillow talk. The practiced oratory of phrasemakers—politicians, lawyers, judges, preachers, teachers, journalists, novelists, speechwriters, songwriters, salesmen, waitresses, funeral directors—and the unconscious eloquence of the unlettered. Figure this one out: The South has more great writers *and* more illiterates per capita than any other region of the country (that's a perfect example of the mystifying contradictions that abound in this schizophrenic land of paradox and irony and abiding ambivalence). In this and other ways, we are some kind of kin to the Irish, another historically downtrodden aggregation of strivers eternally obsessed with words, violence, and spirits—liquid and ethereal.

A precious few eccentric geniuses are our guiding stars—William Faulkner, Richard Wright, Flannery O'Connor, and a handful of others. Bob McDill caught the essence of it in one line of a great country song: "Those Williams boys, they sure mean a lot to me—Hank and Tennessee." (Had he been a nonfiction writer instead of a poet, McDill might have added Claude and Cootie.) The lone wolves, the haunted souls, the village characters who got off in some corner and did whatever it was they did—these were the models who inspired the rest of us, who gave us permission. If old Bill Faulkner could be a college dropout and a fired former postmaster who drank too much—and wrote great novels—then why couldn't we with similar flaws and far less talent at least give the old word game a serious try?

By some inscrutable law of compensation, southern wordsmiths have discovered not only the courage to write, but the confidence to defend their work in the marketplace and in the uncompromising circle of honest critics.

This was Tennessee Williams in a radio interview in Los Angeles some years back, responding to the probing questions of an interviewer who was pushing him to the edge of privacy and propriety and patience:

"Have you been drinking?"

"Yes."

"Do you need to?"

"Yes."

"How much?"

"A lot."

"Think how much better you would write if you were sober."

And at that, Williams reached across the table to pat his questioner gently on the hand and said: "Improve on 'A Streetcar Named Desire.'"

Nobody said we had to *be* Tennessee Williams or William Faulkner, or be as good with words as they were, or as bad to drink. As far as the writing goes, the message was and is simply this: "It's okay to try." Think of it as an invitation, a challenge. Southerners have been rising to it for the past six or seven decades.

Somehow, the rich and variegated and enduringly distinctive voices of the South arise from this grant of permission. Whatever else we have, good and bad, we Southerners have an appreciation, a feel for language, and it is as much a part of our regional identity as any other element of our character. Maybe *more* than any other.

As one of the grantees as a son of the South and a lifelong resident thereof, and as a scrivener by vocation—I take all this unconventional history to heart. It happens that the particular genre I chose to work in is singular, requiring of me nothing more than that I show up alone with a pencil and pad at whatever event is unfolding—say, a murder trial or a funeral or a civil war—and try to extract from it the raw material of my craft. Theater, on the other hand, requires a company of dedicated souls—people who are willing not only to work at a creative venture, but to do it cooperatively, with all the advantages and limitations that collective efforts afford.

Alternate ROOTS is such a collective effort. Actually, it's a large number of small companies allied under the ROOTS mission. It is self-consciously and intentionally regional, dedicated to the support of the performing arts suffused with southern accents and flavors. It is a richly diverse and eclectic union of men and women and children whose bonding commonality is a love of creative and original expression—distinguished, in this case, by the spirit and traditions of the contemporary South.

Here are the versatile and wide-ranging and ever-changing voices of the South, coming to you from a hundred stages, from a thousand throats. Listen! Can't you hear that? This is your own mind and soul, your own voice, trying to make sense of a place too deep to fathom, too complex to unravel, too distant to reach, too close to encompass. The South echoes from these stages like your own voice thrown back from a well or a canyon. Ladies and gentlemen, brothers and sisters, listen.

searching for roots in southern soil

RUBY LERNER

When I returned to my native South in 1981 to become the Director of Alternate ROOTS, I decided to embark on a search for its "roots." I was curious to see if there were historical antecedents, to see if ROOTS could be placed somewhere on a socio-artistic continuum. Was this organization, one which grew directly out of both the social change and alternative art movements of the 1960s and the 70s, wholly unique, or was it simply the contemporary manifestation of a recurring cultural ideal of an art relegated not to culture palaces, but relevant to daily life, an art whose home is in the streets, in schools, church basements, city parks, and other institutions dear to community life?

Among many other revelations, I discovered Frederick Koch, founder of the University of North Carolina Playmakers, whose contributions to the American theater were critical during the period from 1920 well into the 1940s and whose writing provided a language and a framework for talking about what ROOTS was trying to accomplish in the 1980s. When the debate about the need for a "national" theater was raging in the earlier part of the century, Koch wrote that when every community in America had its own native group of plays and producers, speaking to its own community's hopes and aspirations, only then would we have a true national theater. I discovered Lewis Mumford, Howard Odum (a colleague of Koch's at the University of North Carolina) and contemporary Kentucky poet and essayist Wendell Berry's writings on regionalism, all of whom clarified regionalism's possibilities not as parochial, xenophobic, regressive philosophy, but as a positive way of thinking about the future of life in particular places with their peculiar and individual histories and their specific needs. Through these writings, coupled with my own more direct experiences and study of the alternative theater movements of the 1960s and 70s and the civil rights, antiwar and women's movements of the same era, I began to see ROOTS as both unique and simultaneously capable of being "located" in an historical framework.

Alternate ROOTS is an arts service organization, a problem-solving system for southeastern performing artists, creating opportunities for constructive dialogue about developing work and avenues of exposure for completed work. But to define ROOTS solely as an arts organization would be reductionist. It is also a grass roots cultural movement, peculiar to the South, whose aim is to be part of the transformation of the region—by acknowledging and critically assessing its past, particularly with regard to race, uncovering its buried history and untold stories, and celebrating its heroes. What might it mean to be responsibly Southern now and in the future is an unspoken question at the heart of much of the work.

It is probably no accident that ROOTS was born at a meeting hosted by the Highlander Center in 1976, a place noted for its unswerving commitment to citizen action for social change. It is also probably no accident that ROOTS is structured as a membership organization wholly "owned" by all of its members who comprise the organization's board of directors. I doubt that there is another arts organization in America with over 200 people on its board. To become a ROOTS member you must "be present to win." You must attend an annual meeting; you must speak to the assembled about why you want to join (described by some as "witnessing"). It is not an organization to which you anonymously send your annual dues. It is possible to understand the unique organizational structure as a perfectly logical outgrowth of the kind of artistic work undertaken by ROOTS artists and also as congruent with those deeper, transformational goals articulated above.

The work selected for this collection is both thematically and stylistically diverse, reflective of the region's unique history and culture. Several of the works were collaboratively developed by ensembles over considerable periods of time (*Dark Cowgirls and Prairie Queens, Blind Desire* and *Red Fox/Second Hangin'*); several are attempts to recover buried history

(*Preacher with a Horse to Ride, Junebug Jabbo Jones, Dark Cowgirls,* and *Red Fox*); several employ a presentational storytelling style (*Blind Desire, Junebug,* and *Red Fox*); and several are attempts to understand moments of profound change in the history or current life of the region, as in *Junebug's* exploration of the massive migration of African-Americans from the rural South to the industrial North or the changes affecting life in Upper East Tennessee as portrayed in *Blind Desire.*

What all the work shares is a strong evocation of place. The underbelly of New Orleans is palpable in Jim Grimsley's *Mr. Universe;* one can sense the closeness of the central Appalachians enveloping *Red Fox,* the oppressive heat and racism of the Mississippi Delta in *Junebug,* the strip mall of contemporary East Tennessee in *Blind Desire,* and the union battle-fatigued coal mining region of eastern Kentucky in *Preacher with a Horse to Ride.*

So, we are back to place, to the specificity of particular moments in time. Wendell Berry states it clearly in his essay "The Regional Motive": "The regionalism that I adhere to could be defined simply as *local life aware of itself.* It would tend to substitute for myths and stereotypes of a region a particular knowledge of the life of the *place* one lives in and intends to *continue* to live in. . . .

"Without a complex knowledge of one's place, and without the faithfulness to one's place on which such knowledge depends, it is inevitable that the place will be used carelessly, and eventually destroyed. . . . I look upon the sort of regionalism that I am talking about not just as a recurrent literary phenomenon, but as a necessity of civilization and of survival."

The works in this volume reflect Berry's "complex knowledge" and the publication of this volume assures that the ethereal moment of live performance will be forever preserved.

What I began to understand on my "quest" for the roots of ROOTS was that alternative movements are rarely interested in institutionalizing—the very nature of "movement" can be hobbled by the bureaucratic structures that seem so endemic to institution-building. But without institutions that proceed through time, each generation must struggle anew to achieve legitimacy. It appears that without a history, a lineage, there can be no legitimacy. And little possibility of a legacy that might inspire future generations.

It is clear that new kinds of arts institutions are necessary, providing young artists in regions all across America with a value-based training, encouraging a commitment to place, engendering ongoing critical dialogue, and maximizing financial support to artists by creating a diversity of meaningful opportunities. Throughout its history, ROOTS has struggled to become such an institution for performing artists in the Southeast. This volume is therefore more than simply a collection of plays. It assures the important work of ROOTS' artists a legacy that can serve as an inspiration for future generations of artists.

southern american drama and the communal context of story

BETTY JEAN JONES

Esther Merle Jackson, distinguished theorist/critic of the American theater and drama, wrote the following in her landmark comprehensive study, *The American Drama and the New World Vision* (1981): "The fact is that the American playwrights are, to a surprising degree, dramatists of social, moral, and aesthetical ideas, and one in particular; that is the right of every individual to identify as a separate and unique person." Professor Jackson further observes that the American drama as a distinctive form expresses a single important theme—"the significance of democratic ideals for the future of modern man." She acknowledges the poet Walt Whitman as a significant voice in articulating the essence of this democratic form when he wrote in his Preface to *Leaves of Grass* (1885): "the United States themselves are essentially the greatest poem." In his long prose work *Democratic Vistas* Whitman argued for an American drama that was "bold, modern, and all-surrounding," reflecting the vastness of the land and the uniqueness of each individual.

As poets of the theater, American playwrights celebrate the individual while capturing the primal rhythms of the group (social), the sense of right and wrong (moral), and the journey toward truth and beauty (aesthetics), thus capturing what Professor Jackson calls the democratic new world vision of the drama. Unlike its European counterparts, American drama emerged out of pursuit of a complex concept called "freedom" which led to a drama of realism built on the exaltation of the common person. In the American cultural idiom, *common* should be understood to mean individual/separate but still part of a democratic mass struggling with the complex challenges of freedom. American playwrights shape these real-life dramatic dilemmas into a language of the theater that is often grounded in both the mechanics and the aesthetic of the very process we know as story or storytelling.

The prominence of story in southern drama often shapes the structure and houses character, action and place in a tapestry of fluid joining that compels the listener/audience to come into the dramatic moment in a true process of communing.

The mature American drama of the early decades of the twentieth century built its structure and popular acceptance from the roots of local color writing—a form based on story, shaped by place. Contributing to this genre are fiction writers as diverse as Mark Twain (1835–1910), the New Englanders Sarah Orne Jewett (1849–1909) and Margaret Wilkins Freeman (1862–1930), and the social consciousness plays of African American Harlem Renaissance writers Angelina Weld Grimke, Marita Bonner, and Alice Dunbar-Nelson. From these writers emerged characters endowed with properties aligned with the land. Though they may hold values and beliefs that can be described as universal, they could not actually exist anywhere else in the real world except the setting in which they are portrayed.

Twain's biting humor did not deny a sense of history and belonging in the captivating yarns that ultimately raised to glory the value of the American as individual. Jewett's stories reflect a nostalgia for the immediate past and her devotion to *place* (locale) sustained the action in her stories of characters meeting the challenge of a changing America from rural to industrial life. Freeman's stories are often critical of the old ways and her characters confront the conflict directly while still cradling the best in what is deemed traditional.

Grimke, Bonner, and Dunbar-Nelson are all African American women writers of the decade between the end of World War I and the stock market crash in 1929. Bonner, in her play *The Purple Flower* (1928), did not seek to ask if there would be mass rebellion by American Blacks, but instead, with compelling allegory, firmly instructed us as to its inevitability. At the close of World War I in 1918 Dunbar-Nelson sounded the alarm in *Mine Eyes Have Seen* exploring the irony of destruction to a people bound to a land they will defend without having a true place in it—the double-edge sword of American patriotism still faced by persons of color, women, and groups of what are seen by many as those choosing non-traditional societal orientation. Grimke's *Rachel* (1916) is a woman's platform play about the still very present challenge of ethnicity and gender versus nationalism in American culture.

The treatment of character and conflict in regional literature of the 1900s and early twentieth century was an essential component in the emerging mature drama of decided realism evidenced in the work of southern playwrights in the first half of the twentieth century. This group of playwrights includes Georgia's Carson McCullers *(The Member of the Wedding)* and North Carolina's Paul Green *(In Abraham's Bosom)*. Virginia's S. Randolph Edmonds *(Six Plays for a Negro Theatre)*—later of colleges in Maryland and Louisiana— was a pioneer of great importance in educational theater and southern regional drama. Edmonds' southern colleague of the drama was Frederick H. Koch at the University of North Carolina whose Carolina Playmakers influenced the development and survival of a truly American theater through folk drama. Louisiana's Lillian Hellman *(The Little Foxes)* and Mississippi's own Tennessee Williams *(A Streetcar Named Desire)* both took the sense of story and lineage in southern life and culture to theatrical moments of intense personal and group identification. The prominent use of story in southern regional drama is often a form of what I call lyrical American stage realism, a dramatic form which ties character to place and time in a seamless rendition of action and dialogue that is based on reality but envelops the audience in the forever-questioning mysticism of life. This same dramatic legacy is found here on the eve of the twenty-first century in the regional voices of southern playwrights included in this volume.

The American drama of the last half of the twentieth century exploded into the next level of experimentation in a form which sought to reconcile the country's complex heritage with time-honored functions of theater—i.e., explorations of persons/situations/places within a democratic or "free" framework. American drama and theatre styles/genres can be linear, non-linear, realistic, non-realistic, filmic, and posed. Whatever the theatrical shape, American dramatists have continued to exhibit a firm belief in the power of drama to represent profound truths while elevating the commonplace. The actions of characters grow out of cultural conflict. The conflict is a direct function of character and is also related to locale. This building of character informed by place affects not only the physical and psychological facets of the characters, but also dictates a different plot progression. Plot emanates from character rather than the reverse. Another result is a different hero/heroine whose sense of self is imbedded in the morality of one's own *story*.

To know who you are is to know where you are. Place/location/setting is essential to the dramatic process of *being*. It is through the connectedness of place that one's journey to any sense of truth and beauty (aesthetics) begins. We are bound by what might be termed a natural desire to have knowledge of our setting. In the process of the drama, a human exercise in expression and exploration, the poet/playwright examines the consequences of setting. The southern drama often creates this sense through language with its great power of calling forth mind-pictures that transport the speaker (actor) and the listener (audience) into a panorama of thoughts—literally a landscape within the mind. [Consider Don Baker and Dudley Cocke's *Red Fox/Second Hangin'*—mountain legend and fact in open story form.] The theatrical experience becomes a process of being told the story of characters in a particular dilemma, then becoming absorbed to a point of seamless identification.

When we come to the theatrical experience, we knowingly enter a kind of sanctum, willing to lend our collective experience of place to the journey toward some level of truth— i.e., some knowledge reconfirmed, newly gained, or with future promise. [Consider Rebecca Ranson's *Blood On Blood*—a love triangle where three become one with woman as flesh and fibre center.] This journey is not without challenge, and often is not pleasant. But at its most dynamic level the theatrical experience of true transport is unmatched by many other experiences of cathartic beauty. The use of scenic reality in the American drama goes beyond the European nineteenth century sense of the impact of heredity and environment. The American drama is about the poetic transposition of the actual into a coded, dramatic and human mythology of past/present/future, subsumed in the telling of the story. [Consider *You Can't Judge a Book by Looking at the Cover: Sayings from the Life and Writings of Junebug Jabbo Jones: Volume II* by John O'Neal, with Watkins/Kent/Raphael—heritage and critical commentary in the voice and experience of an African American folk hero.] Southern regional drama is a prime example of Professor Jackson's designation of the American democratic character. Southern drama grows out of a region where the democracy of personage is a legacy running the gamut of shame, struggle and success, and back again.

Characters in the American drama embody the sense of right or wrong (morality) while pursuing the individual right to be separate and unique, and at the same time forge a bond with the group. Within this pursuit lies the essence of what it means to be American. Perhaps it is through the drama that this most social of desires can be most evident to the American consciousness. [Consider Linda Parris-Bailey's *Dark Cowgirls and Prairie Queens*—song and drama crack cultural myths and reveal black women rising.] Connected closely with character is the process of thought which reaches its highest manifestation in action. We think and are propelled toward action. And deciding not to act is in itself an active choice. So, illuminating the process of character building through the use of story becomes a particularly American process of self creation and analysis—with all the triumphs and pitfalls therein. [Consider Jim Grimsley's *Mr. Universe*—the irony of tragic normalcy in alternative American lifestyles.] American character within the drama is, then, one of active, vital creation. The playwright constructs character out of the actual "stuff" of life, and then places it in the crucible of theatrical process known as story. Dramatic characters are subjected to a communal test of becoming as the "telling" (i.e., dramatic action) mixes *is* with *what if* and *maybe*. [Consider Jo Carson's *A Preacher with a Horse to Ride*—regional challenges to self-worth in an industrial war.]

When we watch characters evolving, static, tragic or comic, we are, ourselves as audience, going through the process of self-building in the moment of the action we are watching. We may not be conscious of this process in a technical sense, for that would interrupt our joining of the journey. We are, however, struck by the very fiber of storytelling because we enact our own internal narrative as we observe the telling before us on stage. [Consider The Road Company's *Blind Desire*—a woman's journey of self-creation in a dehumanizing, plastic society.] We literally collect and organize events, edit language, underscore themes, and look for the "moral of the story." We do this particularly actively as Americans because we are often driven in the "theater of life" by pursuit of "the bottom line." We do it particularly actively as human beings because of our long association with imitation (i.e., storytelling/dramatization) as a means of education and delight.

We can know that the process of story is prominent and compelling in much of the American drama even if the storytelling is not in the form of direct-address to the audience, and even if the storytelling is not housed in a primarily realist, linear style of theatrical presentation. Story at its basic level relates or recounts something to the listener/audience. This process of recounting implies history, which implies a sense of self, a specific location, and an order of events—or in terms of the drama, a sense of character, setting, and action. Events in the drama are not presented just in terms of pure plausibility, but rather in terms of the relative probability aligned with the truth of the dramatic moment—the same process we know in folklore, oral traditions, and actual life itself!

This volume of plays is a historic whole look at some of the most striking drama in the American theatrical canon. That these pieces represent the southern region of the United States of America is perhaps more nationally characteristic than it may seem on first consideration. Growing out of a sense of place and story, these pieces represent the essence of the American drama. That these pieces evolved and thrive within an arts organization (Alternate ROOTS) that itself is dedicated to the priority of place and story with no destructive homage to commercialism and the creative strictures therein, is more remarkable still! Yet I would venture that the most viable American theater and drama of the twenty-first century will be built on the Alternate ROOTS model—marked by a vitality of community, region, and peoples then flowing out to the world—which is the only way *any* drama truly remains dynamic, viable, alive.

members of the road company ensemble
margaret baker   john fitzpatrick
emily green   robert h. leonard
christine murdock   eugene wolf

blind desire

artists' statement

Conceptual development of *Blind Desire* began in the late fall of 1982 with a six-week period of open improvisations. Where most previous work of the ensemble originated with preestablished themes, *Blind Desire* began as an open study of the acting conception of "condition." The ensemble used a variety of exercises, based on several years of exploration of Viola Spolin's Improvisation for the Theatre and Steven Kent's work with the Provisional Theatre. A fantasy emerged that was first presented to the public in early 1983. A full script was then developed and performed, after which the piece was laid aside for a year. By the time the collective rewriting process began in the summer of 1984, Kelly Hill had joined the ensemble replacing John Fitzpatrick.

The development of the original fantasy was assisted by the haiku of Marlene Mountain. The dance concepts were inspired by the poetry of Anne Kent Rush in *Moon Moon*. The marriage ceremony, taken from *Woman and Nature* by Susan Griffin, is used by permission of the author. The entire ensemble is indebted to the invaluable critiques offered at the 1984 Alternate ROOTS Festival, which served to light the way to effective cuts and rewrites.

production history

The earliest version of *Blind Desire* was presented at the Down Home in Johnson City in February 1983. A full script was then developed that was performed in the summer of 1983 at the Veterans' Administration Memorial Theatre, Mountain Home, Tennessee, and at the Alternate ROOTS Annual Meeting in Ozone, Tennessee. In 1985 The Road Company toured *Blind Desire* through Tennessee, Georgia, Louisiana, Alabama and Florida.

Blind Desire was nominated for *Plays in Process* by Robert

H. Leonard, Producing Director of The Road Company, Johnson City, Tenn. It was presented at the Alternate ROOTS Festival in Atlanta and on tour in Georgia and Tennessee from September 10–21, 1984.

Robert H. Leonard directed. Set and lights were designed by Leonard, costumes by Kelly R. Hill, Jr. and movement by Susan Spalding. The cast was as follows:

Margaret, Linda, Madge, Brick Woman, Peg
and others . . . . MARGARET BAKER

John, Bud, Mark, Brick Man, Preacher
and others . . . . KELLY R. HILL, JR.

Emily, Jean . . . . EMILY GREEN

Christine, Cleo, Snake
and others . . . . CHRISTINE MURDOCK

Eugene, Herb, P. Charming and
others . . . . EUGENE WOLF

production notes

There is an incongruity of style in this play. The dynamic of the play may be found, in part, in the tension between the styles of the separate scenes. This is especially true in the second act.

The ensemble sees the production design of the play as being minimal in nature, leaving much to the creativity of the audience. The Road Company production used a large mobile hanging in the performance space as the sole set piece. Costumes were variations of white with single broad strokes of color applied without reference to the distinction between shirt and pants, blouse and skirt.

characters

Blind Desire is intended to be played by five actors, three women and two men. Each of the five roles involves playing "self" or "actor" in addition to various "characters." For the sake of clarity, the "actors" in the play have been given the first names of the original ensemble rather than generic labels such as "Actor 1," "Actress 2."

MARGARET, who plays LINDA, MADGE, BRICK WOMAN, PEG

JOHN, who plays BUD, MARK, BRICK MAN, PREACHER

EMILY, who plays JEAN

CHRISTINE, who plays CLEO, SNAKE

EUGENE, who plays HERB, P. CHARMING (P.C.)

The following characters may be assigned to any of the five actors except Emily, who plays the part of Jean only:

CUTE-TOP WOMAN
WONDER-WHISK MAN
SHOELACE MAN
TELL-ME-A-STORY WOMAN
GIRLFRIEND MAN
ADVICE WOMAN
I-NEED-SEX MAN
JOGGERS
BARTENDER
WAITER

time

The not-too-distant future.

place

McMankind World, a fully computerized society and Jean's interior world.

act 1

VOICE. *(In the darkness)* Attention. Attention. This is a test. This is just a test. In the event of a catastrophe, the play that you are about to see will probably be of no value what so ever.

JOHN'S VOICE. *(In the darkness)* Ah . . . you got the igonkculators set?

MARGARET'S VOICE. Yeah.

JOHN'S VOICE. O.K.

MARGARET'S VOICE. Fly in the Goddess.

JOHN'S VOICE. All right. The moon's here.

MARGARET'S VOICE. What about the digitals?

JOHN'S VOICE. Yes. Bring up the first digital.

MARGARET'S VOICE. O.K.

Light and sound up and out. Sound may be electronic or created by the Actors, live or recorded.

MARGARET'S VOICE. *(Continued)* Is that tweaked?

JOHN'S VOICE. That's tweaked pretty good. You got the mummy wrapped over there?

MARGARET'S VOICE. Yeah. It took three rolls of adhesive tape.

JOHN'S VOICE. Three rolls! How about the second digital?

MARGARET'S VOICE. O.K. Ready.

JOHN'S VOICE. Bring it on up.

Sound and light up and out.

JOHN'S VOICE. *(Continued)* Oh. Nice.

MARGARET'S VOICE. How is that?

JOHN'S VOICE. That's good. We're ready for the magical third digital.

MARGARET'S VOICE. Ha. Yeah.

JOHN'S VOICE. Tweak away.

Sound up and out, light up and hold.

JOHN. *(Continued)* Ah.

MARGARET'S VOICE. Is that it?

JOHN. Yes. That's it.

MARGARET'S VOICE. Holding.
JOHN. Good. All right. You ready?
MARGARET'S VOICE. Yeah.
JOHN. Actors ready?
ACTORS' VOICES. Yes.
JOHN. Great. Ready, Ritualistic Beginning. Ritualistic Beginning, Go.

Light out. Ritual begins with voices in the darkness: a cantata of sound with the moon and the Goddess as theme. Actors move through house to stage. A light discovers them in a group.

CHRISTINE. Snake is your soul. Snake is your intuition.
JOHN. Layer
EMILY. On layer
EUGENE. On layer
MARGARET. Of rock.
EMILY. A cavity holds
EUGENE. The full moon.
EMILY. Snake is your soul.
MARGARET. Snake is your intuition.
EUGENE. River
EMILY. River
ALL. River, river, river, river, river . . .
EMILY. Passes over moss
JOHN. Into sudden
EUGENE. Darkness.
EMILY. Snake is your soul.
MARGARET. Snake is your intuition.
KELLY. Within the cave
MARGARET. Moist odor
EUGENE. Of a forgotten ritual.

Cantata continues as Actors leave Emily Center. Christine becomes the Snake. There is snaky music and Emily and the Snake dance together to celebrate the moon. Soon the Others are drawn into the dance. Eventually the dialogue resumes.

EUGENE. *(Continued)* Where are you?
EMILY. Moongazing. For a moment I change my name.
MARGARET. Is the moon made out of old seashells?

EMILY.   The moon is a big seashell. It sings. She sings. The moon sings songs to us that we think are dreams.

EUGENE.   What does the moon do?

EMILY.   The moon loves to play tricks. Catch me if you can. Mother may I. Trick or treat. Charades. Ball. All kinds.

JOHN.   Does the moon smell?

EMILY.   The moon smells good. The moon is made of warm snow. The moon smells like . . . me!

JOHN.   *(Tags Emily)* You're it!

Emily tags everyone so They are frozen. She goes Center and begins a new game.

MARGARET.   What are you doing?

EMILY.   Dividing iris. Not knowing where I will be.

MARGARET.   Not knowing?

EMILY.   Fog obscures the mountain that is home.

JOHN.   What's pretty?

EMILY.   Calling her son Forest, an unmarried woman in the woods.

CHRISTINE.   That's pretty?

EMILY.   Rush hour. A woman in the median picking wildflowers.

EUGENE.   What's alone?

EMILY.   Alone in a cotton gown.

JOHN.   That's alone?

EMILY.   Alone. The butterfly's true flight.

EUGENE.   Alone?

EMILY.   Isolation. I work out with the moon who I am.

ALL.   *(Chanting)* Isis, Astarte, Diana, Hecate, Demeter, Kali, Inanna. Isis, Astarte, Diana, Hecate, Demeter, Kali, Inanna.

Christine, Emily and Eugene form a procession Off as John and Margaret become Bud and Linda.

BUD.   Linda! What in the world was that? You're a woman. Tell me what was that all about.

LINDA.   Well, Bud. You've put me on the spot again, as usual, but I still think that this evening's edition of *Guess and Speculate* will hold our viewers riveted.

BUD.   That's right. This is Bud Ellis and Linda McCormack for

McMankind's *Guess and Speculate.* This evening we are discussing a bizarre . . .

LINDA. Not bizarre, Bud. A bit bohemian, perhaps.

BUD. Ritual beginning. Linda, what I saw left me stunned. Not so much for its depth, but for . . . well, frankly, I think those people are mad. Off their rockers!

LINDA. Oh, Bud. Your perceptions are so narrow-minded. You are a man, but still. . . . Rituals are a little intense. They're supposed to be.

BUD. All those circles and patterns. This is the moon image I suppose?

LINDA. I saw the moon, Bud, didn't you?

BUD. And that snake! The snake is a well-known symbol of evil.

LINDA. But, Bud, a giggling snake, evil? And that tongue business was just nonsense. No, this is obviously a case of reverse mythology and, I might add, a rich poetic.

BUD. Poetic, Linda? Bull hockey. Too much for my taste.

LINDA. You certainly are in fine form this evening, Bud. I think you might be more cautious considering we're just a few minutes into this.

BUD. Right, Linda. Good advice. I'll hold my tongue. But, what do I see coming up on my offscreen monitor? Why, yes. It's that woman from the ritual.

Emily enters as Jean. She walks to Center with a stool. She sits.

BUD. *(Continued)* Linda, I'm fully prepared to withhold my judgment until she has had a chance to regain herself. I certainly hope she will.

LINDA. That's awfully big of you, Bud.

BUD. And stay tuned for more *Guess and Speculate* as the situation warrants.

Bud and Linda exit.

JEAN. *(To the audience)* Hi. My name is Jean. And I don't have a job. I was working as a waitress, but this highway came through and they tore that restaurant down. So now I'm out of work. I have been looking for a job for about two months now. You probably know some people who are looking for work, so you know how hard it is. I'm from here originally.

Well, actually a little closer to Nashville. My daddy, he's a farmer there. And he runs the farm just like his daddy before him . . .

The Actors walk Onstage as They provide Jean's female genealogy. Jean sees them, but doesn't really hear what They say.

MARGARET. Your mother was a baker of bread and a teller of stories.

JEAN. Um. . . . Yeah. See, my family, they go back in Tennessee a long way. My great-great-great-great-grandfather was the first Baptist preacher in Tennessee.

CHRISTINE. Her mother was also a teller of stories and a healer, whose mother was a granny woman.

JEAN. That's how my grandmother got in the DAR.

JOHN. Her mother was a granny woman who knew great secrets.

JEAN. Anyway . . . before that, my family came down from Virginia. And before that, they came over from England where most were shopkeepers and tradespeople. That kind of thing. It seems like somebody in my family was knighted by some king or other.

CHRISTINE. Her great-great-great-grandmother was burned at the stake as a witch for she knew these secrets and she worshipped the great Goddess. Before men silenced them.

JEAN. But, most of them were pretty ordinary people.

MARGARET. Once your ancestors worshipped Isis and Hathor and the Goddess whose name shall not be spoken.

EUGENE. Everywhere you look there are fragments.

CHRISTINE. When we learn to come together, we are whole.

JEAN. Whole. I need a job. That's what . . . yeah. So if any of you know of anything. If your uncle or your brother or anybody needs an employee . . .

Margaret becomes Madge. John, Christine and Eugene exit.

MADGE. Fill out these forms please.

JEAN. What?

MADGE. You want a job, don't you?

JEAN. Oh, yes I do!

MADGE. Then just fill out these forms.

JEAN. O.K. *(She starts to do as She is told)*

MADGE. Uh-uh. No pencil. Voiceprint only.

JEAN. Oh. *(She puts her voiceprint on the paper)*

MADGE. Let's see. Your file came up in today's late printout. But there seem to be some gaps in your profile. Do you like ice cream?

JEAN. Yes, ma'am, I sure do.

MADGE. *(Punches in answer)* Have you ever peeled grapes?

JEAN. Well, yes. Once I did. See, my boyfriend came over . . .

MADGE. Uh, Jean, have you ever peeled grapes professionally?

JEAN. Oh. No.

MADGE. *(Punches in answer)* Picked crabs?

JEAN. Once on vacation in Ocracoke I did.

MADGE. Jean, they are looking for full-time professional peelers and pickers down at Pyramid Profit Management. Now, do you have the qualifications?

JEAN. No.

MADGE. Good answer. Good answer. *(Punches in)* Do you like my hair? The cut of it. The cut of it.

JEAN. Yes. Yes, it has a sense of humor.

MADGE. Good answer. It says here that your mother. . . . Let me check. *(Punch)* She grew up here didn't she? Doesn't her line go back? Doesn't it Jean?

JOHN. Jean.

JEAN. Yes?

JOHN. I'm lost.

JEAN. You're onstage.

JOHN. Oh. Thanks.

MADGE. Doesn't it, Jean?

EUGENE. Jean, Jean I can't find that key. If I don't get that key I can't get back in here.

JEAN. It's in the locket. In the locket. If you'll just wait until it comes by then you can get it and come in. *(To Madge)* Yes, I believe it does.

Eugene is puzzled, waits a while, then pulls the key out of the air.

MADGE. It's not in the record, though. That's the gap. Damn! A void.

JEAN. I know.

MADGE. Jean, you have a void. What are you going to do about it?

JEAN. Fill it.

MADGE. Good answer. Good answer.

CHRISTINE. Jean, I'm almost on. Can I just wait here for my cue?

JEAN. Sure.

CHRISTINE. Great.

MADGE. Jean, I have been noticing that you are filled with good answers. I think I might have just the place for you.

JEAN. Really?!

MADGE. They are looking for some I.A.'s over at McMankind International.

JEAN. I.A.'s?

MADGE. Information Accessor. You know, you just punch in your personal and the perfect product appears on the screen. . . .

JEAN. Oh! The buyer's guide to every need! Me?

MADGE. You have the raw talent. You answer questions.

JEAN. Well, when I have the answers.

MADGE. At McMankind you won't need the answers. We give them to you. Jean, you will have to relocate.

JEAN. What, leave home?

MADGE. Here or Memphis, what's the difference. It's all L.A. anyway.

JEAN. Memphis sounds great.

MADGE. It's where all the young people are going these days.

JEAN. McMankind here I come.

MADGE. And, Jean, there will have to be just a few changes.

JEAN. Changes?

MADGE. Herb!

JEAN. What do you mean changes?

Eugene becomes Herb.

HERB. What, Madge? Oh, my God. Madge. Who's this one for? And don't say McMankind. I mean, I'm great. Cleo's great, but . . .

MADGE. McMankind, Herb.

HERB. I.A.?

MADGE. I.A.

HERB. Cleo!

CHRISTINE. I'm on, Jean! I'm on!

HERB. Cleo!

JEAN. Well, start.

CHRISTINE. Oh. *(She becomes Cleo)* Oh.

HERB. McMankind.

CLEO. Ooooooohhhhh.

HERB. I.A.

CLEO. OOOOOOOHHHHH.

HERB. When Madge?

MADGE. Today Herb. McMankind needs an I.A. today, and when McMankind needs, McMankind gets.

HERB. Yes, yes, yes. God knows we're the go-getters this time. Me and Cleo. We come in here, take this little ragamuffin and make an I.A. out of her.

MADGE. Herb! How would you like to be gluing thermometers to calendars down in the Y section?

HERB. You're hard as nails, Madge.

Madge exits.

CLEO. Well, come on Herbert. It's time to get to work. Time to take this drab little body and make a few improvements.

HERB. Improvements! We're talking major overhaul. Let's see. . . . Let's have some chin. Tip up the chin.

Jean does.

HERB. *(Continued)* O.K. Raise the chest.

Jean does.

HERB. *(Continued)* Did you not hear me? Well, I guess we'll just have to work with what she has.

CLEO. Now, she has a charming personality. *(She squeezes Jean's breasts)* Oh, I'd say about a B cup.

HERB. B cup?

CLEO. B with assistance. All right dear, thrust.

JEAN. What?

CLEO. Thrust. *(Slaps Jean on the ass)* From here. Thrust.

JEAN. Oh.

HERB. Nice line.

CLEO. That's a charming little frock, dear. Did you make it yourself?

JEAN. Yes, I did.

CLEO. Take it off.

JEAN. Oh. O.K.

CLEO. I'm thinking the little . . .

HERB. Oooo. . . .

CLEO. With the stripes. . . .

HERB. Cleo, I'm reading your mind. The little red sweater-dress-type-thing. . . . Oh yes! Now, Jean, step up on this stool.

Jean does.

HERB. *(Continued)* Let's have some chin. Well, Cleo, there is a chin. We have something to work with. At McMankind, darling, the policy is go with your assets. We'll just go with your chin. Ah. *(As He applies the makeup)* Make it strong. Determination. Ooh. What do you think, Cleo?

CLEO. Yes. Here you are, dear, just slip this on.

Jean slips on dress.

HERB. Good color. Good color.

CLEO. Yes, I think it will do very nicely.

JEAN. You think?

HERB. Never think! Go with your assets.

JEAN. O.K.

CLEO. Yes, dear, now for the assistance. Lean down here. Oh! That's better. We're getting there.

HERB. Let's see those cheekbones. Oh, yes. We'll do something with that little oval face of yours. Looking much better. What do you think, Cleo. Look at this.

Herb and Cleo "ooh" and "aah."

HERB. *(Continued)* Now, let's try those eyes. Let's see those eyes. Cleo, you are right. There is personality!

CLEO. And for the hair, I'm thinking something . . .

HERB. Keep it short, smart.

CLEO. You know . . .

HERB. Frame the face. Like I said, Jean, you do have personality. All yours needs is a little help. Say thank you.

JEAN. Thank you.

HERB. No, no, no, no, no. Like you mean it. Thank you.

JEAN. Thank you.

Herb applies lipstick to Jean's pursed lips.

HERB. Oh ho. There you go.

JEAN. Thank you.

CLEO. All right dear, step down. *(She puts wig on Jean)*

HERB. Just the right shade, too, Cleo.

JEAN. Thank you.

HERB. That is a start. Just hold it, hold it, hold it.

John as Mark, a photographer, runs Onstage.

MARK. HOLD IT! Hold it. Hold it right there, Jean. Look at you. You are the picture of personality. Information access screen here you come!

JEAN. Thank you.

MARK. Jean, you make me want.

JEAN. Yes?

HERB. No, no, no. Yes, may I hep you?

JEAN. Yes, may I help you?

HERB. No, HeP you.

JEAN. Hep you.

HERB. Hep you.

JEAN. May I hep you?

MARK. Yes you may. More chest. Yes. More hips. Yes. You make me want. Can she walk?

HERB. Walk.

CLEO. Walk.

JEAN. Walk. Of course I can walk.

HERB. Well.

CLEO. Then walk, dear.

Jean does.

CLEO. *(Continued)* Shoes.

HERB. Where is the personality now?

MARK. Go with your assets. Go with your assets. . . . Height.

HERB. Height.

CLEO. Shoes! All right, dear, if you'll just slip these on.

Jean slips into extremely high heels.

CLEO. *(Continued)* Now, try that walk again.

MARK. Yes. More shoulders. Yes. More knees. Yes. More you. At
McMankind we give more you.

HERB. Jean. Let's try that walk one more time and this time let's
try a little hesitation in the step.

JEAN. A little what?

HERB. *(He demonstrates)* A little . . . hesitation. Keep it subtle.
Make it flow.

JEAN. May I hep you? Thank you.

CLEO. Have a nice day!

JEAN. Have a nice day!

CLEO. Madge! Madge!

Madge enters.

MADGE. Oh, my. Turn around. Let's have a look-see. Wonderful!
Take a walk for me there, Jean.

HERB. Hesitate, hesitate.

JEAN. Thank you! Have a nice day!

MADGE. Personality!

JEAN. Hi! May I hep you?

MADGE. Desire in a package! Bravo, team, and right on time.
Congratulations, Jean. You are a graduate. You have a job.

JEAN. Thank you!

MADGE. Let's all go out for drinks. On me.

All but Jean exit with great congratulations.

JEAN. *(To audience)* Hi! My name is Jean. I have a job. May I hep
you?

CHRISTINE. *(Off)* Her great-great-great-grandmother was burned
at the stake as a witch for she knew these secrets and she
worshipped the great Goddess.

JEAN. Hi! My name is Jean. I have a job. May I hep you? Hi. My
name is Jean. I have a job. May I hep you?

Bud and Linda appear.

LINDA. Well! Jean certainly turned out to be the plucky one,
didn't she?

BUD. Plucky, Linda? That little woman has no backbone at all.
She's become a product, not a wage earner. And I want to

know what happened to the moon and the patterns and all that stuff.

LINDA. A product, Bud? What are you or what am I, for that matter. No, McMankind remake teams like Herb and Cleo are responsible for keeping you in your place and me in mine. I'm afraid you haven't got a leg to stand on on that one, Bud.

BUD. And what a difference a hairstyle can make, eh, Linda? Still, she seems to have that combination of innocence and sex that will take her far at McMankind.

LINDA. Image is the key, Bud. Image is the key.

BUD. Right, Linda. But what about the snake?

Cute-top Woman enters.

LINDA. Well, it looks like Jean's about to step back into the action. We'll have to let the snake slide for now, Bud.

BUD. I agree, Linda. But not for long. I'm not a patient man. And I do disagree about plucky. Lucky maybe, but not plucky.

Bud and Linda exit.

JEAN. Good morning, shoppers! This is the early morning special announcement. For the next five minutes, your get-up-and-go needs can be satisfied by a simple call to McMankind. Remember. Just punch in your personal! Be listening for updates throughout the day. Thank you! Have a nice day!

Cute-top Woman punches her personal.

JEAN. *(Continued)* Hi! My name is Jean. I have a job. May I hep you?

CUTE-TOP WOMAN. Yes. I'm looking for a cute top.

JEAN. Something to go with that cute bottom?

CUTE-TOP WOMAN. Yes!

JEAN. We have cute tops in solids, stripes, and prints. Name brands and off brands. Long sleeved or short sleeved. May I hep you?

CUTE-TOP WOMAN. Yes. Stripes. Short sleeved. Name brand.

JEAN. Oh! *(She produces the product out of the air)*

CUTE-TOP WOMAN. That's the cutest top I've ever seen!

JEAN. Cash or charge?
CUTE-TOP WOMAN. Charge it.
JEAN. Thank you. Have a nice day!

Cute-top Woman exits as Wonder-Whisk Man enters in a quandary.

WONDER-WHISK MAN. I need a wonder whisk. I need a wonder whisk. *(He punches in his personal)*
JEAN. Hi! My name is Jean. I have a job. May I hep you?
WONDER-WHISK MAN. I need a wonder whisk.
JEAN. Deluxe or embossed?
WONDER-WHISK MAN. Deluxe.
JEAN. A housewares special! *(Produces product)*
WONDER-WHISK MAN. Great! Thank you.
JEAN. Cash or charge?
WONDER-WHISK MAN. Charge it.
JEAN. Will there be anything else? Something from the Junior Miss for your little angel? There is a special.
WONDER-WHISK MAN. No. Uh-uh.
JEAN. Thank you. Have a nice day!

Wonder-wisk Man exits as Madge enters.

JEAN. *(Continued)* Madge! How am I doing?
MADGE. Fine Jean. But, we need to be more delicate. Think "lady." Be a "lady." The customers want to see a "lady." *(She exits)*
JEAN. Lady. Right.

Jean ponders this advice as the Shoelace Man enters.

SHOELACE MAN. *(Yelling to Offstage)* All right, honey. Look, why don't you just go ahead and start the car and hush about it. I'll be there in a minute. *(He notices that his shoes are untied. As He begins to tie them, the laces break)* Oh, damn. *(He punches in his personal)*
JEAN. Hi. My name is Jean. I'm a little lady and I have a job. May I hep you?
SHOELACE MAN. I just broke my damn shoelaces, and I can't. . . . *(He looks up)* Oh. *(Calls Offstage)* Honey, they got a new one over at McMankind. She's kinda cute.

JEAN. We have shoelaces in many tasteful lengths and colors. May I hep you?

SHOELACE MAN. Yeah. I need some for these shoes right here. . . .

As the Shoelace Man steps in to show her his shoes, a buzzer sounds.

JEAN. Please step back.

Shoelace Man does.

JEAN. *(Continued)* I believe this length will do very nicely. *(Produces product)* Will there be anything else?

SHOELACE MAN. Well, I got some other shoes back in the . . .

Tell-me-a-Story Woman enters and punches her personal.

JEAN. Excuse me. *(She goes to Woman)* Hi. My name is Jean. I'm a little lady and I have a job. May I hep you?

TELL-ME-A-STORY WOMAN. Yes. Tell me a story.

JEAN. Oh! Once upon a time there was this lovely lady, and she lived in this castle that was just covered with vines. One day this handsome gentleman came along, he climbed up the castle tower, kissed the lady, and she gave him the castle and planted rose bushes. They lived happily ever after.

TELL-ME-A-STORY WOMAN. That's awful. That is the worst story I have ever heard. It's stupid. It's old-fashioned and I won't pay for it.

JEAN. I am sorry, ma'am. It happens to be the only one we have at the moment.

CLEO. *(Enters)* Jean! Jean, sell it with sex. Think SEX. Steamy sex. *(And She is gone)*

JEAN. Sex. All right. *(In her sexiest manner)* How about this one? Once upon a time there was this beautiful woman, and she lived in this castle that was just covered with vines. And one day, this handsome prince came along, he climbed up the castle tower, kissed the woman, she gave him the castle and planted rose bushes. They lived happily ever after. Cash or charge?

TELL-ME-A-STORY WOMAN. *(Hot)* Charge it.

JEAN. Thank you. Have a nice day.

Tell-me-a-Story Woman exits.

JEAN. *(Continued)* Oh. It's hot in here. *(She notices the Shoelace Man still waiting)* Oh. Will there be anything else?

SHOELACE MAN. I do have some boots that I need . . .

The Shoelace Man steps too close. Buzzer sounds.

JEAN. Please step back.

Shoelace Man does.

JEAN. *(Continued)* I believe this length will do very nicely. *(Produces product)* Anything else?

SHOELACE MAN. I've got some steel-toed shoes that . . .

Girlfriend Man enters and punches in.

JEAN. Excuse me. *(To Girlfriend Man)* Hi. My name is Jean. I'm a lady with sex appeal and I have a job. May I hep you?

GIRLFRIEND MAN. I'm on my break.

JEAN. Oh. Would you like a sweet?

SHOELACE MAN. *(Overlapping with Jean)* Break already!! *(Calls Off-stage)* Honey, they are double-linked over at McMankind again. I'll be there in a minute.

GIRLFRIEND MAN. *(Overlapping with Shoelace Man)* No. I was thinking about getting some jewelry for my girlfriend.

JEAN. Isn't that sweet! How long have ya'll been dating?

GIRLFRIEND MAN. Six months tomorrow.

JEAN. Really! Are you gonna take her out?

CLEO. *(Enters)* Move the sale, Jean. Move the sale.

JEAN. She might like our Night in Egypt line. Diadem watch-bands make her feel like a legend.

GIRLFRIEND MAN. I was thinking of something more like a ring.

JEAN. Oh.

CLEO. Smile, Jean.

JEAN. Oh! The Desert Dawn comes with a full year warranty. *(Produces ring)*

GIRLFRIEND MAN. That's pretty.

JEAN. Cash or charge?

GIRLFRIEND MAN. Charge it.

JEAN. Thank you. Have a nice day.

Girlfriend Man exits.

SHOELACE MAN. *(Imitating Jean)* Thank you. Have a nice day.

MARGARET. Isis.

SHOELACE MAN. What a whore.

JOHN. Osiris.

JEAN. What?

CHRISTINE. Sexual intercourse used to be revered as the highest form of spirituality.

Jean ponders a moment. She surfaces to see the Shoelace Man looking at her.

JEAN. Oh. Yes. Your bootlaces.

SHOELACE MAN. Never mind the bootlaces. We've done those. What time do you get off work?

JEAN. What?

SHOELACE MAN. *(Touching Jean)* Nice ass.

Buzzer sounds.

JEAN. Sir! Please don't do that. I'm a lady.

SHOELACE MAN. A lady! You're kidding! Look at yourself. You're begging for it. I'll see you later. *(Calls Offstage)* Honey, I'm coming. . . . *(He exits)*

MARGARET. *(As She crosses the stage)* Is the moon made out of old seashells?

Mark runs On.

MARK. Excellent, Jean. Excellent! You've got them wanting. That's just what you've been paid for. You've been selected "Accessor of the Week"!

JEAN. Oh!

MARK. Yes.

JEAN. Oh, you're kidding!

MARK. No.

JEAN. I don't know what to say! I didn't even try! Well, I mean, I did try to do what you said, but . . .

Cleo and Madge enter.

CLEO. Jean, Jean don't rattle. Your linkage is fine. It's not what you say at McMankind that's important, but how you say it. And remember, courtesy is convenience.

JEAN. Courtesy is convenience.

MADGE. And Jean, don't let them run over you. You've got to have balls, girl, balls. Get tough!

Madge exits and Cleo becomes the Advice Woman.

JEAN. Balls. Right.

ADVICE WOMAN. Ohhhhh! I don't . . . what . . . *(She punches in)*

JEAN. Hi. My name is Jean. I am a no-nonsense lady with sex appeal and I have a job. May I hep you?

ADVICE WOMAN. Yes. I need some advice.

JEAN. Ah. turn more than RPM's. Turn some heads. Seek out new horizons at the Post Office. Invest your money in an IRA. And remember, this is the best of all possible worlds.

ADVICE WOMAN. What?!

JEAN. It's true. Cash or charge?

ADVICE WOMAN. Cash.

JEAN. Thank you. Have a nice day.

ADVICE WOMAN. What a bitch.

JEAN. What?

EUGENE. Inanna, the young woman, was also the Goddess of rage.

The I-Need-Sex Man rushes On and punches in his personal.

JEAN. Hi. My name is Jean. I am a no-nonsense lady . . .

I-NEED-SEX MAN. I need sex!

JEAN. Ah. Well, sir, I don't believe we have sex at the moment . . .

HERB. *(Enters)* Jean! Jean, full bins mean profit sales.

JEAN. Ah. Sir, I believe I was wrong. I believe you can find sex in . . .

HERB. Notions.

JEAN. . . . notions at this time of day. Will that be cash or charge?

I-NEED-SEX MAN. Cash.

JEAN. Do you have a charge account with McMankind?

I-NEED-SEX MAN. I said I need sex, not a charge.

JEAN. If you just put your thumbprint right in the L spacer, a charge account will immediately be in place for your convenience.

I-NEED-SEX MAN. I said I need sex. How'd you get your job? Sleep with marketing? *(He exits)*

HERB. Smile, Jean, smile. You've just been selected Accessor of the Year! Take a walk!

JEAN. Oh! I can't believe it! Service is our business. Progress is only the icing on the cake of customer satisfaction. Thank you. Have a nice day.

CHRISTINE. She looks cheap.

EUGENE. Yeah, sticks her chest out far enough.

MARGARET. It gets her by.

CHRISTINE. An eight-by-ten on the bulletin board.

JEAN. May I hep you?

CHRISTINE. Back to work.

JOHN. Can't even get a cup of coffee.

JEAN. Thank you. Have a nice day.

MARK. *(Runs On)* Jean. Jean. We knew we'd done right by you. You've been upgraded to Executive Accessor, Chief of Information Sector!

Cleo, Herb and Madge gather round as Jean screams with delight.

CLEO. Bottoms up, Jean. You're a success.

HERB. Well, I never. Who's to believe it. Congratulations, Jean. You owe it all to us. I mean, we did it all for you. Your progress is our best product. You'll have to have drinks with us sometime. How about next week. Fine.

All exit in a bunch, leaving Jean alone.

JEAN. *(To the audience)* Hi. My name is Jean. I have a job. May I hep you? Hi. My name is Jean. I have a job. May I hep you?

Jean continues silently to repeat her phrase over and over. John enters as the Brick Man and moves his bricks from one corner of the stage to another. Margaret enters as the Brick Woman. She is confused.

BRICK WOMAN. Uh . . . What did I, uh . . . where uh . . .

BRICK MAN. Huh?

BRICK WOMAN. I, uh . . .

BRICK MAN. Come on. You're supposed to be doing this too.

BRICK WOMAN. Yes, but my personal is lost, or missing, or . . .

BRICK MAN. Just misplaced.

BRICK WOMAN. Yes, but I . . .

BRICK MAN. Come on over and do your job.

BRICK WOMAN. Right.

BRICK MAN. Damn right.

Brick Woman tries to work.

BRICK WOMAN. I can't. I just don't feel right without it. What if I need something. Right away. Need a thing or something.

BRICK MAN. Look. If you don't move your brick, you don't get your check. If you don't get your check, you can't pay for your products.

BRICK WOMAN. Then I wouldn't need a personal.

BRICK MAN. Right.

They return to work.

BRICK WOMAN. I need my personal. I cannot be expected to function without it. I really need it.

BRICK MAN. I really need some help here.

BRICK WOMAN. I bet I left it on the slow cooker. God, it's going to melt.

BRICK MAN. God, you're addicted.

BRICK WOMAN. I'm pretty sure it's on the cooker.

BRICK MAN. That's a relief, isn't it? Now, come on.

BRICK WOMAN. Huh?

BRICK MAN. Come on over and do your job.

They work.

BRICK WOMAN. I really need something shiny and new and smelling of vinyl.

BRICK MAN. Look, now.

BRICK WOMAN. Or the leather look. The leather look, the leather look, the leather look. . . .

BRICK MAN. Look, look, look, look here. Use mine.

BRICK WOMAN. What?

BRICK MAN. Use my personal. You can order something and

when we get home you'll get yours again, so what's the difference?

BRICK WOMAN. I couldn't.

BRICK MAN. Come on, use it.

BRICK WOMAN. That looks like mine.

BRICK MAN. They all look alike. Use it.

BRICK WOMAN. No. It's yours.

BRICK MAN. Please. Use it.

BRICK WOMAN. We have work to do.

They return to work.

BRICK WOMAN. *(Continued; stopping suddenly)* They have new rubber garden hoses.

BRICK MAN. Order one.

BRICK WOMAN. Fifty Festive Feet!

BRICK MAN. Lady, you are hooked.

BRICK WOMAN. Don't you think I need a new rubber garden hose?

BRICK MAN. I think you need a rubber room.

BRICK WOMAN. Fifty Festive Feet!!

BRICK MAN. Order one, damn it, and let's get back to work. *(He holds out his personal)*

BRICK WOMAN. No. *(She starts to go back to work, but the draw of the personal is too much for her)* Give me that!

The Brick Woman furiously punches the personal and Jean snaps out of the circuits.

JEAN. Hi. My name is Jean. I'm Chief of Information Sector. May I hep you?

BRICK WOMAN. Yes . . . I. . . . What's good in appliances?

JEAN. We have appliances in Avocado and Aztec Gold.

BRICK WOMAN. A refrigerator in Aztec Gold.

JEAN. Oh! *(She produces product)*

BRICK WOMAN. I'll have another! In Aztec Gold!

BRICK MAN. What are we going to do with two refrigerators?

JEAN. Oh! *(She produces product)*

BRICK WOMAN. It's beautiful! A washer-dryer in Aztec Gold!

JEAN. O.K. *(She produces product)*

BRICK MAN. But, honey, we've got one that works perfectly fine.

BRICK WOMAN. A bath mat in Aztec Gold!
BRICK MAN. A bath mat we could use.

Jean produces product.

BRICK WOMAN. Oh! I'll take fifty.
JEAN. Fifty bath mats?
BRICK WOMAN. In Aztec Gold!
BRICK MAN. But dear, we've only got two bathrooms.
BRICK WOMAN. Some for me, some for my sister.

Jean produces product.

BRICK MAN. How about some chloroform?
BRICK WOMAN. Chloroform! In Aztec Gold!

Herb and Cleo have entered and stand watching with pride.

JEAN. Do we have chloroform?
HERB. We sure do.
JEAN. O.K. *(Produces product)*
BRICK MAN. Thank you.

Brick Man muffles Brick Woman's screams of delight with chloroform. He drags her Offstage.

CLEO. Well done, Jean.
HERB. Some of your best work I've seen to date.
CLEO. Yes. I think that might be the sale of the week.
HERB. Month.
CLEO. Year.
JEAN. You liked that?
CLEO. Yes. You know Jean, there might be an office in this for
   you. Upstairs.
JEAN. Really!?
HERB. Keep up the good work, Jean. You are on your way to the
   top.

Herb and Cleo exit.

JEAN. *(To the audience)* Hi. My name is Jean. I have a job. I do a
   good job. Service is our business. Progress is only the icing
   on the cake of customer satisfaction. Thank you. Have a
   nice. . . . Wait a minute. I need a break.

Jean breaks Downstage and speaks to the audience with as much of herself as She can find at this point. Joggers run behind her, every now and then touching her.

JEAN. *(Continued)* Did you hear that? I may get my own office. That's great! You know, I really don't think that offices are very exciting or that selling things is very . . . *(To a Jogger)* Hi! How are you? . . . selling things is very good work. I don't think I enjoy working with people. As a matter of fact, I don't much like people right now. I don't mean you. You're fine. I guess I mean the people at McMankind. . . . *(To a Jogger)* Hey! Great to see you! . . . I can't think very well. Must be the full moon. I need a drink.

Christine breaks from the Joggers and becomes a Bartender.

BARTENDER. Can I get you something?
JEAN. Yes. Scotch on the rocks, please.
BARTENDER. Here you go.
JEAN. Thank you. Oh. Why did I say that? Um. You know they have stress-management seminars. I think I'm going to do one of them.
BARTENDER. Trouble at work?
JEAN. Umm. Yeah.
BARTENDER. Umm.
JEAN. You don't know who I am do you?
BARTENDER. No.
JEAN. That is so great. I have been looking for someone to talk to . . .

Enter P. Charming (P.C.).

P.C. Scotch, please.
JEAN. Hi.
P.C. Hello. Wait. Wait. Jean. Jean, McMankind, access screen, Chief of Information Sector. . . .
JEAN. Yeah.
P.C. Am I right? I'd know that smile anywhere. I'm P. Charming. My friends call me P.C. Chief of Information Sector, huh?
JEAN. Yeah.
P.C. How long have you been at McMankind?

JEAN.   A year.

P.C.   A year! That's all? And you're already Chief of Information Sector?

JEAN.   Well, yeah. It's not any harder than what I used to do. I simply deal with more important people.

P.C.   Isn't that something? That's great.

JEAN.   Thank you.

P.C.   Thank you. I love that. Thank you. Wait, do it. What is it? Thank you. I can't do it.

JEAN.   Thank you. Have a nice day.

P.C.   I love that. That's wonderful.

JEAN.   Thank you.

P.C.   You're wonderful.

JEAN.   Thank you.

P.C.   Will you have dinner with me tonight?

JEAN.   I'd love to.

P.C.   No.

BARTENDER.   No!

JEAN.   Yes.

P.C.   Really? This must be my lucky day.

JEAN.   *(To Bartender)* Another time, maybe. *(To audience)* My face hurts.

> *P.C. turns to become Herb. Bartender turns to become Cleo.*

HERB.   Cleo! Madge! Let's see now . . . "date."

MARK.   *(Enters)* Yes, she's going out on a date. What we need from you on a date is sex. Allure. A sense of urban sophistication. Panache. Style.

CLEO.   Muss the hair.

HERB.   Think low in the hips.

CLEO.   Yes. Lower the voice.

JEAN.   Lower.

CLEO.   Lower the voice.

HERB.   Plunge the neckline.

CLEO.   Lips. Lots of lips, dear. Wet those lips. Yes.

HERB.   Let's try that walk.

CLEO.   Slow seductive.

JEAN.   Thank you. Thank you.

CLEO.   I'll have what you're having.

JEAN. I'll have what you're having.

Cleo does a low throaty laugh which Jean imitates.

CLEO. Good.

MARK. Excellent.

JEAN. Thank you. I'll have what you're having. *(Laugh)*

CLEO. Madge! Madge!

MADGE. *(Enters)* Turn around, Jean.

Jean does.

MADGE. *(Continued)* Oh, my. Everything seems to be in order. Let's have an equipment check. Lipstick. Tissues. Diaphragm. All seems to be in order. Congratulations, Jean. Here is your clutch. You have a date.

JEAN. Thank you.

Herb becomes P.C. again. He and Jean are at a table. There is music. A Waiter moves in and out with their food and drink. P.C. tells a silent joke, Jean laughs.

WAITER. A light white wine. And would you be having an appetizer this evening? We have calamari in a light white wine sauce.

P.C. Sounds wonderful. What do you think, Jean?

JEAN. I'll have what you're having.

P.C. Two.

WAITER. Excellent.

P.C. and Jean toast. P.C. tells a silent joke. Jean laughs.

WAITER. *(Continued)* Your calamari. And the entre for the evening is baked filet of sole à Robert, in a light white wine sauce.

P.C. Ummm. What do you think?

JEAN. I'll have what you're having.

P.C. Two.

WAITER. Excellent.

P.C. looks deep into Jean's eyes. They are drawn together. They kiss.

WAITER. *(Continued)* Your sole.

P.C. and Jean laugh. P.C. takes Jean's hand and goes down on his knees.

P.C. Marry me.

A pause. Everything stops.

JEAN. Why not.

Wedding march begins as All sweep around to get Jean ready for marriage. John becomes the Preacher. During the following dialogue Christine and Margaret dress Jean in a dress of cardboard and plastic.

PREACHER. Dearly beloved. You have come here to be united in this holy estate.

CHRISTINE. You are the empty vessel.

PREACHER. It behooveth you then to declare in the presence of God and these witnesses.

MARGARET. You are the body and the flesh.

PREACHER. The sincere intent you both have.

CHRISTINE. You are one with him.

PREACHER. Who gives this woman to be married to this man.

JEAN. He is the one.

PREACHER. Will you have this man to be thy wedded husband.

MARGARET. You bear his name.

PREACHER. To live with him after God's ordinance in this holy estate.

CHRISTINE. His knowledge is your knowledge.

MARGARET. What he asks of you, you give.

P.C. Matter impressed.

CHRISTINE. You are the background, the body.

JEAN. I receive.

P.C. Matter impressed with heat.

PREACHER. The enlarging of the molecule. The polymerization of material.

P.C. The formation of plastic.

MARGARET. You remember the story of the foolish virgin who was not always waiting for the bridegroom.

JEAN. I wait.

P.C. The making of plasticity. The material molded to desire.

PREACHER. The synthesis of polymide. The coupling of hexamethaline dymine with adipic acid. Nylon.

MARGARET. The bride wore a formal gown of white bridal satin.

P.C. The material shaped.

MARGARET. The fitted bodice featured a portrait neckline and was overlaid with . . .

PREACHER. Phenol mixed with formaldehyde.

JEAN. I comply.

PREACHER. Bakelite.

P.C. The material shaped at will.

PREACHER. Ethylene reacting with chlorine. Polyvinyl chloride. Polystyrene. Plexiglass. Polythene. Polyethylene.

MARGARET. Reembroidered Alecon lace and pearls. The renaissance-design sleeves were adorned with lace appliques.

P.C. The material easily shaped.

JEAN. I obey.

PREACHER. Artificial rubber. Artificial wood. Artificial leather.

P.C. Easily used.

PREACHER. Teflon. Silicon. Corfam.

P.C. Malleable.

PREACHER. Cellophane. Polyurethane foam.

P.C. Mutable.

PREACHER. Glass fiber resins.

P.C. Bent to use.

PREACHER. DDT-24D. Ammonic detergent.

MARGARET. The semi-fitted skirt had appliques of lace and scalloped lace hemline border that extended into a cathedral train with matching lace highlights.

P.C. Your leaf shall know no decay. You shall always be as you are now, and I shall wear you for my crown.

PREACHER. Benzene. Hexachloride.

JEAN. I yield.

PREACHER. Dichlorobenzene solvents. Polypropylene plastics.

P.C. Design. The formation of the earth in strata. The convenient stratification of the elements. The utility of the complexities of the earth. The conveniences of resources. The availability of treasure.

CHRISTINE. You exist for his needs. You are a necessity.

PREACHER. Mineral salt. Coal. Metallic ores.

CHRISTINE. It is in your nature to be needed.

P.C.   The production of soil for agriculture. The general dispersal of metals useful to man. The disposition of certain animals for domestication. The provision of food and raiment by plants and animals. The size of animals in relation to man. The convenience of the size of goats for milking. The convenience of the size of ripened corn. The value of labor. The labor theory of value.

PREACHER.   Her labor married to his value.

MARGARET.   She wore a turn-of-the-century hat.

PREACHER.   Her labor.

MARGARET.   With a waltz-length veil.

PREACHER.   Disappearing.

MARGARET.   Overlaying a full-length veil of lace.

PREACHER.   Her labor not counted in his production.

CHRISTINE.   You are the empty vessel, the background, the body.

PREACHER.   His name given to her labor. The wife of the laborer called working class. The wife of the shopkeeper called petit bourgeois. The wife of the factory owner called bourgeoisie.

MARGARET.   Since it is in your nature to be needed.

PREACHER.   Wilt thou love him, comfort him, honor him, obey him.

CHRISTINE.   That his need is your need.

PREACHER.   And keep him in sickness and in health.

MARGARET.   That his happiness is your happiness.

PREACHER.   And forsaking all others, keep thee only to him.

CHRISTINE.   In all things.

PREACHER.   So long as you both shall live?

MARGARET.   And if you should suffer at his hands.

PREACHER.   In the presence of God and these witnesses.

JEAN.   I take thee.

CHRISTINE.   You must have wished for this suffering.

JEAN.   To be my wedded husband.

MARGARET.   That his sins are your sins.

JEAN.   And plight thee my troth.

CHRISTINE.   That without him you are not.

JEAN.   Till death do us part.

> *Jean and P.C. kiss. Jean throws her bouquet. Christine and Margaret wrestle each other to the ground over it. The lights fade as the Others watch them furiously wrestling.*

act 2

In the darkness we hear a waltz. The lights come up and Jean and P.C. dance Onstage. Bud and Linda enter.

BUD. Well, Linda. I noticed some semblance of wedding rite in that last bit of obscurity.

LINDA. Obscurity, Bud? I saw no obscurity.

BUD. Obscurity tends to be low on visibility, Linda.

LINDA. I saw a rather well-drawn metaphor for the plasticity of womankind in the arms of man the earthraper, man the womanraper.

BUD. Really, Linda. You women and your rape fantasies. How you can possibly twist a simple mockery of the synthetic nature of female frippery into an erotic vision is more than this brain can ponder.

LINDA. Well, Bud, I wouldn't want your brain to work overtime, but wouldn't you guess that Jean is in for some MANipulation.

BUD. If you mean that that little husband of hers, P.C., can convince her that she cannot possibly be wife, mother, and Chief of Information Sector, then, Linda, for once I think we agree on something.

LINDA. Let's not start any new trends now, Bud.

BUD. Especially during ratings week, eh, Linda?

LINDA. It looks like the waltz is coming to a close.

BUD. That's right. This is Bud Ellis and Linda McCormack for McMankind's *Guess and Speculate*.

CHRISTINE. *(Offstage)* Inanna was the Goddess of rage.

BUD. There's one of those irritating little voices again, Linda. What the hell is Inanna? Some sort of premenstrual syndrome?

Bud and Linda exit. Jean and P.C. finish their waltz. Christine, Margaret and John enter. During the following dialogue, They form a tight grouping called "the Condo" which is reestablished whenever They enter their own separate apartments. The Three Actors (and later Jean and P.C., once They are "moved in") create a sense of the routine of their individual lives by accompanying the lines of dialogue with specific nonverbal sounds and movements. These sounds and movements are not specified in the text as they are best discovered and orchestrated by individual performers and directors. Once the Condo "routine" is established, it is repeated exactly the same each time the Actors enter their apartments, but at varying speeds. Even when the Condo is reestablished without the text, or with only some of the original dialogue, the sound-and-movement which accompanied the original dialogue will still be performed. For example, whenever Christine enters her apartment, her first action will be to repeat the sound-and-movement she invented for her line "Beer" (opening the tab on the can, making the fizzing sound of the beer).

CHRISTINE. Beer.
JEAN. *(Outside the Condo, looking at it)* Oh, honey Look!
MARGARET. Channel 9.

P.C. and Jean move towards the Condo.

P.C. Watch the traffic.
JOHN. Gin and tonic. VCR.
CHRISTINE. Book.
JEAN. *(Still outside)* I love that tree!
P.C. Ohhh.
MARGARET. News, sports and weather.
P.C. Big yard.
JEAN. *(Stepping into her apartment space)* White walls. I love that.
P.C. Pleasant neighborhood.
JEAN. Curtains.
P.C. *(Joining Jean in the apartment)* Big rooms.
JEAN. Throw rugs.
JOHN. Pretzels.
P.C. Personal computer.
MARGARET. Reruns.
JEAN. Stove. Refrigerator.
P.C. Tools.
JEAN. Picture.
P.C. TV.
JEAN. Dining-room set.

MARGARET. Laugh track.
JEAN. *(Invitingly)* Bed?
MARGARET. Good old movie.
P.C. *(Picking up on it)* You bet.

Jean and P.C. kiss and have sex, then turn over and go to sleep.

MARGARET. Johnny Carson. David Letterman. *Nightline.*

All are asleep. Pause. The alarm rings.

MARGARET. *(Continued)* Good Morning, America.
JEAN. Toothbrush.
P.C. Cigarette.
MARGARET. Coffee.
JOHN. Coffee.
CHRISTINE. Make bed.
MARGARET. Sugar, no cream.
P.C. Coffee.
CHRISTINE. Tea.
JOHN. Danish, microwave.
CHRISTINE. Exercise.
MARGARET. Refill.
JEAN. Honey?

Jean and P.C. smile at each other. They kiss and have sex.

JOHN. Done.
P.C. Shave.
JEAN. Makeup.
JOHN. Eat.
P.C. Aftershave.
JEAN. Here kitty, kitty, kitty.
MARGARET. *(Leaves Condo for Workplace)* Traffic.
JEAN. Where's my keys?
P.C. On the desk.
CHRISTINE. *(Leaves for Workplace)* Almost late.
P.C. Where's my shirt?
JEAN. On the chair.
P.C. Bye.
JEAN. Bye.

P.C. and Jean kiss.

P.C. Love you.
JEAN. Love you.
P.C. Be careful. *(Leaves for Workplace)*
JOHN. *(Leaves for Workplace, joining P.C.)* Off to work.
JEAN. *(Leaves for Workplace)* Subway.
P.C. Vega.

All are at work.

P.C. *(Continued)* Sonitrol off.

The Workplace is created in the same way as the Condo, through
sound and movement accompanying the dialogue. The Workplace
is an active, full-stage routine—a kind of explosion of the
Condo. It should be extremely complex and high-tech, involving
innumerable buttons, levers, pulleys, ID cards, retina checks, etc.
As with the Condo, the Workplace routine, once established, is
repeated exactly each time it occurs but at varying speeds.

JOHN. So, I was telling him the other day what I thought of . . .
JEAN. Screen on.
MARGARET. Time. 9:31 A.M.
JEAN. Hi. My name is Jean. I have a job. May I hep you?
JOHN. Good morning, Jean. Here's the 0900 readout.
JEAN. Item. Radiation levels secure in the Persian Gulf, the
    China Sea, and the Hudson Bay. Status A-OK. Red Zone
    secure. Screen off.
EUGENE. Eighteen-percent returns with twenty-percent produc-
    tion, that's two-percent shrinkage. Watch that.
CHRISTINE. Begin labor unrest in section G. Get rid of radical
    elements. Avoid operatives. Update status hourly.
MARGARET. Reconfirm eminent domain in the third world.
    Status pending.
EUGENE. Official McMankind statement concerning subtropical
    depression.
JEAN. Screen on. McMankind is doing it all for you again in the
    Gulf of Mexico. Due to unexpected tropical storms we have
    pushed all systems into overtime to correct this situation.

Vacationeers need not change their plans. Weather outlook is excellent for the next five years. So enjoy! Screen off.

JOHN. Attention. Attention. Red Zone. Red Zone. Notify Arctic Sectors A through F. Brace for severe radiation-zone activity. Export status A-1 Priority. Alter schedules C, D, E and F. C, D, E and F on my mark. Mark.

CHRISTINE. Here endeth the 0900 readout. Thank you. Have a nice day.

MARGARET. Relocation committee recommends retaining Midwest aquifer until next biannual convenes. Thank you.

JEAN. Screen on. Cost overruns warrant shutdown of solar resources in Lower South regions. Dismantling operations two thirds complete. Screen off.

MARGARET. Close out request.

JEAN. *(Returns to Condo)* Groceries.

As the Actors go home to their apartments, they reestablish their Condo routines.

MARGARET. Time. 5:31 P.M.

JOHN. Goodnight Constance.

MARGARET. Answer request.

EUGENE. Vega. *(Returns to Condo)*

MARGARET. Goodnight Rupert. *(Returns to Condo)*

JEAN. Dinner.

P.C. Guess who.

JEAN. Ralph.

P.C. Ralph?

JEAN. Just kidding.

P.C. Oh. Extra lime.

MARGARET. Channel 9.

P.C. What's for dinner?

JEAN. Stew.

JOHN. Close down all systems through Double X. Close down all systems through Double X.

John and Christine return to Condo, separately.

P.C. Not too spicy. Mow the lawn.

JEAN. Honey, dinner.

MARGARET. Reruns.

JEAN. Food.

P.C. Mmmmm. This is delicious.

JEAN. Thank you.

P.C. Bridge?

MARGARET. Laugh track.

JEAN. Not tonight.

P.C. Movie?

MARGARET. Good old movie.

JEAN. What's on the tube?

JOHN. Gin and tonic.

MARGARET. Reruns.

CHRISTINE. Book.

JOHN. VCR.

P.C. Soaps.

JEAN. That sounds good.

JOHN. *Cannonball Run 13.*

JEAN. Clean up.

P.C. Honey, look.

JEAN. What?

> *Jean looks at the TV. P.C. and Jean laugh.*

JEAN. *(Continued)* Another drink?

MARGARET. Johnny Carson.

P.C. Mmmm, honey. . . .

MARGARET. David Letterman.

JEAN. Bed.

P.C. Yes.

MARGARET. *Nightline.*

> *Jean and P.C. kiss. They have sex. All are asleep. Pause. Alarm.*
> *The routine picks up speed a little.*

MARGARET. *(Continued) Good Morning, America.*

JEAN. Toothbrush.

P.C. Cigarette.

MARGARET. Coffee.

JOHN. Coffee.

CHRISTINE. Make bed.

MARGARET. Sugar, no cream.

P.C. Coffee.

CHRISTINE. Tea.
JOHN. Danish, microwave.
JEAN. Coffee.
CHRISTINE. Exercise.
MARGARET. Refill.
JEAN. Makeup.
JOHN. Done.
P.C. Shave.
JEAN. Clothes.
JOHN. Eat.
P.C. Aftershave.
JEAN. Here kitty, kitty, kitty.
MARGARET. Traffic.
JEAN. Where's my keys?
P.C. On the desk.
CHRISTINE. Almost late.
P.C. Where's my shirt?
JEAN. On the chair.
P.C. Bye.
JEAN. Bye.
P.C. Love you.
JEAN. Love you.
JOHN. Off to work.
JEAN. Subway.
P.C. Vega.

All are at work.

P.C. *(Continued)* Sonitrol off.
JOHN. So, anyway, I was telling him just the other day . . .
JEAN. Screen on. Hi. My name is Jean. I have a job. May I hep you?
JOHN. Good morning, Jean. Here's the 0900 readout.
JEAN. Hawaii. Beautiful beaches. Gorgeous women. And two cops that are having the time of their lives. Tonight on vid channels 12–36.
EUGENE. Commence destruction of arcane-knowledge records.
JEAN. Screen off.
EUGENE. Circa 3000 B.C.

JOHN. Remake team to Statue of Liberty. Stat. Remake team to Statue of Liberty. Stat.

CHRISTINE. Internal readout for ears only.

All stop and listen.

JEAN. Break.

Jean breaks out of the routine and walks Downstage. Margaret becomes Peg and joins her. They are in an employees' lounge.

PEG. Damn! I need a cigarette.

JEAN. I'd offer you one, but I quit.

PEG. I did, too, but I still need one every now and then.

JEAN. I know what you mean. Things get so tense in that office. I could smoke a whole pack at one time.

PEG. I have smoked a whole pack at one time.

JEAN. Most people think . . . well, my husband, he thinks I have so much will power. He just doesn't know how many times I've cheated.

PEG. If he knew he'd probably divorce you and join a monastery.

JEAN. No. I'm serious though. See he expects too much from me. I'm not perfect.

PEG. Me either. I'm not even close.

Buzzer sounds.

JEAN. Oops. Gotta go back. I made it through another break without a cigarette. I guess I owe you one.

PEG. Yeah, I do too. Wait a minute. I knew I recognized you. You're Jean on the screen. You look different in person.

JEAN. Thank you. Look, I really have to go. You're . . .

PEG. I'm Peg.

JEAN. Peg.

PEG. Yeah. Catch you later.

JEAN. O.K.

PEG. Bye. Have a nice day.

JEAN. Isn't that funny. *(Back to work)* Screen on. On a personal note: The winner of the Wee Miniature Little Miss Tiny Girl Debut Model Rhododendron Pageant is Miss Velvet Chastity Johnson. Congratulations, Velvet. McMankind loves you.

Item. Repeat. Radiation levels secure in Persian Gulf. Red Zone status A-OK. Screen off. *(Leaves for Condo)* Groceries.

MARGARET. Time. 5:31 P.M.

Jean, on her way to the Condo, walks Downstage and speaks to the audience. The Others silently continue the routine of leaving work. P.C. arrives "home" and finds Jean out talking with the audience. He comes Downstage to her just as She finishes.

JEAN. *(To audience)* Hi. I want to talk again. See, I don't seem to have much to say these days. Seems like all I do is go to work and come home again and go to work again. I do talk to P.C. We watch the news and we talk about politics a little bit. And we talk about what interesting things happened during our day. Cleo and Herb still think I'm doing just fine. It's funny. I wanted a job, but I never thought it would be a career. Anyway, P.C. went somewhere last Sunday and I had a whole afternoon to myself. And I decided that I should do something important with the afternoon so I sat down and I tried to think of important things, but nothing would come into my head. So, I called up a few people on the screen just to talk and all I could do was babble at them. So I sat down and I decided that the fact that I had nothing important to say was important. But I'm not sure why. I'm lonely. That's all.

P.C. Guess who.

JEAN. Hi, honey. Dinner.

MARGARET. Channel 9.

JOHN. Close down all systems through Double X. Close down all systems through Double X.

P.C. Mmmm. This is delicious.

JEAN. Thank you.

MARGARET. News, sports, and weather.

CHRISTINE. Beer.

MARGARET. Good old movie.

P.C. Honey, look. *(Laugh)*

JOHN. Gin and tonic.

CHRISTINE. Book.

JOHN. VCR.

MARGARET. Reruns.

JOHN. *Cannonball Run 15.*
JEAN. Bed.
MARGARET. Johnny Carson.
P.C. Night.
MARGARET. David Letterman. *Nightline.*

All are asleep. Alarm rings. The routine is repeated very fast.

MARGARET. *(Continued) Good Morning, America.*
JEAN. Toothbrush.
P.C. Cigarette.
MARGARET. Coffee.
JOHN. Coffee.
CHRISTINE. Make bed.
MARGARET. Sugar, no cream.
P.C. Coffee.
CHRISTINE. Tea.
JOHN. Danish, microwave.
JEAN. Coffee.
CHRISTINE. Exercise.
MARGARET. Refill.
JEAN. Makeup.
JOHN. Done.
P.C. Shave.
JEAN. Clothes.
JOHN. Eat.
P.C. Aftershave.
JEAN. Here kitty, kitty, kitty.
MARGARET. Traffic.
JEAN. Where's my keys?
P.C. On the desk.
CHRISTINE. Almost late.
P.C. Where's my shirt?
JEAN. On the chair.
P.C. Bye.
JEAN. Bye.
JOHN. Off to work.
JEAN. Subway.
P.C. Vega.

All are at work.

P.C. *(Continued)* Sonitrol off.

JOHN. So, I was telling him the other day what I thought of . . .

JEAN. Screen on. Hi. My name is Jean. Screen off. Break. *(She breaks Downstage to the lounge)*

PEG. Oh boy, could I use a cigarette.

JEAN. You can have one of mine.

PEG. I didn't influence you to start did I?

JEAN. No. They did. Them. In that office. They expect me to sell things. Things that people don't need. Lots of them.

PEG. And the harder you sell, the more I have to work.

JEAN. Why? Where do you work?

PEG. I work down in Double X. I'm part of the uncertain-matter response team.

JEAN. Oh. That sounds fascinating!

PEG. It's a blast.

JEAN. What's uncertain matter?

PEG. Nobody knows.

JEAN. No, really, what is it? Some sort of residue?

PEG. Yeah. From all those gizmos they sell up there. We decontaminate it, we hope, then we spray it and contain what won't evaporate, then we ship it out.

JEAN. Why, I had no idea. And that happens in Double X?

PEG. It's ugly. With a capital Ugly.

JEAN. Well, at least it doesn't talk back to you and say: "Smile Jean" or "Status A-OK" or "We needed that last Thursday." I'm not in shipping. I don't know what we've got. How am I supposed to know?

PEG. You know, Jean, I think we need something stronger than cigarettes. I think you and I need to take a drink.

JEAN. Well, sometimes I do have a cocktail before dinner.

PEG. No, no. I mean right now. During break. Slug 'em back.

JEAN. Oh, Peg.

JOHN. Alter schedule C, D, E and F.

JEAN. See you later. *(She reenters work routine)*

JOHN. C, D, E and F on my mark. Mark.

EUGENE. C, D, E and F altered.

JEAN. *(Answering phone)* Hello? Hello. Yes, trouble in Double X? I'll put you through.

CHRISTINE. Labor unrest update. Inform operatives. Status A-OK.

EUGENE.   Employee pilferage up a staggering 3.8 percent. Watch Constance.

MARGARET.   Information request, Double X. Information request, Double X.

JOHN.   Attention. Attention.

Stage washes in red.

JOHN.   *(Continued)* Red Zone. Red Zone level Double X. Level Double X.

EUGENE.   Red Zone dispatch to Double X. Red Zone to Double X.

JOHN.   Commence cleanup operations level Double X.

JEAN.   Information request. Information request, level Double X.

EUGENE.   Information blackout.

JEAN.   Information request. Chief of Information Sector, level Double X.

EUGENE.   Information blackout.

JOHN.   Security to level Double X.

MARGARET.   Information request.

EUGENE.   Security dispatch to Double X.

Jean tries to go through a door. It is locked.

CHRISTINE.   Don't go in there. This entrance closed.

MARGARET.   Authorized personnel only.

JOHN.   Red Zone update. Red Zone update.

JEAN.   Information request. Information request level Double X.

JOHN.   Yellow vapor. Yellow vapor.

MARGARET.   Yellow vapor Double X.

EUGENE.   Information blackout.

Jean tries another door. It, too, is locked.

CHRISTINE.   Don't go in there. This exit closed.

MARGARET.   Authorized personnel only.

JOHN.   Attention. Attention. Red Zone secure.

Normal light is restored.

JOHN.   *(Continued)* Red Zone secure.

MARGARET.   Everything is under control.

JEAN. Information request. Information request, level Double X.
EUGENE. All levels of McMankind resume operations as normal.
MARGARET. Everything is under control.
EUGENE. Resume operations as normal.
MARGARET. Everything is under control.
JEAN. *(Leaving for Condo)* Groceries.
MARGARET. Time. 5:31 P.M. Close out request.
JOHN. Goodnight Constance. And thank you.
JEAN. *(On phone in Condo)* Hello?
MARGARET. Answer request. Goodnight Rupert.
JEAN. Hello?
MARGARET. And thank you.
JEAN. Hello?
P.C. Vega.
JEAN. Dinner.
P.C. *(As He turns on TV)* Click.
JEAN. Trouble in Double X.
MARGARET. Channel 9.
JOHN. Close down all levels through Double X.
P.C. Hmmmm?
JOHN. Close down all levels through Double X.
JEAN. Red Zone. Peg's level.
MARGARET. News, sports and weather.
P.C. She O.K.?
JEAN. I don't know. *(Trying phone again)* Hello?
MARGARET. Sit-coms.
JEAN. Hello? *(Pause)* Hello?
MARGARET. Good old movie.
JEAN. Clean up.
JOHN. Gin and tonic.
P.C. Goodnight.
JOHN. VCR.
MARGARET. Johnny Carson.
JOHN. *Cannonball Run 17.*
MARGARET. David Letterman. *Nightline.*

All but Jean are asleep. She gets up and goes to phone.

JEAN. Hello? Hello? *(Pause)* Hello?

Jean goes back to bed with her eyes wide open. She falls asleep. Alarm. All go through the morning routine very fast except Jean. She groggily walks through hers.

MARGARET. *Good Morning, America.*
P.C. Cigarette.
MARGARET. Coffee.
JOHN. Coffee.
JEAN. Toothbrush.
CHRISTINE. Make bed.
MARGARET. Sugar, no cream.
P.C. Coffee.
CHRISTINE. Tea.
JOHN. Danish, microwave.
CHRISTINE. Exercise.
MARGARET. Refill.
JOHN. Done.
P.C. Shave.
JEAN. Clothes.
JOHN. Eat.
P.C. Aftershave.
MARGARET. Traffic. *(Instead of going to work, She goes Downstage and becomes Peg)*
CHRISTINE. Almost late.
P.C. Where's my shirt?
JEAN. Here kitty, kitty, kitty.
P.C. Bye. Love you.
JOHN. Off to work.
P.C. Vega.
JEAN. Subway. *(Instead of going to work, She takes the subway to Peg's apartment)*
P.C. Sonitrol off.
JOHN. So, I was telling him the other day what I thought of . . .

The Workplace routine continues silently behind Jean and Peg.

JEAN. Why is it so dark in here?
PEG. I don't know. Sunlight depresses me.
JEAN. Have you been at home?
PEG. No, I've been on a vacation. The Bahamas.

JEAN. 'Cause I've been trying to call. I was worried. Were you on Double X yesterday? I heard they had an accident.

PEG. Not an accident. They don't call them accidents.

JEAN. What do they call it then?

PEG. A glitch. A glitch in the system. A wrinkle in the fabric. More like a pick in the polyester. Some uncertain matter reacted in an unknown way and created an enigma.

JEAN. What happened?

PEG. I breathed yellow vapor.

JEAN. What does that do to you?

PEG. Nothing. If you get a shot. So they say.

JEAN. Did they give you a shot?

PEG. Yeah. Some word this long. No vowels.

JEAN. Are you O.K.?

PEG. Yeah. Just take two aspirin, little lady, and a couple of days off and you'll be fine. I'm O.K.

JEAN. I'm sorry. I wanted to make sure you were all right.

PEG. I'm glad you're here. Really. They don't exactly encourage you to talk about it.

JEAN. Well, as long as you're O.K. We don't have to talk about it.

PEG. I'm O.K. I took my aspirin and got my shot.

JEAN. *(Turns to the audience)* I went out to Peg's last night. We drank Scotch and she took some of those pain pills that went right to her head and she started crying and hurting real bad. Those pills never help. I don't know why she even bothers to take them. I rubbed all over her body because I didn't know what else would help. She told me that she probably created the pain herself because she kept too much anger inside all these years. I stayed up all night with her. She slept after she got drunk enough. *(She returns to Peg)* Now, if it was dangerous they'd tell you.

PEG. I don't know that. There was this guy a couple of weeks ago and he caused a Red Zone alert. We never heard if something leaked or exploded or what, but he was back at work a few days later. "Hi. How are you doing. Everything's fine." Then he got transferred up to C level and he quit hanging out at the snack bar. Then I heard he got sent to Nashville.

JEAN. Why? What's in Nashville?

PEG. That's where they bury uncertain matter.

JEAN. That's one guy. That doesn't mean anything. If it was serious, they'd tell you.

PEG. They, they, they, they, they. The big sacred They. Jean, they lie to you all the time.

JEAN. Why, they've never lied to me.

PEG. They told you that you looked good in that wig, didn't they?

JEAN. Why . . .

PEG. I rest my case. Ah. I'm getting my sense of humor back. I'm glad you came over. Why don't you stay for dinner?

JEAN. O.K.

PEG. And a drink. I could use a drink. Could you use a drink?

JEAN. Yeah?

PEG. Let's have a drink.

JEAN. O.K.

PEG. O.K.

Christine, John and Eugene continue the Workplace routine in silence for a moment.

JOHN. Goodnight Constance.

Jean and Peg have been drinking.

JEAN. You know they sent me to school. Taught me how to walk.

PEG. Jean, I really hate to break this to you, but I learned how to walk when I was this high.

JEAN. No! No, in these things. *(Holds up shoe)* In these.

PEG. Oh, the circus stilts. I can't believe you put up with those.

JEAN. I'm such a wimp.

PEG. Wiggle your fanny, Jean. More to the left.

JEAN. That's not funny.

PEG. More to the right. I'd like to see Herb in a pair of these.

JEAN. "Oh, Madge, how do you girls do it? You are such acrobats."

PEG. He wouldn't wear them. Men never have to wear the stupid shit. Like hose.

JEAN. Louis the Fourteenth.

PEG. Like girdles. Do women still wear girdles?

JEAN. My mother does.

PEG. Madge does. That tight ass.

JEAN. Does she?

PEG. Jean, grow up. I bet you sell a million of them.

JEAN. Yep.

PEG. And then there's makeup.

JEAN. Louis the Fourteenth again.

PEG. Jean, I'm not talking about fashion, I'm talking about pain. Louis the Fourteenth didn't have to walk around in these spikes. They are instruments of torture. We just wear them because they make our butts stick out and then get mad because men gawk at us.

JEAN. Wait a minute. What do you mean we'll wear anything.

PEG. Easy, Jean, I was being sarcastic. But, look at you. Look at that dress. That dress makes your butt stick out.

JEAN. So that gives some man the right to pinch my ass?

PEG. Nooo. They dress me up like an escapee from the loony bin and men still gawk at my ass.

JEAN. I wonder why they do that.

PEG. They're assholes.

JEAN. Nope. You know what I think. I think they don't like us.

PEG. All of them?

JEAN. Most of them.

PEG. Does P.C. like you?

JEAN. P.C. loves me.

PEG. Without the wig and the Louis the Fourteenth pantyhose?

JEAN. I don't know.

PEG. Jean, has P.C. ever seen you without all that crap?

JEAN. Uh-huh. He likes it better on.

PEG. Sometimes I have to get down to me. I mean, I'm this bottom layer, I'm naked. I don't mean I want people to see me naked, I just mean . . . I don't know what I mean.

JEAN. You know, I look better naked than with clothes on. It's true. I look in the mirror and my body looks better with no clothes on.

PEG. Who thought of wearing clothes anyway?

JEAN. Some Eskimo.

PEG. Not to keep the cold out. Fashion clothes. Who was it said wear a bra so your boobies won't bounce?

JEAN. I don't know. I don't even have any. McMankind gave me new ones. They saw that I had no tits so they slapped some on me. And then they saw that it was good.

PEG. They saw it, all right. You are the talk of the screen. McMankind said: Hmm. I like big tits. And lo, big tits appeared on the screen.

JEAN. And the morning and the evening were the first day.

PEG. Well, God created us in his image. Maybe God has big tits.

JEAN. No, just enough to fill a champagne glass.

They laugh. Jean turns to the audience.

JEAN. *(Continued)* I don't have the patience that I used to have. It seems like I get angry sometimes for nothing. I've taken to blaming it on blood, and it does seem like the week before I bleed there's nothing that can make me happy. P.C. always gets the worst of it. He does real good staying out of my way when I get cranky, but I need to find out where it's coming from so I can stop all this silliness. You see, I know it's not blood. I've had a deep-down anger ever since I started this job. Not at P.C. No, he's so good I really couldn't be angry at him. Angry at the world. I don't know. *(Back to Peg)* Wait a minute. . . . There were WHAT?

PEG. There were women. . . . There were Goddesses, they are in the history books. You have to kind of dig for it.

JEAN. I know all about them Greeks. I read about that stuff.

PEG. No, that's Gods and Goddesses. Before that people just worshipped Goddesses.

JEAN. What, you mean they prayed to women?

PEG. Not just prayed to them. Their whole society was focused on the female.

JEAN. Big deal. So is ours. Eighty percent of the products I sell are for women.

The Condo (John, Christine and Eugene) wakes up behind Jean and Peg. It is morning.

PEG. Different, different. All of the big shots, the everybodies, the Thomas Jefferson types were women. The poets, the statesmen, the athletes. It's so opposite with us. This is how it is now. Name three powerful women. *(A pause)* Thomas Jefferson. Thomas Aquinas. Thomas Paine. Tom Sawyer. Tom Thumb.

JEAN. But those are men.

PEG. Napoleon, Caesar, Shakespeare . . .

JEAN. Uh. Eleanor Roosevelt.

PEG. Freud, Ronald Reagan, Ronald McDonald . . .

JEAN. Harriet Tubman.

PEG. Walter Cronkite, Dan Rather, Boris Karloff . . .

JEAN. What's her name . . .

PEG. Winston Churchill, Henry Ford, Jerry Falwell . . .

JEAN. Golda Meir.

PEG. Mr. Rogers, Mr. Magoo, Mr. Ed . . .

JEAN. Miss Piggy!

PEG. Al Capone, Matthew, Mark, Luke, John, Paul, George, Ringo . . .

JEAN. Ah . . . the Virgin Mary.

PEG. Doc Watson, Doc Holiday, Gandhi, God.

JEAN. God?

CHRISTINE. Once her ancestors worshipped Isis and Hathor and the Goddess whose name shall not be spoken.

PEG. God's a biggie.

JOHN. Hecate.

EUGENE. Tiamat.

JEAN. Why should God be a man?

CHRISTINE. Kali.

EUGENE. Mami.

JOHN. Inanna.

JEAN. I don't want to go to work. *(She struggles with her shoes and begins to work)* Screen on.

MARGARET. Time. 9:31 A.M.

JEAN. Why do I feel overworked? *(She stands looking at screen)*

EUGENE. Never think, Jean. Go with your assets.

CHRISTINE. It is in your nature to be needed.

JEAN. Screen off.

> *From this point on, Jean drops out of the work routine. She moves about the Workspace, unseen and unrecognized by the others, no matter how directly She puts her questions to any one of them. The Other Actors continue their Workspace routines even when the text They speak is not their normal Workspace dialogue.*

JEAN. *(Continued)* How come I never heard about a Goddess before?

JOHN. In the presence of God and these witnesses.

CHRISTINE. His knowledge is your knowledge.

MARGARET. His happiness is your happiness.

JEAN. Do a lot of people know about that?

EUGENE. And God made man a helpmate.

JEAN. Why are women supposed to be weak?

JOHN. Yellow vapor alert.

EUGENE. What a whore.

CHRISTINE. Without him you are not.

MARGARET. You need to be more delicate. Think lady.

JEAN. Why do I feel so powerless?

CHRISTINE. You are the empty vessel.

EUGENE. Information blackout. Information blackout.

JEAN. Why don't they talk about it in the history books?

MARGARET. Everything is under control.

JEAN. Does no one think it's important?

JOHN. So, primitive legend conceived of the man in the moon as a dominant male.

JEAN. Are all our images male?

MARGARET. I've seen God, and comrades, she's black.

JEAN. Don't we have any female images?

MARGARET. Everything is under control.

JEAN. Who do I look to as a model?

CHRISTINE. I don't want to get married when I grow up, I want to be somebody.

MARGARET. Everything is under control.

JEAN. Do people look at me on the screen and try to be like me?

CHRISTINE. She looks cheap.

EUGENE. Well, at least she has a chin, Cleo. We have something to go on.

MARGARET. Under control.

JEAN. Why do I wear this stupid wig anyway? *(She throws it off)* Why do I have to wear uncomfortable clothes to work? *(She takes off her shoes)*

CHRISTINE. We'll have to make a few improvements.

EUGENE. We're talking major overhaul.

JEAN. Why don't I have control over my own body?

JOHN. Defense spending equals a thousand dollars per second since Jesus was born.

JEAN. Why can't I go out alone at night?

EUGENE. Twenty-five percent of the men interviewed said they would rape a woman . . .

MARGARET. Everything is under control.

JEAN. Why do I see women in chains on the newsstand?

EUGENE. . . . if they could get away with it.

CHRISTINE. Thirteen million barrels of oil used in California in one day.

JEAN. How come I can't have control over my own body?

JOHN. Her labor married to his value.

JEAN. Nobody ever taught me to question what was taught.

MARGARET. Everything is under control.

JEAN. Why do I wear this stupid dress? *(She removes it)*

EUGENE. When you're the only woman with two men, you can't help but get attention.

JOHN. Her labor married to his value.

MARGARET. Everything is under control.

CHRISTINE. I'll have what you're having. *(Laugh)*

JEAN. How can I get back some of my own power?

EUGENE. The material easily shaped. Easily used.

JEAN. Do I have to give up something to get it?

EUGENE. Mutable.

JEAN. Why am I ashamed of my own body?

EUGENE. I shall wear you for my crown.

JEAN. Why are women raped?

MARGARET. Everything is under control.

The Workplace routine, which has continued unabated to this point, clicks to a termination with the Actors at a neutral rest, together in a group, separate from Jean, waiting without expectation.

JEAN. How can you change any of that? Where in the world do you start? *(She removes her makeup in a long silence)*

PEG. *(Materializing out of the group and moving towards Jean)* Jean?

JEAN. Peg! Peg, I can't stop thinking about what we were talking about the other day. . . .

PEG. Oh, I was kidding about the wig. . . .

JEAN. No, I'm serious. I think I need to go and sit and look at the moon for a long time.

PEG. I think you'll like what you find.

Jean and Peg embrace.

JEAN. *(Speaking to the audience from the embrace)* All my life I was
told about God the father. And I always carried an image of
a grandfather-like man with the flowing beard, and whenever I would look into the sky I would see that image in my
mind. I was taught that Eve was weak. When I was a child I
was told to look up to my father and respect him for the
distance that he kept. I was told to be nice to men because
they will hire you and if you are lucky they will marry you.
I was taught to compete with other women for a man's
attention. I was taught not to trust another woman. I was
taught that blood was shameful, smelly, dirty, and not to be
talked about. I was taught to be pretty and I was taught to
say feminine things. I was taught that women were to be all
things to all people and they weren't supposed to complain
or be angry. And I saw pictures of women looking out of
magazines, and they taught me that I was an actor and if I
played the role I would go far. I was taught that power comes
from above and not from within myself. . . . And if I look
around me . . . and I start to see with new eyes . . . I begin
to see that these things that I was taught are not true. That
I have lived a life based on facts that are not true. And I
don't know what to do about it. I'm lost because all frames
of reference are gone and I have no images to hold onto.
And I get frightened because no one I see on the street
seems to know that there is something drastically wrong. I
want to grab someone by the face and scream at them that
I am important. And Peg is important. And all the silent
women in all the dusty corners of McMankind are important
and they have their own power. And we've all been duped
and we don't even know it.

*During Jean's speech Peg and Christine have changed places.
Christine becomes the Snake. John, Margaret and Eugene speak
the following lines from a stationary position Upstage, making a
collage of stories, words and sounds to which Jean and the Snake
dance. The dance is a progression, reflecting Jean's awareness of
the Snake and her elusive search for contact with the Snake.
Each time contact is made Jean and the Snake rejoice, their
laughter punctuating the collage.*

SNAKE. Snake is your soul. Snake is your intuition.

JOHN. Layer

EUGENE. On layer

MARGARET. Of rock.

JOHN. A cavity holds

EUGENE. The full moon.

JOHN. Snake is your soul.

MARGARET. Snake is your intuition.

EUGENE. River

MARGARET. River

EUGENE, MARGARET AND JOHN. River river river river river river

MARGARET. Passes over moss

JOHN. Into sudden

EUGENE. Darkness.

JOHN. Within the cave

MARGARET. Moist odor

EUGENE. Of a forgotten ritual.

JOHN. My great-great-great-great-grandmother stayed on the farm while the men went off to fight for the South. They had one milk cow, and the Union soldiers kept trying to steal it. She kept running them off. At night when she went to bed, she tied one end of the rope to the cow and the other end to her ankle. If the cow moved, she woke up.

MARGARET. I had an aunt. She was a real big, real strong woman. My mother said she looked like an Indian. Dark and proud. She didn't get married until she was nearly fifty years old. She used to travel around the country with a black woman at a time when black and white women didn't travel together. Her name was Dot. Aunt Dot. She died last year from breathing asbestos when she worked in a ship factory during World War II.

JOHN. My grandmother worked at Oak Ridge. She helped build the atomic bomb. Of course, she didn't know that. They didn't tell them what they were working on. She was a chemist and she worked with all kinds of different compounds. She spilled some once, and she has a scar that looks like a dinosaur on her forearm.

The collage puts the Storytellers in motion. They travel across the stage. Jean and the Snake, dancing together, join them.

JEAN. My grandmother—Inanna was the Goddess of rage—was a teller of stories and a healer and a dancer. She danced in her garden, under the moon. . . .

The dance becomes a chanted ritual of sound and movement, celebrating the moon and the Goddess. The Actors' bodies are united, lifting Jean into their collective protection, pulsing. She emerges in a visual echo of birth. She sits for a moment in silence. P.C. materializes and breaks the silence.

P.C. Jean? Jean, where have you been?

Jean thinks a moment, laughs, looks at P.C., looks at Snake. The Snake and Jean exchange a moment. She thinks again and turns to P.C.

JEAN. Well. . . .

Blackout.

don baker and dudley cocke

red fox/second hangin'

artists' statement

I am a native of far southwest Virginia, a peculiar place. I have always been fascinated by the politics of ambivalence and the recurring themes evident in our struggles to merge our communal family and individual selves. To study those struggles, which happen in the neck of the woods that I was given, seems to me a reasonable task and one to which I might be able to offer at least a peculiar perspective and voice.

about the theater

Roadside Theater began in 1975 with the challenge to find a form and dramatic content that made sense to the rural people who live around the theater's home in the Appalachian Mountains of eastern Kentucky, southern West Virginia, upper east Tennessee, and southwest Virginia, a people for whom there was no written body of dramatic literature or tradition of attending the theater. Roadside's members, all natives of the region, called on their heritage of storytelling, oral history, and the drama of indigenous church services to develop a theatrical form, which combines a natural storytelling style with acting and music. *Smithsonian Magazine* has described this content and style as "dramaturgy with a difference; a hybrid form of play-acting as organic to this hardbitten coal country as the Cumberland walnut, an Appalachian oral history carefully crafted into down-home docudrama."

Roadside views its efforts as an imaginative dialogue with its culture, a dialogue that includes the past, present, and future. The theater wants to vitalize its indigenous theatrical traditions for another generation of Appalachian people—as this vitality was given to it as a gift by the people who are its members' forbearers. This passing along is important because it helps the region maintain a critical measure of self-definition. This purpose challenges Roadside to find deeper and more complex connections to its history while pushing the theater to meet the considerable challenges of the present and the foreseeable future. Theater is a wonderful medium for this exchange, because it is a communal event. Roadside's theater includes the audience as part of the show; there is no fourth wall, dense sets or effects. The actors and audience are free to improvise within the text and the moment.

production history

Red Fox/Second Hangin' premiered in Whitesburg, Kentucky in 1976, toured throughout the Appalachian Mountains where it was often performed in community centers, churches, and in a portable tent, was performed off-Broadway in New York City at Theatre for the New City in 1977 and the Manhattan Theatre Club in 1978, and toured regionally and nationally until 1988.

stage

Upstage a 8' x 11' screen for projected images. A straightback chair, wooden stool, small table or box for water pitcher and three glasses.

cast

3 Storytellers. Each is physically and temperamentally different. All three are natives of the Cumberland Mountains.

place and time

Here and now.

A series of 24 introductory slides. They are copies of old photographs from Wise County, Virginia and Letcher County, Kentucky, 1885–1895. The photographs were researched and collected with the assistance of the Southwest Virginia Historical Museum, Big Stone Gap, Virginia; the Alice Lloyd College Photographic Archives, Pippa Passes, Kentucky; and the family collections of many individuals in Wise and Letcher counties.

D. H. (Alone onstage, comments on several of the introductory slides in passing, perhaps asks that one or two be backed up for a closer look)

prologue

D. H. Hello. For those of you who haven't read your programs, we come from the coalfields of Appalachia, the Cumberland Mountains where Virginia backs up on Kentucky. And we've come here to tell you folks a tale. It's a true story about a man who lived down home back in the 1890s, time of the first big coal boom. Kind of a wild, raw story told from court records and 100 years worth of memory. Now that ain't my memory. But in a way it is. And for the three of us, it sort of helps to explain that place where we grew up, live, and work.

You know, old pictures like these are always kind of brown and faded. And sometimes it seems like them old people, theirselves, must have walked around in a brown, faded world, don't it? But when you listen to them talk about the way things used to be; sit back, hear them spin them old yarns, slowly wind them threads out, they'll weave a story for you about a time full of color.

Of all the old people down around home that love telling bits and pieces of this story, I reckon I'd rather listen to an old man from up on Kingdom Come Creek over in Kentucky. (enter Gary Dale) Everybody up Kingdom Come Creek called him Pap, and to tell you our story, we've got to tell you a little bit about Pap and his time . . .

act 1

Slide: family on porch of log cabin

GARY DALE. Pap, we'd go to his house, and he'd sit by the fire and tell us things.

D. H. He'd tell us how in his family they was eight of them.

GARY DALE. Then he'd stop, study a minute, mumble,

D. H. *(As Pap)* "No, there was two boys and, le's see, seven girls, I believe."

GARY DALE. And then he'd count them off on his fingers.

D. H. And he'd tell how his granddaddy had twelve and raised them til they's all growed.

GARY DALE. And ol' Gid Isom, they was fourteen in their family,

D. H. and twelve in ol' Doc Cornett's family.

GARY DALE. Bad Henry Adams, why he had 23 younguns.

D. H. And folks plumb give up trying to count how many Devil John Wright had.

GARY DALE. People used to raise big families back then, and, when they'd go to the field to go a-workin',

TOGETHER. they could flat do some work.

GARY DALE. Said people was friendly back then, and everybody seemed like they enjoyed theirselves more than what they do today.

D. H. That's 'cause they had time to stop with one another.

GARY DALE. Didn't have to punch no time clock, nor have no hired work.

D. H. They'd just make their crop, you know. They'd go visit one another on weekends, stay a night or two. Back then people had plenty of beds. Maybe just one or two big rooms. But they'd be 4 or 5 beds in every room. Cook, eat, sleep all in one room. Back then, they'd have 'em big get-togethers

GARY DALE. and they'd have more fun a-workin'.

D. H. They'd hunt for them ole stewballs at corn shuckin's, and at them log rollin's the corn whiskey

GARY DALE.   and apple brandy

D. H.   made
the work go

TOGETHER.   awful good.

D. H.   And them big stout men would get to trying to out do
one another,

GARY DALE.   to see who could carry the heaviest load,

D. H.   til
pretty soon

TOGETHER.   all the work was done.

D. H.   Yessir, now at a-workin' everybody would gather in;

GARY DALE.   the
women folk would work about twice as hard as the men,
gather in a bunch of 'em and cook a big dinner,

D. H.   and
everybody'd eat'

GARY DALE.   and then they'd start a-passin' that jug of
stimulants around again.

D. H.   Then like as not they'd have 'em a wrasslin' match,

GARY DALE.   and
somebody would git a little tipsy and drag an ole banjer out
of the corner and start a-pickin' on it

D. H.   and then they would
light the pine knots what they used for lamps,

GARY DALE.   and they'd
be dancin',

D. H.   and singin'

TOGETHER.   and carryin' on

D. H.   'til finally they'd get
tired

GARY DALE.   and go on home to maybe do the same thing the
next day at somebody else's little ole log house.

D. H.   All you'd see nearly, was log houses.

GARY DALE.   Ever now and then you'd see one of them houses
with plank boards on the side of it, but they just wadn't many
saw mills back then.

D. H.   They just flat laid the logs on you know.

GARY DALE.   Couldn't hardly buy no nails.

D. H.   What nails they was, was cut nails, they called 'em.

GARY DALE. Now cut nails, you hit one of them little boogers, and it would just go a-zingin' through the air

TOGETHER. like a bat-outa-hell.

GARY DALE. And you had to be awful careful of them cut nails, or they'd flail off in your eyeball.

D. H. My daddy, why he wouldn't hammer no cut nail so long as he lived, said,

GARY DALE. *(As daddy)* "The woods is full of them one-eyed fellers, and I ain't got no intention to jine 'em."

D. H. Hit was a sight how many they was with only one eye.

GARY DALE. Sight, wadn't it.

D.H. And, you know, ever' one I'd see when I's little, well, I got to a-saying, "Cut eye one nail, ole cut nail one eye," and one time they's this one-eyed man come up to the house to see Daddy bout somethin or nother.

GARY DALE. One-eyed Doc Mullins, was his name.

D. H. Yeh, and I's inside, and I got to singin' that over and over to myself, you know, the way a child will.

GARY DALE. *(Sings as child)* "Cut eye one nail, cut nail one eye."

D. H. *(Referring to Gary Dale)* Sorta like that.

Pretty soon I musta got to a-singin' it out loud without realizin' it. 'Cause one-eyed Doc left, and after a bit Daddy he come in off the porch with a big stick in his hand *(As child)* yanked me up and looked me right square in the eye, says,

GARY DALE. *(As daddy)* "Don't you never . . . what time you live and breathe, don't you never ever let me hear you make fun of nobody like that again."

D. H. And then he lit into me, and with me a'hollerin' *(As child)* "I never meant to, Daddy!" ever breath, he flailed the living daylights out of me. Law, I thought I's awful ill-treated to a-got that whuppin' and I pouted for a solid week.

GARY DALE. Bet you never did much talk to yourself after that, did you?

D. H. *(Derisively to Gary Dale)* No, nor never made fun of nobody less fortunate than me neither.

Slide: 40 children in front of a log school house

GARY DALE. Pap taught school nine year.

D. H. Taught for $26 a month;

GARY DALE.   had to furnish his own bucket,

D. H. his own dipper,

GARY DALE.   broom,

D. H.   coal,

GARY DALE.   all that on $26 a month.

D. H. *(As pap)* "Yeh, I worked hard,"

GARY DALE. Pap'd say,

D. H.   "and hit weren't a case of work or starve. Honey, hit was work and starve."

GARY DALE. Pap got tired of teaching school, decided to go get him a honest job. So he went to work in one of them stave mills where they made wood barrels that they put whiskey in. Pap was a timber cutter.

D. H. Used to be all sorts of timber back down home like what they ain't now.

GARY DALE. Virgin timber.

D. H. Why, in them days hit weren't nothing to see a poplar tree six ner eight foot through and straight as a arrow

TOGETHER.   for 200 foot or more.

D. H. They had to use sometimes six, eight, maybe even ten yoke of oxen to snake them logs out of there.

GARY DALE. Hit was a sight to see twelve, sixteen or twenty of them big ole oxen hitched to a log that big around

D. H.   with a man a-crackin' one of them big ole long ox whips over their heads.

GARY DALE. *(As driver)* When that whip would come down, you could see the fur fly!

D. H. *(As driver)* Just as soon as that driver man started to whirling that whip

GARY DALE.   them oxen

D. H.   Would start to shake their heads,

GARY DALE. *(As ox)*   bow over,

TOGETHER. *(As Oxen)*   twist and squirm,

GARY DALE.   and them yokes would start to creak . . . *Hoyt "moos" from offstage (maybe sitting among the audience)*

D.H. *(To Hoyt)* Thank you, Hoyt.
. . . and them logs
would start to move.
GARY DALE. Yessir, now they had to work hard a-cuttin' that
timber and training them actors to imitate them oxen,
D. H.   and
they still didn't have much money.
GARY DALE. Why, in them days if a man made $1,000 he's a
wheel-hoss,
D. H.   cause it was so hard to get, ya know,
GARY DALE.   and if you's
to see a feller go by in a buggy *(both D. H. and Gary Dale see
man in buggy)* you'd say, "Well, looky yonder, there goes a
rich man."
D. H. Yeh, but now I'll just tell you,
GARY DALE.   for all that,
D. H.   I'd ruther be
back there.
GARY DALE. I reckon I heard Pap say it at least a thousand times,
D. II. *(As Pap)* "Can't be modren, hit costes too much."

Slide: Cumberland Mountain

HOYT. Yeah, Pap, bless his heart, he could tell all kinds of tales
like that, 'bout old times and the way people used to do, if
you could ever get him started. If you could get him started,
he almost always winded up talkin' 'bout a feller by the name
of Doc Taylor
D. H. The Red Fox.
HOYT. Now, if you know much about a red fox, you know he's
a slippery feller. Past master at throwing off the trackers.
Why, he'll double back, sidetrack, run along fence tops,
through creeks, skim over thin ice. You know those ole
snake-rail fences like they used to have, an ole red fox will
just walk along the top of 'em.
    One time when Pap was a boy, the foxes around home got
to stealing chickens so bad that they got up a big posse of
over a hundred men to set out a-scouring the hills, huntin'
fer them ole red-coated chicken thieves. Well sir, accordin'
to Pap, two men got shot up real bad in that hunt,

D. H.   twelve
hounds kilt dead as a door nail.

HOYT. There wadn't nary a fox caught. But now, they said that
some of them men had tracked this big ol' daddy fox right
up to this woman's house. Lost track and had finally give up
and gone on. Directly, that woman went to do her bakin'.
When she opened the oven door *(Gary Dale screams)* . . . that
fox jumped outta there, scared her so bad, she had to put
off her bakin' 'til the next day.

D. H. On top of that, her bread fell.

GARY DALE. Pap remembers the first time he ever seed Doc
Taylor, the Red Fox. He was just a boy an' one mornin' his
mommy and his sister was down at the creek a-battlin' their
clothes.

D. H. Used to, you had to battle your clothes, they'd get so
smelly and rank, nearly knock you down.

GARY DALE. Anyhow, Pap's mommy, she went on back to the
house to fix the noon meal

HOYT.   and left his little sister at the
creek

GARY DALE & HOYT. to finish up the wash.

D. H. His sister, *(As girl batting clothes)* she washed along for a
while, and directly she happened to look up *(Startled)* . . .
and seen a man a standin' by the thicket across the creek

GARY DALE. a-watchin her.

D. H. *(As girl)* He had long red hair

GARY DALE.   and a big red beard

D. H. *(As girl)*   and a
great big mole on his cheek

GARY DALE.   and in his hand was the biggest
rifle she'd ever seed

D. H. *(As girl)*   and going this-a-way acrosst his chest was
two big belts of bullets, just a-gleamin' in the sun.

GARY DALE. Her mouth dropped open

D. H.*(As girl)*   her eyes popped out

HOYT. and she took off a-runnin' to the house just as fast as she
could go. Ran in the house, slammed the door, and hollered

D. H. *(As girl)* "Mommy! Mommy! There's a man snuck up down
at the creek, Mommy, had long red hair, a big red beard,

Mommy, he had a big gun, it looked like a cannon, Mommy, oh Mommy, he's goin' to kill us!"

GARY DALE. *(As mama)* "Daughter, if you don't stop shakin' like that you're gonna pee in your pants! That's just Old Doc Taylor, honey. He'll be on up to the house d'rectly, to get him sumptin to eat. I hope."

D. H. Sure enough, hit was old Doc.

GARY DALE. And, sure enough, he come up to the house for sumptin to eat.

D. H. And, sure enough,

GARY DALE.   he got it.

HOYT. And her Ma seemed right glad to see him.

GARY DALE. Her and Doc set and talked a long spell about

D. H. & GARY DALE.   this and that and the other.

HOYT. Pap's little sister, she got plumb struck on Ole Doc long afore he left.

D. H. *(As girl)* Oh, she thought he had the gentlest voice she'd ever heared and the most fascinatin' way of talkin'

HOYT.   and after he left that day, she started in a-wishin'

D. H. *(As girl)*   "Hope he comes back tomorry."

GARY DALE. *(As young pap)* "Nah,nah,nah,nah, nah,nah, Sissie's got a sweetheart."

D. H. *(As girl with fist)* "You shut up!"

Now, that's the way hit was with ole Doc Taylor.

GARY DALE. The women folk would rather listen to Doc Taylor talk about the spirits as to eat gingerbread come election time.

HOYT. *(Charming woman in audience)* Seems like he could just cast a spell over 'em—or somethin' like that, anyways.

GARY DALE. *(Joining Hoyt)* He was a woman's man, now!

D. H. & HOYT. Lord, was he ever.

GARY DALE. An' he done some spell casting all right.

D. H. He's the very one all the women all called on when it came to birthin' babies.

HOYT. Just couldn't be beat at birthin' babies and a-curin' the flux.

D. H.   *(Holding his behind)* Oh God, the flux.

GARY DALE.   Hit's a deadly disease of the bowels;

D. H.   starvation
dysentery's what it was. Killed people by the dozens back
here in these mountains when it was so bad.

GARY DALE.   Pap used to say the flux reached into the best and
finest houses around there. And once you got the flux, you
better learn to live with the flux 'cause weren't nothin' you
could do about the flux.

D. H.   Pap also said Doc Taylor could do something about the
flux.

GARY DALE.   Doc was a natural at curing folks,

D. H.   always had been.

GARY DALE.   One time, when Doc was a boy, 17 or 18 years old,
before he ever got any formal doctorin' training . . .

D. H.   Now
he did get some formal doctorin' training later on, up there
at Louisville Medical College.

GARY DALE.   . . . he walked out in his backyard there and saw
one of his little brothers a-running along with his nose cut
just about clean off with the sharp edge of a double edged
axe.

D. H.   He took one look at that boy

GARY DALE.   and another look at
that nose

D. H.   went back in the house there, got one of his mama's
silk handkerchiefs, unraveled that handkerchief, made him
a thread,

GARY DALE.   got him a needle, went back out there, and held
that little boy down and sewed that nose back on so good

D. H.   after it healed, they said you had to look twice to see airy
a sign of a scar.

GARY DALE.   Doc Taylor, he couldn't be beat sewin' noses and
birthin' babies.

D. H.   An he hardly ever charged for none of his curin' neither.

GARY DALE.   Just had a special way about him. Like that story
Pap would tell about an ole pack peddlar selling pots and
pans from back of his wagon, got waylaid

D. H.   back in 1890.

HOYT.   *(As pack peddlar)* "I uz coming across the Pine Mountain

and over there at that spring at Scuttle Hole Gap there's a
bunch of rogues ambushed me, shot me up with pistols, cut
me up with knives, and throwed me over in an ole laurel
thicket and left me there for dead. When I come-to, I
thought I shore enough was dead and had gone to heaven—
'cause I wadn't in that laurel thicket no more. An' I could
hear somebody a singin' that sweet old hymn, 'How Firm
the Foundation Ye Saints of the Lord'. . . . Well, I just laid
there a listenin', and a feelin' right proud of myself for
havin' made it up to heaven; and I could hear what sounded
like a rockin' chair a creakin'. I got to lookin' around to see
what heaven looked like (it was a little bit darker up there
than what I had figgered it to be). D'rectly that singin
stopped. The creakin' stopped. A door opened. Somebody
come in. Lit a lamp. And a man come, stood over me, put
his hand on my forehead, and stood there lookin' up,
straight up for, oh, the longest time. And I breathed good.

Well, now the next thing I remember, it was daylight and
I could see I uz in a bed, in a cabin, and a hangin' from
the rafters over me was all sorts a dried plants, herbs and
stuff. An I had about figgered out I hadn't died, much less
gone to heaven, when this feller I had seen standin' over
me come in an asked me how I was. Told me as how he'd
found me there in that laurel thicket and brought me back
to that place. Told me as how I uz going to be all right. That
the Lord had told him so. Now that feller fed me, doctored
me, and uz right good to me. It uz old Doc Taylor, you know.
When I got my strength back, I'd join him out on the porch
of a evenin'. He'd sing to me and talk to me. I asked him
what he'd used to cure me. An he told me he used the
spirits. Said he give me a little rattle snake meat and some
jillica to he'p them spirits along a bit, but how hit was the
Holy Spirits what he used to do the curin'. He'd read to me
from out of the Bible and this big book on religion by a
feller named Swedenburg. Most of the words now uz too big
for me to understand, but ole Doc could whittle em down.
He told how the Lord's holy angels could appear to me, talk
to me, and he'p me, if I'd let em. An' you know, before I'd
left that cabin, I had seed the Lord's angels. You fellers may
think I'm crazy, but them old spirits have appeared to me

time and time again. An I've allus thanked that Red Fox, old Doc Taylor, for a brangin' em to me."

D. H. Doc sure did have a way of preachin' about the spirits all right. He ought to of had a way, cause he was a preacher. Been a preacher ever since the Civil War. Like everybody else, Doc, he j'ined up. But it weren't long before he seed what was going on and quit, and set into preachin' that this war was too ungodly a business for a man to be a-takin' a part in.

Slide: two men, possibly an uncle and nephew, side by side with firearms

GARY DALE. They's alot of folks around home what didn't think that war's too ungodly a business.

HOYT. Now back during the Civil War around home folks didn't go off so much and jine up with the big armies.

GARY DALE. Most of the fightin' here was little gangs of men from up one holler, or down one creek

HOYT.   fightin' another little gang of men from up another holler or down another creek.

GARY DALE. They wadn't fightin' some enemy soldier so much as they was a-fightin' and killin'

GARY DALE. & HOYT.   their neighbors.

GARY DALE. There's an awful lot of hate built up with that war. An' after the war, people around home just had to settle down with that hate and not do nothin' about it and look a man you hated right square in the face every day or so.

HOYT. A man you knowed had kilt your daddy

GARY DALE.   or your brother

HOYT. or your son.

D. H. All them ole feuds you heared about, the Hatfields and McCoys, Frenches and Eversoles, old Clabe Jones War, and the like, they all come about on account of these here old Civil War grudges.

GARY DALE. Now, durin the war the bloodiest and

D. H. & GARY DALE.   **nastiest**

GARY DALE.   of

the fightin' around home all happened right there below

Pound Gap, south of the Cumberland Mountain and right
there was bottled up some of the worst

D. H. & GARY DALE. **hate**

GARY DALE. ya could ever hope to see.

D. H. Now right there at the foot of the mountain

HOYT. on the
Virginia side,

D. H. there's a little stretch of road

GARY DALE. called the Mud
Hole

D. H. where the road used to go right smack dab through a
long swampy place there

HOYT. fer about half a mile.

D. H. After the war, when the pack peddlers would come through
there with their goods all loaded down on wagons,

HOYT. and
they'd knowed they'd be going through the Mud Hole,

D. H. what
they'd do was get together over there aroun' the Wise Court
House

GARY DALE. ya know, get six or eight wagons together in order
to go through there.

D. H. Well, when they would get to the Mud Hole,

HOYT. they'd take
all the teams loose,

D. H. hitch 'em all together,

TOGETHER. *(Pulling the wagon)* and then pull one wagon
through.

GARY DALE. Then they'd go back,

D. H. hitch up to the next 'un,

TOGETHER. *(Pulling the wagon)* and
pull hit through;

D. H. keep on like that until the very last one was
through,

GARY DALE. and then they'd go on across the mountain . . .

D. H. "See ya Gustav!" . . . and go their own way.

HOYT. You can sure see that the Mud Hole was a natural stop-
pin' place.

GARY DALE. If any of you good folks ever been mired to your
hind-end in mud, you know what we're talkin about.

D. H.   So right there, there got to be a bunch—now, I ain't talkin'
about four, five, six, or seven

GARY DALE.   (he's talkin' about a bunch)

D. H.   of
what they called public houses.

HOYT.   *(As old time preacher)* "What's the world coming to today.
It has got so a man can't go through the Mud Hole without
getting his head cut off or his wagon robbed. Lord . . . they
gamble, sell whiskey, keep loose women, God Almighty!"

D. H., GARY DALE & HOYT.   *(Singing)*
"Don't raise them nicotined stained hands
To the Lord in prayer
Don't try to hide in the closet
'Cause He will find you there
Whiskey, beer, wine, and gin
It's the devil's recipe for sin
Come on down
Come on down
Come on in"

HOYT.   *(As old time preacher)* "There must be 10, 15, 20 . . . too
many of them public houses"

D. H. & GARY DALE.   right there on that half-a-mile
stretch.

D. H.   Now, like I said, right in there was a whole hellava-lota
hate built up. And so what with all that drinkin'

GARY DALE.   an' gamblin'

HOYT.   an carryin' on

D. H. & GARY DALE.   an' all that hatin'

D. H.   they was bound to be
trouble.

GARY DALE.   It got so there's a shoot-out a day in the Mud Hole.

D. H.   Nervous fellers stayed outa' there.

HOYT.   The Mud Hole come to be a rough neighborhood,

D. H.   and
it took a lota liquor

GARY DALE.   an' a lota apple brandy

TOGETHER.   an' a lota
moonshine to satisfy it.

D. H.   I guess there ain't no need in tellin' you folks,

GARY DALE.   (go ahead
and tell 'em anyway.)

D. H.   they's a lota satisfaction

GARY DALE.   (ya know,
money, cash, jingle in your pocket)

D. H.   to be made from shinin' the Mud Hole,

HOYT.   and
there's a lot of men would kill to get that satisfaction

D. H.   and did.

GARY DALE. In 1888, Doc Taylor had took the job as U.S. mar-
shall to try to stop some of that killing, clean up some of
that mess.

HOYT. And right from the first of his marshallin', he started
crossin' some of the baddest of that bad Mud Hole lot.

D. H. The baddest bad man of the mountains was a feller by the
name of

ALL TOGETHER. Bad Talt Hall.

D. H. Now, everybody all around home had heared about bad
Talton Hall. And they's stories as how he'd kilt 99 men
during his career.

GARY DALE. Talt, ya see, got started killin' young. When the Civil
War got started, Talt, he's just a boy 'bout 13 or 14 years
old. The war had been goin on awful hot for a while, and
Talt's daddy had got him the name of

D. H. & GARY DALE.   "Bad" Dave Hall.

GARY DALE. Well now, Talt, he wanted to be like his daddy . . .

HOYT. *(As Talt)* "More n' anything in the world, I wanna be like
my Daddy!"

GARY DALE. . . . an' he was jest a itchin' to get him a bad name

HOYT. *(As Talt)* "jest like my Daddy."

D. H. Talt had fell in with a gang of full growed men that was
fightin' on the Confederate side . . .

HOYT. *(As Talt)* "kinda runnin' and hidin' and ambushin' in the
mountains."

D. H. Well, this gang come across one of Talt's uncles

D. H. & GARY DALE. *(As confederate gang)*   who's
a-sidin' with the Yankees.

HOYT. *(As Talt)* "That's Mama's brother, Henry Maggard. You a
Yankee, Uncle Henry?"

GARY DALE. So they decided they's goin' to

D. H. & GARY DALE. *(As gang)*   kill Henry Maggard.

HOYT. *(As Talt)* "Oh, let me do it. Let me shoot my uncle."

GARY DALE. Well, knowin' as how Talt had been a-hankerin' to get him a bad name, they talked it over and decided

D. H. *(As gang member)* "shore, why not!"

D. H. & GARY DALE. *(As gang)* "Let the boy do the killing!"

D. H. *(Holding Gary Dale)* So they held Uncle Henry,

HOYT. *(As Talt getting ready to shoot)*   and Talt, he up with his hog rifle . . .

D. H.   "Hurry up, boy! We ain't got all day!"

HOYT. . . . and blowed his head off!

D. H. He'd been jest a-itchin' to kill him a man

GARY DALE.   and after that he jumped up on a ole log a-layin' there *(Hoyt stands on stool)*

D. H. and flapped his arms

D. H. & GARY DALE.   and crowed like a banty rooster.

HOYT. *(As Talt)* "From now on they'll call me Bad Talt Hall! Ain't nobody goin' to call me boy agin."

GARY DALE. After that's when Talt fell in with what was to become his lifelong buddy

D. H. & GARY DALE.   Devil John Wright.

D. H. *(Posturing as Devil John)* Now, Devil John, he was 19 and something of a soldier,

D. H. & HOYT. *(As bad Talt and Devil John)* and they got along good.

D. H. *(As John)* D'rectly him and Talt was being hunted by a bunch of Yankees.

HOYT. *(As Talt)* "Must be a hundred and fifty of 'em, John! And no tellin' how many blood hounds!"

D. H. *(As John)* Now they knowed it wouldn't be long 'til they'd catch up with em *(While they talk)* . . . so they talked things over and decided

HOYT. *(As Talt)*   to put up a fight

D. H. *(As John)*   and not be nobody's prisoner

D. H. & HOYT. *(As John and Talt)* and sell their life for as much as they could get out of them.

GARY DALE. *(Standing on chair making thunder storm)* Hit had come a hard rain the night before,

D. H. *(As John)*   and when the fight got started

HOYT. *(As Talt)* why, their durn ole guns had gotten soakin' wet and wouldn't shoot . . . "Ain't worth the tits on a boar hog, John!"

D. H. *(As John)* So there wadn't nothin left for them to do

D. H. & HOYT. *(As John and Talt)*   but run *(They run)*

D. H. *(As John)* They hit the brush; John, he got away

HOYT. *(As Gary Dale captures him)*   but Talt, he got hung up in the brush and got captured.

D. H. *(As John)* When John seen they had his buddy he come in the next mornin' and give himself up *(D. H. gives himself up)*

HOYT. "Ho, John."

D. H. "Hello, Talt."

GARY DALE. *(As captain to D. H.)* "Come over here, stupid."

D.H. *(As John)* Who me?

GARY DALE. *(As captain)* Yeh, you!

D. H. *(As John)* As luck would have it, the captain of that posse

D. H. & HOYT. *(As John and Talt)* what took 'em . . .

GARY DALE. *(As captain)*   (That's me.)

D. H. *(As John)* . . . turned out to be another of Talt's uncles

HOYT. *(As Talt)* "on dad-burn Daddy's side."

D. H. *(As John)* He wanted to kill Wright.

GARY DALE. *(As captain)* "I want to kill you."

D. H. *(As John)* "I know."

HOYT. *(As Talt)* "If you kill my buddy, you've got to kill me, too."

D. H. *(As John)* "Yeah!"

HOYT. *(As Talt)* "Shut up, John."

GARY DALE. *(As captain)* "Now you little boys is Rebel soldiers ain't ya?"

D. H. & HOYT. *(As John and Talt)* "Yes sir."

GARY DALE. *(As captain)* "Me, I'm an officer in the Union Army. See them stripes on my shoulder?"

D. H. & HOYT. *(As John and Talt)* "Yes sir!"

GARY DALE. *(As captain)* "I know you boys like to chase them little ole girls up there in them woods and shoot off them little ole guns, don't ya?"

D. H. & HOYT. *(As John and Talt)* "Yes sir."

GARY DALE. *(As captain)* "And you want to keep on doin' that too, just as long as you can, don't ya?"

D. H. & HOYT. *(As John and Talt)* "Yes sir!"

GARY DALE. *(As captain)* "Well, I'll tell you what, if you fellers don't jine up with me in my army, I'll send both of you up to Confederate heaven! Don't make a damn bit o' difference to me."

D. H. *(As John)* So there wasn't nothin' else left for 'em to do but

D. H. & HOYT. *(As John and Talt, lock arms with captain)* to switch sides and jine up with the Yankees.

GARY DALE. *(As captain)* I reckon they didn't much know ner care who ner what they's a-fightin' by this time.

D. H. *(As John)* They's just

D. H. & HOYT. *(As John and Talt, jam elbows into captain's ribs)* into that fightin'!

GARY DALE. So Devil John and Talt made em some real good enemies on both sides of that there war

D. H. & HOYT.   don't ya see.

Slide: Devil John Wright mounted on horseback

GARY DALE. That's a picture of the growed up Devil John Wright.

D. H. The growed up Devil John Wright got to be a rich man in all that feudin', fightin' and commotion after the war. He got to be a land buyer for some of them coal and land companies over in Big Stone Gap. Pretty persuasive feller, if you know what I mean. And Talt, he'd always do John's dirty work. But then John'd always watch out for Talt. Whenever Talt'd get into something too hot, John'd just buy him a train ticket, send him out west somewheres 'til things kinda cooled off.

GARY DALE. One time Talt, he done somethin' or 'nother, and John sent him packin' out west, and he stayed out there for about a year. But he kindly got homesick. Started missing the mountains. Reminded him of his mommy. When he got back, he headed right straight over to Nan Justice's saloon in Norton,

HOYT. *(As Talt)* ordered him up a big drink of moonshine.

GARY DALE. Nan, she sidled over.

D. H. *(As Nan)* "Long time, no see, Big Boy. How things been?"

HOYT. *(As Talt)* "Pretty tough, Nan. Pretty tough. I seen lots of botherment since I left here."

D. H. *(As Nan)* "Reckon ya might stay awhile this time?"

HOYT. *(As Talt, eyeing Nan)* "No, I'm headed for Kentucky . . . but maybe I can stop . . . an' see a couple-a my old friends."

D. H. *(As Nan)* Uh huh!

GARY DALE. Well, they got acquainted with one another all over again.

D. H. Directly one of Talt's ole drinkin' buddies

GARY DALE. *(As drinkin' buddy)* heared he's in town and come a-lookin' for him.

GARY DALE & HOYT. *(As characters)* They tied on a biggun.

D. H. Directly, the sheriff of Norton come in and said he was goin' *(As sheriff)* "to arrest Talt's drinkin' buddy for stealin' a watch."

GARY DALE. *(As buddy)* "Who, me?"

D. H. *(As sheriff)* "Yeah, you!"

GARY DALE. *(As buddy)* "I can't even tell time. What the hell good would a watch do me?"

D. H. *(As sheriff)*"Beats me, buddy, but you're under arrest."

HOYT. Talt Hall shot him. *(He does)*

GARY DALE. *(As buddy)* "Shoot, Talt, you shot the sheriff!"

Sheriff dies elaborately.

GARY DALE. Now, that grossly over acted killin' right there was Talt's mistake. Hit was the last one he did, and it done-him-in.

HOYT. And Pap, he always said that the reason it done-him-in

D. H. *(As Pap)* "was that it put him right square on the wrong side of ole Doc Taylor."

Slide: Hattie Salyers as a young woman

GARY DALE. Now Doc, he had him four children by his legal wife,

HOYT. three girls and then a boy,

GARY DALE. Sylvan,

HOYT. the youngest.

D. H. Doc, he always was partial to Sylvan,

GARY DALE.   would give him just
about anything he wanted.

D. H. Well, when Sylvan up and married a young girl from up
at Wise Courthouse named Hattie Salyers,

HOYT.   Doc just about
busted with pride,

GARY DALE.   'cause, ya see, Hattie was just about the
prettiest and cleverest girl that they ever was around home.

D. H. Doc, he'd go up there and visit with 'em, set and talk fer
hours

HOYT.   with Hattie.

GARY DALE. He thought the world of her.

D. H. Now, what Hattie would talk about,

HOYT.   like as not,

D. H.   was none
other than

TOGETHER.   Bad Talt Hall.

D. H. 'Cause Hattie knowed that Bad Talt had shot and kilt her
uncle in Floyd County, Kentucky in 1885,

GARY DALE.   took his wife,
stole his horse and run off with 'em both.

D. H. Well, when ole Bad Talt up and kilt Hattie's brother-in-law,
who's that p'or sheriff ya just seed die right before your very
eyes, Hattie set in to a-beggin'

D. H. & HOYT. *(On either side, alternating as Hattie)* "Doc, don't
let him get away with killin' another one of my family. He's
kilt my uncle, shot my brother, and he ain't goin' to be
satisfied 'til he's kilt ever last one of us."

GARY DALE. So Doc, he (layed hands on Hattie and cured her
schizophrenia,) took up Talt's trail and tracked him clean
out to Memphis, Tennessee.

HOYT. Doc hadn't been in Memphis long 'fore he had him
together.

Slide: train tracks in the winter

D. H. They brought Talt back on the train Christmas Eve, 1891.
Folks was out singin' Christmas carols.

GARY DALE & HOYT. *(As carolers sing)* "O Come All Ye Faithful"

D. H. When they heared the train pull up, they changed their tune and went to the depot in mobs

HOYT. *(As mob)* trying to get at Talt to lynch him.

GARY DALE. *(As mob)* "String him up!"

D. H. Huh uh! Doc, he'd just stand there, right in front of Talt, that big ole Winchester of his 'un

GARY DALE. *(As Doc)* "jest a darin' any man to take another step."

D. H. They got Talt locked up, locked up in the jail at the Wise Courthouse, and the rumors started a-flyin' around that old Devil John

HOYT. and his gang

D. H. was goin' to come an' bust Talt out that jail,

HOYT. but Doc,

GARY DALE. *(As Doc)* he was determined that Talt was goin' to stand his trial

D. H. & HOYT. And he weren't the only one neither.

Slide: Big Stone Gap city-slickers dressed in regalia

GARY DALE. You see now about that time, there's an awful lot of rich city folks figured that there was alot of money to be made in these mountains,

HOYT. and they just figured

D. H. & GARY DALE. *(As rich city folks)* they'd be the very ones to make it.

GARY DALE. They knowed for a long time that there was ore and timber and coal back in here, but they hadn't been able to figure out how to get it out.

HOYT. By 1885, they'd about got all the bugs worked outa that little problem

D. H. & GARY DALE. *(As rich city folks)* and was ready to start a-makin' their money.

HOYT. Everybody was expectin' to make' them a king's ransom. Hit was just like the California gold rush.

D. H. Now, they's a little town 25 miles from the Mud Hole called Big Stone Gap,

HOYT. and they's people pourin' into little bitty Big Stone Gap

D. H. & HOYT.   from all over this world.

D. H. *(As a duke)* There's even a duke

GARY DALE. *(As a duchess)*   and a duchess

D. H. & GARY DALE.   from
London, England.

HOYT. Them fellers set about to make little bitty Big Stone Gap

TOGETHER. into the Pittsburgh of the South!

D. H. They's runnin' full page advertisements in the *New York Times*

GARY DALE. *(Reading from paper)* proclaiming as how, "This country has everything to offer to make you a fortune. They have
timber, coal, and iron ore, all in one spot. The natives have
no idea of the money they're sitting on, and there are men
who know how to talk to these natives"

D. H. & HOYT.   like Devil John
Wright

GARY DALE. "and not pay anything for it, either."

D. H. Well, I'll be!

HOYT. Upon my honor!

D. H. Well now, them companies set in to build big factories to
work in

HOYT.   and the owners big palaces to live in

TOGETHER.   right there in
little bitty Big Stone Gap.

HOYT. Oh! They did some fancy livin',

D. H.   had more money than
they knowed what to do with.

GARY DALE. They'd have these little pink tea parties

D. H.   and send
engraved invitations around on little silver trays,

HOYT.   carried
from palace to palace *(Portrays boy carrying tray)*

GARY DALE.   by some little Negro boy that they'd dress up like some Arab shiek

D. H. with a turban on his head.

GARY DALE. Now the only problem was—these fellers was scared
to death to set foot out of Big Stone Gap.

HOYT. Half the time they didn't feel safe outside their own front
doors.

GARY DALE. Seems like the natives,

D. H.   as they called 'em,

GARY DALE.   thought
it was a bushel of fun to come ridin' into town *(Hoyt portrays native, D.H. portrays rich city folk)* down them wood plank sidewalks, reins in their teeth, shootin' their pistols off in the air an a hollerin' and a carryin' on!

Slide: two Mud Hole outlaws shooting, brandishing pistols in the air. Hound with head thrown back, howling

D. H. *(As rich city folk)* This uncivilized behavior didn't set too well with polite society.

GARY DALE. That polite society figured that "the natives" needed to have the fear of God,

D. H.   or rather the fear of law and order,

GARY DALE. struck in to 'em, or their businesses at the Gap would never amount to a hill of beans.

HOYT. *(With Gary Dale as guard, marching)* So they got 'em up a little army to protect theirselves, and their businesses, and they called it the Home Guard.

GARY DALE. Hut, two, three, four.

Slide: the Home Guard at attention

D. H. Now, there had never been a hangin' in Wise County. Never! But this here Home Guard decided that now, by George, was as good a time as any to have one.

GARY DALE. It was a better time than most, seeing as they had the most famous bad man of the mountains layin' in the jail

D. H. & GARY DALE. Ole Bad Talt Hall!

D. H. And what with all them rumors about Devil John Wright and his gang a-bustin' Talt out of jail, that Guard picked up, transported theirselves the 12 miles to the Wise Courthouse, rigged 'em up a fort around the courthouse and jail, and took up a 24 hour watch.

GARY DALE. They kept so many chains on poor ole Talt,

D. H. around his feet,

HOYT.   on his arms an hands,

GARY DALE.   around his neck

D. H. said it would have took a mule to have moved him.

HOYT. *(As Talt)* A big mule at that.

D. H. An', they got him tried

HOYT.   an' they got him convicted

GARY DALE.   and
that new judge done something that no local judge had ever
done before. He sentenced Talt to hang.

D. H. Right after the sentencing, the Guard put Talt on a train
an shipped him half-way across the state of Virginia to
Lynchburg, for safe keeping 'til the day come for him to
hang.

GARY DALE. Doc, he never took too kindly to all them goings
on down at Big Stone Gap. Didn't care for the idea of having
no Pittsburgh at his back door.

D. H. Doc had a lot more sense than them fancy city fellers give
him credit for.

HOYT. He could see this here boom business wouldn't mean
nothin' no more than the end of a natural way of life.

GARY DALE. Doc give up his marshaling job, 'cause he could see
that this here law an' order thing, the way these fellers had
it figured, weren't going to do no more than exchange one
bunch of rogues for another.

D. H. You'd have the Big Stone Gap bunch

HOYT.   in place of the Mud
Hole bunch,

D. H.   and on top of that, on top of all that, he thought
they's goin' to destroy the mountains.

GARY DALE. He'd seed it all in visions and

D. H. & HOYT.   warned agin it.

Slides: series of 4 slides showing the destruction of the mountains

INTERMISSION

act 2

---

*Film: slide of horses and wagon being led into the barnyard
becomes the first frame of the film
Scene of barnyard and loading a man into a jolt-wagon. It is
period 1890, rural Appalachia. Film is toned deep brown.*

D. H. Layin' there in the wagon is the likeness of an old moonshiner by the name of Bad Iry Mullins. Mean as a striped rattlesnake—didn't care about nothin' nor nobody. Now, besides makin' moonshine hisself, Bad Iry used to run liquor from down in North Carolina–don't ask me why he run all the way down to North Carolina when there's plenty to be made at home, but anyhow, he did–made alota money doing it. One time on a run of liquor down in North Carolina, he got in a fight with the law down there, got shot square through the neck, got paralyzed. Said he couldn't even feed hisself after that, much less walk. But he didn't let that stop him—just took all that money of hissen, hired out his work and his killin' done for him.

Film: wagon and gang head out, cross a wide creek, and start up the mountain.

D. II. They carried him around in the back of an old jolt-wagon. Even though, like I said, he's paralyzed, folks around home was all scared to death of him.

This day right here supposed to be May 14, 1892. Bad Iry and his bunch had gone back over to the old homeplace up on Elkhorn Creek in Kentucky to do some dealings. On Saturday morning long about nine o'clock they left out of there headed back across the mountain to Virginia and the Mud Hole. They's seven of 'em that day. Iry's wife, Lourenzy, riding in the wagon there, was as mean as any man. And it was well knowed that she carried all Iry's money, more than a thousand dollars, hid in a little money purse up and under her top skirt. Bad Iry and a year or so back, maybe 1890, Lourenzy hated Doc Taylor. You see, one time, afore Doc Taylor give up his marshalin' job, Bad Iry and his bunch was coming back from North Carolina with a load of liquor, and they got in a big gun battle with Doc Taylor and some of his deputies—right there on the main street of Wise Courthouse. Said folks was skeedaddling ever which way to get under cover somehow, and one of Iry's men was kilt, two of em was wounded and captured, but ole Iry in the wagon got away. Now after that, wadn't nothing but real bad blood between Iry Mullins and Doc Taylor. Iry commenced offering two, three, four hundred dollar rewards to have Doc Taylor kilt—said Doc Taylor, he was a marked man. Doc, he heared about them rewards, and he let it out to folks if he's ever to get in another row with a wagon, what he'd do was shoot the wagon horses first, then said he'd get *what* was in the wagon. Everybody all around home had been just waiting for a couple of years to see who would git who first.

This day Iry and his bunch crossed the top of the mountain and got just a quarter of a mile down into Virginia:

Film: Iry and his gang are ambushed from rocks above the wagon. The wagon horses are killed first. Then a man and a boy. Two run and get away. Lourenzy and Iry, both wounded, are killed last at very close range.
The last frame of Iry lying dead in the wagon is frozen as a slide

D. H.   They's five of them kilt that day up there on the mountain, and the $1000 Iry's wife carried was stole. Iry's boy, John, he got away, said when the shootin' started, he took off a runnin' and never looked back. They shot his gallouses, his suspenders, in two, but he got away—never seed nothin. Iry's sister, Jane, she got away—said they told her to run—and at first she said she didn't have no idea who them men was—that they's way above the road, down in behind some rocks, and had green veils down over their faces.

But now, in a few days, that woman changed her story complete—said she recognized em. Said it was ole Doc Taylor and them boys he run with. Now, everbody all round knowed that there weren't nothing but real bad blood between Doc Taylor and Iry Mullins. And when folks went up on the mountain that day to get the bodies, they found dead wagon horses. Everybody remembered what Doc had said 'bout the wagon horses. So a lot of folks started layin' the blame on Doc; they got up big rewards for him, big posses set out after him, and Doc, he set into scoutin-out.

They's just all kinds of what they call scoutin' out stories about Doc being able to slip through the wilderness unnatural-like. Somebody would see him at one place this side the mountain, and then . . . before they knowed it he'd be clean across the mountain in another place in no time atall. Just like a fox, he'd slip through here and slip through there, and then directly he'd slip in and light with one of his woman friends, whenever he'd need a little rest.

Slide: house

D. H. *(Continues. Gary Dale enters, sits)* Like the time he come up to the Widder Vanover's place, up there on Elkhorn Creek, to rest hisself and a feller by the name of John Venters, who lived about five miles on down the creek, heard Doc was there *(Hoyt enters)* and come to get him to see his little girl, says

HOYT. *(As Venters, to Gary Dale)* "Doc, my little girl is terrible sick. She's burnin' up with a fever. You come up the house and take a look at her."

D. H. Well, Doc, he knowed Venters was a stiller, and that he run with the Mud Hole bunch, and Devil John Wright's gang too, and he was suspicious.

GARY DALE. *(As Doc)* "Yeah, I'll go directly, but now you'll have to wait for just a little bit. I got some things to attend to here. Just pull ya up a chair."

HOYT. *(As Venters)* "All right,"

D. H.   says Venters,

HOYT. *(As Venters)* "No. No, I'll run on ahead cause I'm awful worried about my little girl, and you come on when you're ready."

D. H. Then he turned and high-tailed it outa there. Doc, he sat there a-studyin' for awhile.

GARY DALE. *(As Doc)* "Well now, they're up to something— they're up to something."

HOYT. *(As Widder Vanover)* "Well, how do you figure that?"

D. H. the Widder Vanover asked him.

GARY DALE. *(As Doc)* "I could tell he's a lyin' about that child bein' sick by the way he carried on—said he didn't have time to wait. If she really was so sick—why, he wouldn't have left this place without me for fear I'd take too long a-comin' or not come at all. I reckon he's got a gang of men a-waitin' by the road to ambush me . . . and I reckon I best be a-goin'."

HOYT. *(As the Widder)* "Oh, you'll not go atall,"

D. H.   said the Widder

HOYT. *(As the Widder)* "Why, they'll kill you shore, just like they
done my poor old husband."

GARY DALE. *(As Doc, petting the Widder)* "Don't you worry your
purty self none, Widder. It'd be a awful shame for them men
to set there all night by the road with nothin' to do. And
maybe as how I'm wrong anyways an' his little girl is sick."

D. H. So Doc, he got up—went out to the wood shed there, built
him a little wheel about the size of a bicycle wheel. Fastened
him a light scantlin' pole about ten foot long to the axle.
Rigged him up a little frame to hold one of them ole walkin'
lanterns, what only shines a light in front of you, you know,
so's you can see to walk at night.

Then he waited 'til it got good and dark, afore the moon
come up, gathered up some of his doctorin' tools, got his
old 45 X 75 Winchester rifle, lit that lantern an hung it on
the frame. Then he took holt of the end of that pole, and,
a-pushin that wheel about ten feet in front of him in the
road, set out for Venter's house.

Now let me tell you, it looked exactly like a man carryin'
that lantern the way Doc had it rigged up there on that
frame. And he'd not got but about two mile down the road
when he come to a real dark place there in the wilderness,
big old beech tree off to one side—laurel thicket all around
the base of it. Well sir, when that wheel got smack-dab-even
with that beech tree, they started shootin, and down went
that lantern. Four men jumped out from the bushes.

D. H. & HOYT. *(As gang jumping from bushes)* "We got you now,
you Old Fox!"

D. H. Doc, he let em have it. That big old Winchester of hisn
was a-shootin' flames this-a-way and that-a-way, and them
men hit the brush.

GARY DALE. *(As Doc)* "I reckon your daughter's over her fever
now!"

D. H.   Doc hollered at em. But now, just to make sure,

HOYT.   or at
least to get a good laugh,

D. H.   said he went on up there anyways.
And, sure enough, that child had broke her fever. Said it
was a holy miracle.

Slide: posse with firearms at train station

HOYT. Doc got tired dodgin', scoutin'-out, he'd 'bout determined that all he wanted to do was to just come in and stand
his trial. But his son, Sylvan, said,

GARY DALE. *(As Sylvan)* "Pa, ya ain't got a snowball's
chance in hell of gettin' tried fair. Lawin' costs alota money
since the Big Stone Gap bunch took over running things,
an' we ain't rich folks, Pa."

GARY DALE. *(As Doc)* "Well, what do you expect me to do?"

D. H. *(As Sylvan)* "I've been workin' me up a little plan here.
What we'll do is we'll get us a big dry goods box and put
you in it. Now don't laugh 'til you heared me out. We'll fix
it up with rations an all, fix a little latch so you can get out
when ya want. Then we'll take it down and put it on a train
like it was going to some of Hattie's people up in Cincinnati.
When that train gets to Bluefield, West Virginia, git outa that
box an' get you on a train headed for Florida. You'll like hit
down there, Pa, hit's warm, green all year around."

GARY DALE. *(As Doc)* "I reckon I might. I've heard a fella can
just walk around an pick them sweet things off'en the trees
all year round down there. *(sarcastically)* Why hit might be
the very thing for this here diabetes condition of mine. Let's
give it a try."

HOYT. So Sylvan, he went out an bought Doc a full new suit of
clothes

D. H.   got a big ole box

HOYT.   an' put Doc in it

D. H.   an' wrote

D. H. & HOYT.   **"To Cincinnati"**

D. H.   on the top, took it down an put it on a train

HOYT. an Doc, he's outa' there.

D. H. But now, as luck would have it,

HOYT.   someone had told the
authorities what was afoot.

D. H. And when Doc climbed outa that box in Bluefield

D. H. & HOYT. there's two detectives

D. H.   standin' there waitin' to
grab him.

HOYT.   *(Capturing Gary Dale)* "Kindly tight quarters there Doctor Taylor."

D. H.   *(As detective)* "Was ya headed somewheres?"

GARY DALE.   *(As Doc)* "Well, I was thinkin' about goin' to Florida, but I reckon we'll be headed back to the Wise Courthouse, huh boys?"

D. H. & HOYT.   "Yep."

Slide: front page of Police Gazette with drawing of Doc in jail as Talt is led in a prisoner.

D. H.   That's the National Police Gazette, New York City edition; date on it is August 20, 1892. *(Quoting)* "Two of the most notorious outlaws and murderers in southwest Virginia and east Kentucky are Talton Hall and 'Doc' Taylor, the former soon to pay the penalty of his crimes with his life on the gallows; the other certain to follow him after the legal formality of a trial."

HOYT.   Doc, he'd been there in jail two weeks when they brung Bad Talt back from Lynchburg, fixin' to hang him.

D. H.   Said when Doc heard 'em bring in Talt, he got up and walked over to the door of his cell.

HOYT.   Said the very minute Talt laid eyes on Doc, he tried to break loose from the guards and git at him, reach right through the bars and grab him,

D. H.   but he had them chains on his hands—remember them chains—all he could do was set into hollerin' and a-cussin'

HOYT.   *(As Talt, D. H. restraining him)* "You no count ole varmit, they're goin' to hang you, too. You'll rot in hell, you ole bastard, for puttin' me here. I never kilt no women and children! They tell me you did."

D. H.   All Doc said was just plain and simple.

GARY DALE.   *(As Doc)* "Take him away boys."

Slide: stone jail and guards

D. H.   Them two stayed there in that jail, right across from one another, for nigh onto a month. The Guard, they took up their watch again, and a lull set in like just 'fore a storm.

Rumors was goin' around that Devil John Wright had

patched up his differences with Ole Clabe Jones. The reason Devil John would go so far as to patch-up his differences with a man he'd been fightin' for thirty years was that Clabe, they said, had a Gatlin gun, an' Clabe, they said, had a cannon and Clabe, they knew, had a whole desperate gang of men of his own. And talk was going around that them two was goin' to pool their resources, dynamite the town of Wise, an' batter that jail down to powder, that Devil John Wright *(as Devil John)* meant to have Talt Hall!

HOYT. Well now, you can just imagine what the condition of them guards nerves was. Why, some of 'em was accusin' cows of being spys.

D. H. While all this was going on, Talt's day to hang come closer and closer. He wouldn't eat nothin' at all hardly, they just kept feedin' him more and more whiskey.

In the following speech Hoyt fluctuates from narrator to Talt, from past to present.

HOYT. Talt, see, he kept having these hallucinations about yaller birds a-tearin' at him. 'Cause ya see, right after he'd kilt Hattie's brother-in-law, the sheriff or Norton, and hightailed it into the woods to get away, he had come to a spring there in the wilderness. He got him a drink and laid down to think what he was goin' to do.

All at once the bresh all around him come alive with little bitty yaller birds, hundreds and hundreds of 'em a 'flutterin all around his head, just a-chatterin' and a-scoldin' him. He'd try to fight 'em off, but they wouldn't leave. He'd shake the bush they's on, but as soon as he'd let go of that bush, they'd be right back again. *(Talt crows at the birds)*

D. H. He finally did manage to get away from them birds,

GARY DALE. but he never did manage to shake the sound of them birds out of his ears,

Hoyt is hunkering, caught in his hallucinations and holding his ears.

D. H. *(Closing in)*   and as his day to hang come closer

GARY DALE. *(Closing in)* and closer,

D. H.   them sounds

D. H. & GARY DALE.   got louder . . .
and louder

D. H.   and Talt, he was like a mad man caged up there
in that jail. Said if the guard wouldn't give him whiskey, he'd
set into *(Screaming at Hoyt)* screamin' an' a hollerin', makin'
such a racket

GARY DALE.   'til finally one of the guards would take pity on
him and get him a bottle.

D. H.   Doc, he'd just sit there in his cell

GARY DALE.   right across the hall

D. H.   on
a hammock

GARY DALE.   calm as could be, reading from his Bible, an'
tryin' to sort things out fer hisself

Slide: Talt Hall, haggard, despondent

HOYT.   That's a picture of Bad Talt Hall two days afore they hung
him.

D. H.   They hung him on September 2, 1892. Said you never
seed such a crowd of people in all your life. They's on top
of the houses and the ridge poles was saggin' from the
weight. They's in all the trees. The womenfolk had come all
decked out in gay ribbons. They'd come from all the counties around Virginia, Kentucky, North Carolina, Tennessee.
Hell, Talt Hall was the Jesse James of his day, and Pap said
they come from nigh onto all over the world to see this here
first hangin' in Wise County, Virginia—to see if ole Devil
John Wright, Talt's ole buddy; was really gonna let him hang.
Everybody kept wonderin' that day, "Where is ole Devil
John?" I'll tell you where he was—he's between a rock and
a hard place, that's where he was. On the one hand, he'd
do just about anything to help his ole buddy; but on the
other hand, remember now, he'd been gettin' rich buying
land for the Big Stone Gap bunch. And what do you do
when you're between that kinda rock and hard place? Ya
don't do nothin'. That's what you do. Talt Hall dropped
through that trap door, his neck snapped, and he hung
there like a sack of corn. They said Doc Taylor stood at the
window of his cell, his Bible in one hand and his watch in

the other, and he clocked, an' he watched the Big Stone Gap bunch pull this hangin' off. Watched this here new law start takin' its course.

Slide #1: four men carrying a rough cut coffin with two lengths of split rail fence along a dusty road by a field
Slide #2: courthouse

HOYT. Doc's trial got started on Monday, right after they hung Bad Talt Hall on Friday. Excitement was over now, and folks up at the Courthouse had to get back to business and give them fleas in that ole hemp rug in the courtroom something to chaw on.

GARY DALE. Now, there weren't no place to sit down in there, you know, unless you was the judge or the jury or some of them fancy lawyers.

HOYT. They had little ole wood benches to sit on.

GARY DALE. There's a four foot high picket fence that run crosswise in the middle of that courtroom

HOYT.   an everybody else had to stand all bunched together in back of it.

GARY DALE. Early that mornin folks started gatherin in there.

HOYT. Said there'd been more 'cept Devil John had pickets stationed up there at Pound Gap to make sure nobody come from Kentucky

D. H. *(As Devil John)* unlessen he wanted 'em to. *(as himself)* See Talt Hall at the time of his trial had accused Doc of driving off some of his witnesses at gunpoint. And talk was going around in Kentucky that ole Devil John was gonna give Doc

D. H. & HOYT. the very same dose.

GARY DALE. Directly the law brung in Doc, and the judge said,

D. H. *(As judge)* "Let's git this here thing started."

GARY DALE. Then over a hundred witnesses started comin' up

D. H. & GARY DALE. one . . . by one.

D. H. *(As clerk)* Iry's sister, Jane

HOYT. *(As sister Jane on stand)* "They had green veils down over their faces and they's down in behind the rocks, but I could see 'em from the waist up to where them veils come right at their mouth—it looked like hit might have been Doc Taylor."

D. H.   *(As Sara on stand)* "Me and Jane uz good friends. The next mornin' after the killin' I went around to where they had all the dead laid out. Jane, she said she didn't have no idea who it was done that killin'. I said, 'Jane honey, don't you have no idea atall?'

She said, 'No. They had black somethin' or other over their faces and a green strip across their foreheads.'"

HOYT.   *(As Jane)* "Sara Blevins, I never told you that, neither. And I swear I never told the Grand Jury that they had veils all over their faces. I said, part of their faces."

D. H.   *(As Sara)* "Jane said she uz so scared when the shootin' started she wouldn't have even a knowed my husband Matt if he'd been there . . . and they's real good friends, too."

HOYT.   *(As Jane)* "I told what suited me when it suited me. Why, I'd recognize Doc on a dark night—with his back to me—if his head was cut off. He's bowlegged and has a peculiar walk that no other man could acquire."

D. H.   *(As Sara)* "Last winter me and Jane was a-sewin' an all at once Jane looked up and says, 'There goes that old devil!'

I says, 'Who?' She says, 'Doc Taylor. I've hated that ole . . . bastard ever since he caught my brother, Henderson. I wish he uz in the middle of a kettle of torment.'"

HOYT.   *(As Jane)* "Hit's a lie!"

D. H.   *(As Sara)* "Is not!"

HOYT.   *(As Jane)* "Hit's a lie. I never told Sara Blevins that I wished Doc Taylor was in the middle of a kettle of torment— *(To Sara)* I wish you was in the middle of a kettle of torment! And if hit was I told Sara Blevins I didn't know who hit was, I uz just a-talkin' anyway, wadn't swearin'. Well, I told a lot of 'em I didn't know who hit was. Told 'em what I wanted to tell 'em. I uz afraid to tell who hit was, I uz afeared that they'd kill me."

GARY DALE.   Now there's alota folks wondering how come them fellers to let Jane go,

D. H.   and they's a lot of 'em thought it was mighty suspicious

HOYT.   an' thought maybe Jane, she was in on that meaness, too.

D. H.   *(As judge)* "Proceed!"

GARY DALE. *(As another witness)* "They come up there to get me the day them people got shot up on the mountain. So I went on up there with 'em, and I got to lookin' around up there an' I saw a little pile of leaves, and when I looked up in under, there's six big ole empty cartridge shells, they's 45 x 75 caliber, looked like they'd been put there a pint blank purpose. Yeh, Henry Adams has got a gun that size. He let me shoot it one time, and it like to knocked my shoulder out of wack. . . . No sir, don't know where Henry's at now. They tell me he's a-dodgin the law."

D. H. Now, you remember that Doc's gun was a 45 x 75 caliber Winchester, don't you? Well everbody around home back then did. That's a big gun and they wadn't too many around like it. But now, there's just a little bit more to it than the fact that ole Henry Adams had a gun the same size as Doc's.

HOYT. Ya see, ole Henry Adams had a beard like Doc's.

GARY DALE. An' ole Henry, he was kindly stocky like Doc.

D. H. An' ole Henry, he was known as

TOGETHER. **Bad Henry Adams**

D. H. and
there was real bad blood between him an' Iry Mullins.

HOYT. Ya see, he'd shot and killed Iry's brother Henderson just about a year before.

D. H. Henderson, see, he had a bitin' dog

HOYT. an' it had bit several
people

D. H. And Bad Henry had told him,

GARY DALE. *(As Bad Henry)* "If that goddamn dog bites me, Henderson, I'm gonna kill it."

HOYT. Well, it wadn't long after that, that man Henderson found his dog shot. *(Makes yelping sound of shot dog—Gary Dale spits on dean dog)*

D. H. Course, he figured that it was Bad Henry what had done it. Said he run in on Bad Henry and drawed his guns. *(Accosts someone in audience—D. H. being Henderson)* Bad Henry, now he was settin there at the supper table eating. *(To audience member, "Would you pretend like you're eating? Good. Keep on.")* Now Bad Henry, he never once layed his guns aside, while he ate, while he slept, and he shot that man,

Henderson, without even takin' that gun outa his pocket. Shot him plumb straight up through the table and all. And that man, Henderson, he fell over right there in the supper table gravy, dead.

GARY DALE & HOYT. **Shot over a dog!**

D. H. Well, after that Bad Iry set out rewards for Bad Henry,

HOYT. and Bad Henry, he let it be knowed,

GARY DALE. *(As Bad Henry)* "Rewards, hell. He can stick them rewards where the sun don't never shine. I'll kill Iry Mullins and any of his Mud Hole drunks the first damn chance I get."

D. H. *(After a beat)* Doc, he tried to tell 'em that there in the courtroom,

GARY DALE. but that judge wouldn't listen.

D. H. *(As judge)* "Proceed,"

GARY DALE.   said the Judge.

HOYT. *(As Gooseneck John—sinister and peculiar)* "Saw Doc a week after the killin' in the road on the south side of the mountain, an' he asked if there's any news. I told him, 'No, nothin' 'cept that murder.' He asked me who they was accusin' on this side of the mountain, and I said, 'Why, Doc, you.' Doc, he didn't act exactly natural, seemed to talk kinda whispered like."

D. H. That is ole Gooseneck John Branham. Let me tell you a little bit about *(Mocking him with his goose-like neck)* ole Gooseneck John Branham: Ya see, him and Bad Henry Adams, they's thick.

HOYT. Thick as fiddlers in Hell.

D. H. They run together with John Venters

GARY DALE. *(Quickly moving across stage)* You remember Venters, he's the one come an' got Doc; let on like his little girl's sick—the time that Doc outfoxed them fellers with that lantern rigged up on that wheel.

HOYT. *(As Venters stuttering)* "I seen Doc sometimes after the killing, seen him up on the Widder Vanover's land."

D. H. *(Stuttering)* The Widder Vanover

GARY DALE.   how come her to be a *(Stuttering)* widder

D. H.   was that Bad Iry Mullins,

GARY DALE & HOYT.   dead Bad Iry
   Mullins,
D. H.   hired two of
TOGETHER. *(Imitating Gooseneck)* Gooseneck John Branham's
D. H. brother-in-laws to kill her husband. They issued subpoenas
   for her to appear in this here court trial
HOYT.   but she
   never showed.
D. H. *(As judge)* "Proceed."
GARY DALE. *(As W.M. on stand)* "There's a bunch of us settin' on
   the porch at Flanary's Store a few days afore the killin'. Doc,
   he said while he uz over in Kentucky somebody had shot
   into Iry's bed over here in Virginia. I asked him, 'Well, how
   do you know that?'
       Doc said, 'Spirits told me.'
       And I says, 'Well, how come I can't talk to them spirits
   that a way?'
       Doc, he grinned real sly like, says, 'Cause you don't, W.M.'
   Well that made me mad, fer Doc to make fun of me like
   that, so I just got up and went on in the store and left him
   a settin' there."
D. H. *(As old woman on stand)* "Doc appeared natural as always.
   I told him there's a mob out after him, that I'd heared
   Gooseneck John Branham say he'd shoot a hole through
   Doc big enough for a poor ole thing like me to crawl
   through. Then said he'd set fire to the body and hear the
   grease boil. There's all that Mud Hole bunch with him when
   he said that—they's Floyd Branham, Ed Hall, Ed Cox, Rube
   McFall, Granville Cox, all 'em. They's a rough bunch."
HOYT. *(Gary Dale and Hoyt on stand as "rough bunch")* "We ain't
   no rough bunch, neither. Why, we used to work for Doc in
   the Infernal Revenue business."
GARY DALE. "He didn't pay us no good so we quit him and
   cussed him."
HOYT. "That uz four years ago back in the fall of '89."
GARY DALE. "We ain't never gone along with him since."
HOYT. "Fore we quit him, Doc, he used to try to get us to go
   with him and try to kill Henderson"
GARY DALE & HOYT.   "but we wouldn't do it."

HOYT. "Well," Doc said, "'Bedads,' he'd just go himself then."

GARY DALE. "Said he'd already put a man out of the way once't, and damned if he wouldn't do it again."

HOYT. "Said 'damned', your honor. We thought it was all talk."

GARY DALE. "We never had no idea that Doc meant to do what he said."

HOYT. "But I told Iry about hit just in case."

GARY DALE. "No sir, we don't care for Doc atall."

D. H. *(As Sylvan on stand)* "Pa wanted to come in and stand his trial, but me and Hattie talked him out of it, on account we thought he wouldn't git no fair trial . . . I don't know nothing about no money Iry's wife carried. Pa never had no money on him atall when he come in from scoutin-out."

GARY DALE. Well then, Doc's lawyer brought Doc's ole gun up there,

HOYT.   that big ole 45 x 75,

GARY DALE.   and showed it around. An' showed how Doc's gun, when the firin pin hit the bullet,

HOYT.   it hit it right square in the middle.

GARY DALE. And them bullets they found up there at the killin' had been hit on the edge.

HOYT. They's from a rimfire gun,

GARY DALE.   and Doc's gun, hit was a center fire.

D. H. Then the judge, he asked Doc *(As Judge)* if he had anything more to offer.

GARY DALE. *(As Doc)* "No, I reckon not. They's some others from over in Kentucky that wanted to come an tell what they knowed, but I see they ain't here."

D. H. The judge sent the jury on up to their little deciding room.

HOYT. Directly one of them jury men appeared up at the top of them stairs, hollered down an says,

D. H. *(As jury man)*   "We want to see Doc's ole gun up here."

HOYT. Well, they sent hit up,

D. H.   an' them jury men got to a-takin' it apart, examining it an' all

D. H. & HOYT. *(As jury men)*   an' found thar's some file dust in there.

D. H. An so they determined that Doc's gun had been tampered with.

HOYT. Before that, them jury men had just about determined to set Doc free,

D. H.   but this here gun thing re-determined them,

HOYT. an' they just come on back down an' says,

D. H. *(As foreman of jury)*   "He's guilty."

GARY DALE. Doc, he never got to explain to that jury that he hadn't even seen that gun since the day they arrested him, and all kindsa fellers had had their paws on it.

D. H. You know, they said it was a real sloppy job a tampering with that gun,

HOYT.   an' everybody knew how clever Doc Taylor was with his hands.

D. H. Just a lot of it never made no sense.

When the judge pronounced the final sentence on Doc and asked *(As Judge)* Doc if there was anything more he wanted to say,

HOYT. Doc said,

GARY DALE. *(As Doc)* "No, I don't. But a friend, a witness, will speak for me."

D. H. The judge asked him *(As Judge)* who it was.

GARY DALE. *(As Doc)* "The Lord, Jesus Christ."

HOYT. Now that judge was kinda hard of hearin', deaf you know, and he turned around to the clerk in the courtroom and, just as straight and sober as a judge is supposed to be, said,

D. H. *(As judge)* "Well, bring him around, Charley, and have him sworn in."

HOYT. Doc never flinched an eye at that, just picked up the Holy Bible and started readin' from Psalms,

GARY DALE. *(As Doc, reading)*   "Consider mine enemies for they are many, and they hate me with a cruel hatred. They laid at my charge things that I knew not. Deliver me not over unto the will of mine enemies for false witnesses are risen up against me. . . . I had fainted unless I believed to see the goodness of the Lord in this land of the living."

D. H. *(As judge)* "Readin' from the Holy Bible in my court ain't goin' to help your case none. You are a condemned man, condemned to hang by the neck until dead."

Slide—That's the Judge.
Slide—That's the prosecutor and his wife on their wedding trip.
Slide—That's Doc's lawyer.
Slide—That's the sheriff and his wife; it's not their wedding trip.
Slide—That's the hangman.
Slide—That's the Wise County gallows.
They had Doc's hangin on Friday, October 27, 1893.

HOYT. They let Doc hold a religious service there on the porch of the old jail.

D. H. It drizzled rain off and on that day, but a pretty big crowd of people came anyhow.

HOYT. Pap's whole family went; and when they finally brought Doc out, Pap expected to see that long red hair and that long red beard,

D. H.   but they's both cut real short that day.

D. H. & HOYT. Doc had on a snow white suit.

D. H. Pap's Ma told him how Doc's shy wife, Nancy, had made that suit for him out of an old white linen table cloth

HOYT.   and
how it was an "emblem" of Doc's innocence.

D. H. Pap said he's sure that's the first time he ever heard the word, "emblem,"

HOYT.   'cause he remembered his Ma explaining it to him.

D. H. Explaining as how the Book of Revelations talks about heavenly armies upon white horses, clothed in fine linen,

D. H. & HOYT. clean and white.

HOYT. Doc preached for a long spell that day, talked about how his diabetes condition had him run down.

GARY DALE. *(As Doc)* "But my spirits is good. *(Preaching)* God's angels has been with me there in that jail . . . bein' in jail's been the happiest times of my life."

D. H. Pretty strange thing to hear a fella say, ain't it? Being in jail's the happiest time of his life. But Pap said, "If ya knowed the man, what he had to say that day made sense."

GARY DALE. *(As Doc, reading from the Bible)* "The devil shall cast some of ye into prison that ye may be tried. But be thou faithful unto death, and I will give thee a crown of life. He that hath an ear, let him hear. Behold, I stand at the door and knock. If any man hear my voice and open the door, I will come in to him and sup with him and he with me."

D. H. They had a little table set up there,

HOYT. had bread and wine on it,

D. H. and Doc, he took the Holy Sacrament,

HOYT. him and his wife,

D. H. and then turned and offered it to all them people standin' there,

HOYT. asked them if they would take the Sacrament with them.

D. H. No one did.

HOYT. They just stood there.

GARY DALE. Right after that service, Pap run and got up in that old chestnut tree down by the stables, got out on the same limb he'd been on at Talt Hall's hangin'.

D. H. *(As Pap)* Yeah, said he could remember all the gay ribbons at Talt's hangin',

HOYT. but said he didn't see none of them ribbons now.

GARY DALE. He could hear people down under the tree talkin' about Doc's religion, an' how Doc believed there'd be a new time on earth.

HOYT. About how they couldn't believe he was guilty.

D. H. About all the talk goin' around that Doc said he was going to rise again in three days.

GARY DALE. About his believing he was Jesus Christ.

HOYT. Pap's Ma said something or another about everybody being Jesus Christ.

D. H. Pap said in later years he mulled that thought over, about everybody being Jesus. Said it made a lot of sense when you thought about it. But that day, said he couldn't think of nothing but that suit of snow white.

GARY DALE. At two o'clock they brought Doc out to the gallows.

HOYT. The gallows was completely enclosed.

GARY DALE. A box, 16 foot high,

HOYT. 16 foot square.

D. H. Doc stopped and looked up at that box,

GARY DALE. sorta surveyin' it.

D. H. Seemed like maybe he was tryin' to decide whether it was going to do the job or not.

HOYT. Then he stepped up on the steps to the gallows and knelt and prayed an' read from the Bible real quiet-like.

D. H. They had put newspapers on the gallows steps,

GARY DALE. and all them fellers guardin' him pulled their handkerchiefs out of their pockets and started wipin' the mud off Doc's red patent leather shoes.

D. H. D'rectly they stopped him prayin',

GARY DALE. got him up

HOYT. And tied his hands with a white cloth.

D. H. Led him on up the steps to his eternity.

HOYT. At the trap door, they put the noose around his neck

GARY DALE. and a white hood over his head.

HOYT. His wife made that fer him too.

GARY DALE. Doc never flinched.

D. H. But then, while they was loosenin' the props, they jostled the trap door, and Doc musta thought he was hung, 'cause he just fell in a heap right there on the gallows floor.

GARY DALE. And they had to help him back up to hang him.

HOYT. Everything got deathly quiet.

GARY DALE. Then come two licks with the back of the hatchet. *(Hits floor with boot heel)*

HOYT. They hit two licks with the back of the hatchet before they cut the rope.

GARY DALE. Doc stood stiff as a board.

D. H. And on that third lick, it was just like an apparition. That white suit shot down through that hole . . . *(The actors' hands are choreographed to the action)*

GARY DALE. bounced

HOYT. and started spinnin

D. H. & HOYT. round and round.

D. H. Spun one way til the rope got tight.

D. H. & GARY DALE. Stopped.

GARY DALE. Started spinnin the other way.

D. H. Kept on like that 'til all the
TOGETHER.   twist
HOYT.   come out of that rope,
D. H. and Doc
GARY DALE.   he just hung there.
D. II. Hung there they said for nineteen minutes.
GARY DALE. A couple of Doctors come and pronounced him
   dead by strangulation.
HOYT. Then they cut him down
D. H.   and laid him in a coffin
GARY DALE.   and
   closed the lid. Pap waited around three days to see if Doc
   was gonna rise again. When he never, Pap was kinda disap
   pointed.

Slide: Doc Taylor

HOYT. That's a picture of Doc three days before the hanging.
D. II. Pap said he never heared nothin' no different about the
   hangin' for ten years, 'cept he did hear folks say that Doc's
   body never got cold. But in 10 years Pap was married, and
   his wife was having their first baby. When the Doctor got
   there for the confinement, and was waiting around to birth
   the baby, well, he got to talking to 'em about things and
   found out that Pap's wife was Doc Taylor's niece.
       And then that Doctor told them a story that sorta changed
   things around a bit. Told as how he was one of the two
   Doctors what pronounced Doc dead by strangulation—not
   no broken neck, mind you. Said he was one of Doc's Mason
   brothers; and how nigh onto ever'body inside that *enclosed*
   gallows was a Mason. He said Doc Taylor did *not* die there
   in them gallows atall. Said they had rigged up a little spring-
   like harness under his armpits, and when Doc fell on that
   trap door like that, was when they hitched it up. Said they
   buried a railroad tie up there in that unmarked grave in the
   cemetery, and that Doc he wanted to appear to folks again
   in three days, but that his family talked him out of it and
   wisked him out of there, way out to Saline County, Missouri.
GARY DALE. You know, Pap, he was gettin' nigh on towards a
   hundred, and like alota old people, he liked to sit almost

right up in the fire, bakin' his bones he called it. He'd sit, a-starin' into that fire—directly he'd let loose a big wad of ambeer, damned near put the fire out, look over at one of us younguns, shake his ole head, grin and say,

D. H. *(As Pap)* "Ya reckon that's true?"

Slide: Doc Taylor as a young man
Slide: three men (kin) seated side by side, arms crossed, looking at the camera

HOYT. *(As encore)* One more thing I'd like to tell you before we go. The next spring after they'd hung Doc, the corn was already way up, and on May 19, 1894, she come a ten inch snow fall in Wise County; said the Good Lord dressed that whole county in a suit of snow white. Some folks said it was a judgement on people for hanging a man like Doc. I don't know about that, but I do know one thing—the corn crop weren't fit for nothin' that year, and the moonshinin' business come to a grinding halt.

Slide: twilight—canoe and logs on the river

END

john o'neal and nayo barbara watkins
with
steven kent
with additional words by
timothy raphael

you can't judge a book by looking at the cover: sayings from the life and writings of junebug jabbo jones: volume ii

artist's statement

Theater of its essence is a collaborative venture. This is even
more true or those of us who, out of economic necessity,
work in the solo format. Because this piece was designed for
a solo writer/performer, it seemed important to have other
eyes and ears going into the text. The writing partnership
with Nayo turned out so good that we've already written
another piece together with Q.R. Hand and we plan to do
more. Then there were the valuable collaborations with
other theaters (a very crucial element for a small, really poor
theatre), directors, assistant directors, the numerous people
who submitted to the interviews that gave us stories and
access to the history the play is based on. But the most
valuable of our collaborators have been those nameless
thousands who created the language and those who polished
the gems of image and metaphor that we simply have tried
to interpret and give back as good as was given to us.

production history

You Can't Judge a Book by Looking at the Cover was developed
in 1985 as a co-production between 7Stages in Atlanta and
Junebug Productions. It was written by John O'Neal and
Nayo Barbara Watkins with additional text by Steven Kent
and Timothy Raphael. It was revised and presented the following year in a six-week residency at Wisdom Bridge Theatre in Chicago. Since then it has been a regular part of the
touring repertory of the Junebug Theater Project. Each version of the play has been directed by Steven Kent and performed by John O'Neal.

The following version of the text has been edited for
reading. The performing text is considerably shorter and
contains less descriptive information.

prologue

Po Tatum, Po Tatum
Where you been?
Been to the city and I'm going again.
What you goin to do when you get back?
Take a little walk on the railroad track.
Po Tatum!

Po Tatum, Po Tatum
Have you heard?
Junebug's here and he's spreading the word.
Telling everybody you was his best friend
Telling all about how you's done in.
Telling how you had to leave away from home.
Telling how you had to hit the road alone.

When Po Tatum was just a little bitty baby
His mama was known to be a real fine lady.
His daddy was a man with a special skill
Could make people laugh and he knowed how to build.

'had a nice little farm and a real fine house
As Po growed up he learned to run his mouth.
They was doing pretty well till things got funny
They run out of work and they run out of money.

Need money for the farm, need money for the house
Need money for the cat, 'n for the cat to catch the
    mouse.
Need money for clothes, need money for school.
Even need money to feed the old mule

You run to the city trying to get you some money.
You run to the city trying to find your honey.
When you run out of money come to the end of your
    rope.
You run out of money you run out of hope.
Po Tatum!

act one

GOING TO CHICAGO

That's the "Po Tatum Hambone Blues."

It was because of Po Tatum that I finally come to understand that I was supposed to be a storyteller. I'ma tell y'all how that come about.

Po was the youngest one of Miz Adeline and Mr. Jake Tatum's three boys. There's Ralph, Skinhead and Po.

Now, you might have thought we called him Po cause he's so skinny. He's so skinny that he could get lost behind a telephone pole. But that ain't why we called him "Po." We called him "Po" cause when he was seven years old he ate a whole half a bushel of raw I'sh potatoes by himself. Miz Adeline said to him, "Why you eat all them raw potatoes, son?" He just grinned and say, "Cause I's hungry." Why he didn't gain no weight I don't know, as much as he would eat! That boy could eat some potatoes! That's why we called him Po Tatum.

'Fore Po Tatum left home going to Chicago he was one of the nicest fellows around. He'd go out of his way to try and help people. He'd always speak to people and everything.

I remember one time, Mr. Raggs got drunk and fell in old man Quinland's cesspool. Miz Maybelle, Mr. Raggs' old lady, always beat him up real bad when he got drunk.

At one time Mr. Raggs had one of the nicest little farms in Pike County. But then the city of Macomb thought they could get a plant in there to make bullets for the war if they had Mr. Raggs' property. They told him he had to leave off his land an they took it over. They gave him a little money for it, but they took away his pride. They never did get that ammunition plant in there neither.

Well, this particular time Mr. Raggs was trying to sneak in the back door. He misremembered and walked on them rotten boards over that cesspool and fell in. He made the biggest racket! Well, Po Tatum was the only one would help

Mr. Raggs get out of that cesspool. Miz Maybelle wouldn't even beat him up till he went down to the Bogue Chitto River and washed himself off.

Well, that's the kind of fellow Po was before he went off to Chicago. But he got to the big city and his mind got turned around.

The Tatums come from this place out 'round The New Mt. Zion Community we called "The Bottom." Mr. Jake was the Head Deacon at the New Mt. Zion church and was the best carpenter around at the time. He had learned the carpenter trade from his daddy, Mr. Freeman Tatum, which they say he had been the main one to do most of the building on the Pike County Courthouse and most of the rich white people's homes. Mr. Freeman built two homes for Col. Whitten. The Tatums had scrimped and scrapped for years till they was able to build a real fine home down in The Bottom, in some ways as good or better than any they built for the white folk. And they built it out of scraps of stuff they's able to save off of whatever job they was doing for the white people.

The Bottom was kind of a special place. It was mostly swamp land didn't nobody want, but them that lived there. For years and years white folk just didn't go down there at all. It was said that in years past a bunch of runaway slaves and some Red Indians had laid ambush and killed a bunch of white people there. For a long time after that white folk wouldn't go down to The Bottom for nothing, not even the High Sheriff.

The first white man to go down there in modern times was old man Ebenezzer Winston and he got there by accident. Eb was a sneaky, low lifted sort of fellow, looked like a mangy dog. Come sidling up to you with its tail all sucked up between his legs. You couldn't tell where its intent to lick or bite you.

One day, during the Depression, old Eb had been out looking for work and Eb fell asleep on his wagon and his mule wandered off up in there. When the wagon stopped rocking from the walking of the mule old Eb woke up, figured out where he was at, and hightailed it back to town.

He had the High Sheriff come out there to arrest Mr. Jake, "cause couldn't no uppity nigger afford a house that good no matter how hard him to work!"

But couldn't nobody 'round there figure out where Mr. Jake or his daddy had ever done anybody wrong. They would nearly always finish whatever job they's working on, on time and save people's money on the job too.

Since they couldn't find nobody to bring charges, they had to let him go. But after that Mr. Jake wasn't able to get much carpenter work from the white folk. So, he had to work harder to make something out of that little piece of swamp land they called a farm.

It takes a heap of work and a heap of money to make do on a farm. Aw, you can pretty much stay in something to eat, but you pay hell trying to get ahead without no money.

They did some of everything trying to get ahead. They raised chickens, geese, hogs, some goats and a few cows, they had what was known to be the best bull thereabouts. People used to bring they cows from as far as Chrystal Springs to stud off 'n that bull.

Miz Adeline kept a good sized vegetable garden. They did everything; but soon's they's able to get one step forward, seemed like some big wind would come and blow them two steps back.

Still and all Miz Adeline and Mr. Jake did right well compared to most. Things would probably worked out all right cept for the fact that Mr. Jake was so proud of their intentions that he got to braggin "that boy's going to be the first of our kin to go to college. Po wasn't even out of grade school and already, Mr. Jake seen him as the one who was going to put the family on a new footstand. "It's something about the boy, he just look like a lawyer to me. Besides, he ain't never going to be fit for no *real* work, he's too skinny."

Mr. Jake would get that big heavy dictionary book down and say, "All right son, read me something. If you goin to be a lawyer, you got to know all kinds of things." He'd make Po read three or four pages a night out of that dictionary.

By the time Po was twelve years old, he'd worked his way up to the letter "m" in that dictionary. His mind got stuck on the word "meteorology." He told his daddy he needed a weather vane on top of the barn so's he could see which way the wind was blowing. Mr. Jake didn't have no money to buy no weather vane so he went and *made* one out of scraps he was able to find in the barnyard. One Sunday afternoon after church, Mr. Jake was up on that tin roofed barn to put that homemade wather vane up there when this freakish little summer storm blowed up. A bolt of lightning, just as red as blood, hit him and knocked him plumb off that roof. He had to have been dead before he hit the ground. The body almost landed on young Po.

Miz Adeline wan't nair bit of good after that. Seem like she just lost all interest in living. Miz Adeline was half Indian—long black hair down to here. It's a funny thing about them indians—they get done living they just ups and dies. She lingered on a good while, but she wan't nair bit of good.

Like I said, Po was a nice young man, but with his Daddy dead and his Maw acting funny, Po got kind of lost. Guess he thought it was his fault what had happened.

Miz Caldonia Spencer, which everybody called her "Aunt Callie," had the farm next door to the Tatums. Being a retired school teacher she could see that neither Ralph, Skinhead nor Po's oldest sister, Miss Jeanine, was going to be able to do much with the young Po. Being an old friend of the family, she could see that there was little or no hope that Miz Adeline would ever get straight, so it didn't surprise nobody when she made it her business to try to keep Po from going sour.

Because of her arthritis she had to have help working the land since she was the last of her family. At the time, Aunt Callie had three young calves which she hired Po to take care of. He got into it too. Took to wearing a cowboy hat and everything. I wasn't but a child at the time but I remember wondering how Po thought he could be a Cowboy when he didn't have neither horse or six-shooter.

After a few months working for Aunt Callie, Po was a lot better. He even made up a little song to sing:

I'm an old cowhand from Bogue Chitto land.
My legs ain't bowed but my cheeks are tan.
I'm a cowboy who knows all about a cow,

I raise 'em real good cause I sure know how,
Get out of my way cause I'm acoming now.
Yippee-tie-yo-tia-yea.

One day he come home from school to find all three of
his calves sick. He said, "Aunt Callie, what's wrong with my
calves!" "I don't know son. Go get me Joe Whittie to come
and look at them."

Po ran all the way to Mr. Joe Whittie's place. He looked
at each one of them and said, "it's that red tick fever. You
got to have a perscription from Doc Shultz to fix it. But it's
that red tick fever, that's what it is, all right! That's what it
is!" Po went to Doc Shultz' office. Doc Shultz told him, "Well,
if that's what Joe Whittie said, that's what it is alright. That's
what it is. I'll give you the perscription but it's going to cost
$75 for the treatment to cure all three Cows." Neither Po
nor Aunt Callie could come up with the $75 before all three
cows died.

It wasn't too long after that Po quit school and got a job
at The Rainbow Sign Casino. He swore he wasn't never
going to be without money again.

By the time Po was 17 he'd done got right wild. He took
to fancy dressing and hanging out on the weekends up in
McComb. Up till then I believe I would have followed Po to
the gates of Hell. But now I'd begun to have some doubts.

He did have the gift of gab! That boy coulda talked St.
Peter into letting the Devil pass through the Pearly Gates!
He would make up little rhymes and sayings quick as you
could turn around. And don't talk about no Dozens! That's
a game we play the idea being to get people mad and upset
so you can take advantage of them. The way you suppose to
get them mad is by talking bad about their mamas!

Po could play some Dozens! Everybody else be struggling
to remember one or two bad names to call your mother, Po
be running off a string of bad names—in rhyme! If your
mama's name was "Mary" he might-a said:

Late last nite, snuck in to see Miz Mary
I mighta tried to kiss her but her face was too hairy
Your mama was a fool, got kept in school

For trying to tell the teacher bout the golden rule
The teacher got hot said gimme what you got
Fore I send you back home on your Daddy's old mule!

I ain't never heard of Po being beat at playing the dozens or playing cards but one time. There's this fellow named Tipper Rowe from New Orleans. They called him Tipper cause he always walked around on his tiptoes like he's trying to sneak up on somebody. He always wore these little soft shoes looked like slippers. Said he had bad feet. He would always carry an umbrella rain or shine. Called everybody "Little" something. "Hey, where you at, Lil Bro?"

When I was coming up we used to a "Fall Break" and a "Spring Break." "Spring Break" would come during cotton chopping season and "Fall Break" come when it was time to pick cotton. The white kids didn't get no breaks. We thought we were lucky.

One spring we was on break and it was raining too hard to chop cotton. So a bunch of us fellows had gathered up in the back of Bugs Underground Cafe to play Tunk. Po was acting a fool that day. He was just sounding on folks and putting them in the dozens. But Tipper was hanging right in there with him just as quiet as could be. Finally it come down to just the two of them. Po running his mouth and Tipper just running them cards. Before he knowed what was happening, Po was down to his last money. Po pulled the Queen of Spades, "Doggonit! I told your mama not to send me no more of her ugly pictures."

Tipper pulled a card and just as cool as a cucumber said, "Hey, wait a minute, my son. You can say anything you want to about my mother or anyone of her kinfolks. But if you just look like you gonna say one bad word about your sweet lil mamma, I'm going to be personally offended." He'd laid down three aces and three deuces—ain't no way to beat that in Tunk! "You country hip, Little Daddy, but your game is lame. You ain't nothing but a five pound fish in a ten pound pond. Where I come from, we use chumps like you for batting practice. Now, Mr. Tatum, I'ma take your money, go up front and buy everybody a nice cool R. C. Cola." After that Po ain't had no more to do with Tipper and the dozens. Tipper be in a game of cards or something, Po go shoot some pool.

Fore long, Po got his mind made up that he's goin to the city. Every time you seen him he be saying:

Gonna get me some money honey
I'm going to Chicago, baby, heading for the city.
Chica chica chica chica chica Chicago
Chica chica chica chica chica Chicago
Chica chica chica chica chica Chicago
Gonna catch a northbound train.

One day I asked him, "Why you got to go way to Chicago? They got plenty work right over here in New Orleans."

"And they got the same mean ass white folks down there as they got here. Dan Skinner's got a first cousin down there's a big timer in the Waterfront Union. Dan's down there two or three times a year himself. He comes out to the Rainbow Sign Casino just bragging about 'the mello yellow Creole gals' he finds down there. Col. Whitten's got a brother, four nephews and a son down there. They owns the newspaper and a radio station. No siree, Bob! It sounds too much like home to me. Besides, that's where old jive time Tipper Rowe come from. What kind of rep you think I'm going to make with him around to get on my case. I'm going to get me some money."

I'm going to the city
Where the women's really pretty
And they tell me that the money falls like rain.
Cause I'm tired of picking cotton
Mississippi's gotten rotten
Gonna pack my bag and jump the quickest train.
Chica chica chica chica chica Chicago
Chica chica chica chica chica Chicago
Chica chica chica chica chica Chicago
Let me catch the Northbound train!

Po kept on like that every time you seen him, but after two or three months he just up and disappeared! It was a bunch of rumors as to why Po left town so quick like that.

It was a well known fact in a small circle that him and Becky Sawyers was making time. She was a waitress out there at the Rainbow Sign Casino where Po was busting dishes. Becky Sawyers was good looking in a way but she was on the thin side. She's so thin she could dodge between raindrops in a good sized storm and not get wet. In that way her and Po made a good pair. She always wore these two long braids. Them braids was bigger than her legs. She was thin. But she was also white.

Some of you all might be surprised that it was so much of that type of race mixing going on during the deep down Jim Crow days. But I'm here to tell you that there was plenty of it. See, segregation had more to do with sitting down together. If you was standing up working or laying down working it was alright.

The Sawyers was what we used to call "poor white trash." They wasn't nothing but sharecroppers just like the rest of us, but that's what we used to call them. When she was thirteen Becky'd done had a child for Dan Skinner, Col. Whitten's Overseer and Deputy Sheriff. Dan never made no move to marry her 'cause she had the reputation of being a "bad girl"—due to the child she'd had for him. 'Course Dan wasn't in no shape to get married no way, financial or otherwise. "I'll keep her for fooling around, but you want a wife, buddy, you got to get you a good girl."

So, when Po come along she must have figured, "If he's got the nerve to try me then I sure got the nerve to try him." Plus, she knowed, if they ever got caught she could always claim he's raping her.

They say that one night Dan Skinner had caught ol Po with Becky in the smoke house out back of the Casino, shot him dead and throwed his body in the Bogue Chitto River. For years after Po disappeared, every time a body washed up in the Bogue Chitto River, people would wonder, "Is that Po?"

A more likely story goes that Po had found out where Antonio Dominuis "Stonewall" Whitten was keeping his money hid.

Stonewall Whitten was Col. Whitten's younger brother. Col. Whitten and their older brother, Beaureguard Caesar

Whitten, owned the bank in McComb. Stonewall didn't have a dime's worth of confidence in his brothers or their bank. He claimed that when their daddy died, Col. Whitten and B. C. Whitten had stolen his share of the inheritance. Two or three times a year Stonewall would bring a legal action to try to get his money back. Every time he come down there his case would be thrown out of court. Everytime they thrown him out of court he would haul off and start preaching on the courthouse steps.

"Brethern and Sisteren of the righteous cause of the Confederation. Beware of the sins of sloth, greed and gluttony! Yea, even also the products of my father's seed, issue of my sainted mother's loin, have made league with the devil in hell in rapacious lust for your land and property. Through the devilish device of this Bank, aided and abetted by the officers of this Court, the police jury, the Sheriff, the Mayor and the City Council they are bleeding you dry! Dry! Dry! I say we must rise up against this heathenistic oligarchy! Before the South can rise again, we must purge ourselves of these fiendish devils sporting the cloth and style of gentlemen." He made it plain and clear that he was calling for a rebellion for the white folks. The colored people knew they'd need a passport to get within a block of the Courthouse when Stonewall was out there preaching.

Stonewall would rather have died than put two pennies in that bank. Since it was the only bank around it was said that Stonewall had a way of stashing money in glass jars, strong boxes, anything, in places all over his farm. Po had been heard to say that he knowed where Stonewall was hiding that money and that whenever Po needed some, he'd just sneak out there in the dead of night and take whatever he wanted.

You might can tell Stonewall was somewhat peculiar. Where most folk would have used dogs for the purpose, Stonewall kept a pack of wild hogs on his place for protection. Now that ain't necessarily as dumb as it first might seem. A hog is stronger, meaner and smarter than your average dog.

The story goes that one night while Po was down there rooting for Stonewall's money, the biggest, baddest boar in the pack caught up with Po fore he had the time to get out the hole with the money. That wild pig was said to have put a gash on the left side of Po's face from his mouth to his ear fore he was able to rassle that hog down and cut him bad enough to bleed it to death.

Stonewall loved that hog more than he loved money. He's the first one I ever heard of to quit eating pork. He'd made his wife leave home cause she didn't want that thing sleeping in the bed with them when it was a baby.

After killing Stonewall's favorite wild boar and getting cut like that, Po knew it was time for him to grab his hat.

Po was feeling so low down that the belly of a rattlesnake would have looked like a bridge. He went that night and hopped an I.C. freight train heading for Chicago.

The old freight train's a rocking,
My aching head's a popping
Need me something just to ease the pain.
Had to leave my home and family
Cause this crazy cracker jammed me.
I'm going and I won't be back again.

Going to Chicago, Baby, heading for the City.
Going to Chicago, Baby, heading for the City.
Chica chica chica chica chica Chicago
Chica chica chica chica chica Chicago
Chica chica chica chica chica Chicago
I done gone and caught the Northbound train.

home for the funeral

Well, it was five years mo fore Po was seen again in Pike County. His Mama, Miz Adeline, had done pined and pined till she couldn't pine no more. After Mr. Jake was killed like he was she didn't have much use for the world. Year by year, as their land would go, a piece at a time, she just went more and more into herself. Whilst all her other children was gathered around her dying bed she kept asking to see her baby one more time.

The problem of it was the family didn't know where in the world Po was. They used to get a money order from him once every month for three or four hundred dollars. But they hadn't heard anything for over a year now. They's sitting there trying to figure it out and Skinhead said, "By God, let's go up to Mr. Jimmy Knowles store and call Junebug. Him and Po's tighter than the twine on Aunt Callie's corset. If anybody'd know where to find him Junebug would."

I was running this shoeshine stand at the Pontchartrain Hotel in New Orleans at the time. They's kind of sometimy about me getting phone calls there. But when Long Distance called for me even the switchboard operator got excited.

"Pontchartrain Hotel . . . Long Distance? For Mr. Jones? One moment please . . . I'm sorry we don't have a Mr. J. J. Jones registered at this time. . . . What's that? . . . Junebug? Oh! You mean JUNEBUG? Operator, he's a Nee-ga-row! . . . Alright operator, hold on please. What's this world coming to? Charles, tell the shoeshine boy that he has a Long Distance call!"

"Long Distance? For Junebug? Boy, oh boy! Hey Junebug! Boy, you got a Long Distance telephone call in here. Florine says you'll have to call em back on the pay phone if it takes more than three minutes. She can't have you tying up her lines."

"If it take a week, a week'll do, Turkey. And from now on, it's 'Mr. Boy' to you. You ain't never had no Long Distance call. (Pause) Hello. This is Mr. Jones."

"HEY, LI'L DAVID, THIS IS SKINHEAD."

Right away I knowed who it was. Didn't but one person call me by my given name like that beside my mama. "You keep on like that you going to break the telephone. Hey, Skinhead. What's going on?"

"WE TRYING TO FIND PO. MAMA'S LOW DOWN SICK AND SHE BEEN ASKING FOR HIM."

"Miz Adeline's sick?"

"LOW DOWN SICK. TELL YOU THE TRUTH I DON'T

THINK SHE GON MAKE IT THIS TIME. WE AIN'T
HEARD A WORD FROM PO IN OVER A YEAR."

"I ain't heard nothing from Po in the last little while
myself, but I feel and believe that I can find him."

"ALL RIGHT THEN, YOU GET TO HIM. TELL HIM
THAT HIS MAMA'S ON HER DYING BED AND SHE'S
CALLING FOR HIM."

"I'll do that now, you take it easy, Skinhead. Tell all your
people hello."

"ALL RIGHT, LI'L DAVID. SO LONG NOW."

It hurt me something bad to hear that. By me being so
close to Po and all, Miz Adeline was next to my momma in
my mind. But finding Po was more'n a notion.

The trouble was Po didn't exactly live in no one particular
place. If he got in tight with some woman he'd stay with her
for a while but mostly he'd live in his car. Every now and
then, being as Po was none too swift in the writing department, he'd have this one particular lady friend of his to write
me a letter. Whenever I wanted to get in touch with Po I
had to write to this lady, which her name was Consuela
LeBeaux. She's from Haiti. That's over by Miami in the
Atlantic Ocean.

It took me a while but I's able to get her number from
"Information." The operator put the call through for me.

"Miz Consuela, I'm a trying to reach P—, I mean, Phillip
Anthony Tatum. I need to talk to him quick, fast and in a
hurry."

"You must be the one he calls, Junebug?"

I was knocked out. Not only did she know who I was, she
sounded like the original Honey-dripper!

"Phillipe said you might call someday. Is there anything
wrong?"

"Yes Mam, it is. I need to let Po know that Miz Adeline,
his mama, is on her dying bed and she's calling for him."

It got so quiet on the other end of the line that I'd begun
to think we'd been cut off.

"Hello. Hello, Miz Consuela?"

"Yes, I am here. I'll get the message to Phillipe right away."

I couldn't tell what was wrong but I figured it was something from the way she said that. But when she said that one of them would call back, I decided to leave it alone.

I went on back to work feeling like I had done something worthwhile. Early that next morning the porter came to my shoeshine stand.

"Say boy, you getting to be a regular business man around here. You got another one of them Long Distance calls!"

"Ah, hush up man. You just jealous because you ain't got no long distance telephone call. And from now on, it's 'Mr. Boy' to you. . . . Hello."

"WELL, SHE GONE, LI'L DAVID. DID YOU FIND HIM?"

"Yeah. I found him. Least wise I found somebody said they could get a message to him. I'll call em back. Let em know. When's the funeral?"

"SATURDAY."

"All right, I'll see you, Skinhead."

"I'LL SEE YOU, LI'L DAVID."

I called Miz Consuela right away. She was mighty upset bout Po's dear mama and she was more upset cause she couldn't promise that Po was going to be able to make the funeral that coming Saturday. I didn't say nothing but I did wonder what was Po so tied up in that he couldn't make it to his own mama's funeral. I later found out Po had been in jail at that time.

I got to Four Corners late that Friday afternoon. Next morning at the funeral, they had the front four rows of the church on both sides roped off for the family. Rev. Wright preached a powerful sermon. I reckon he was glad to have a funeral to preach that he didn't have to spend most of his time lying about the poor departed. Miz Adeline was one of the nicest people you ever going to meet.

Rev. Wright was done preaching and Willie Gladstone had just opened up the casket so we could view the remains when it came a great racket outside of a car sliding to a halt. The door to the church house popped open and there stood this lady, on high heeled shoes, which was more strap than shoe, she sorta pranced like a high bred filly without touching the ground too hard. My eye followed her blue stockings up them long shapely legs till I almost embarrassed myself.

Scared I was about to see something that I wasn't supposed to look at, my other eye jumped up to the woman's face which was covered by a little blue veil pinned to a little blue pancake hat tilted over her left eye. She licked her shiny red lips and dabbed her eye with this little blue handkerchief. She turned to hold the door open for Po Tatum!

He had on a white, double breasted gabardine suit with a black silk shirt and a white necktie and this wide brimmed Panama hat with a black and white polka-dot band. As he stepped into the church house, Po dabbed his forehead. And sure enough, a long scar ran from his ear to his lip on the left side of his face, made him look like he's smiling all the time.

He walked straight up to the coffin, raised up the veil bent down and kissed his mama. Then, slow like in slow motion, he slumped down on his knees and cried like a baby.

Up to that point, it had not been such a sad funeral. But it's a sad thing to see a grown man cry. In less than a minute, half the people in the church broke out crying. Skinhead, who ain't never been heard to whisper a day in his life, said, "Well, I'll be a monkey's uncle."

It took Rev. Wright and Willie Gladstone a good while to get the service back under control. They finally got the casket loaded out onto the hearse. That being done, Po became the center of attention again. All his brothers and sisters was hugging him and holding him trying to find out all about him. Me, I turned my attention to the blue lady. Still feeling obliged not to look below the pearl looking necklace she wore, I said,

"How do, M'am? I'm Junebug, you must be Miz Consuela."

"The name my Mama give me was Flora Belle. My Daddy's name was Washington. Do that sound like Consuela to you? Po, Daddy, Po! You ready to go?"

She walked as much as that tight fitting dress would let her to where Po was standing and he loaded her into that brand new 1951, powder blue Cadillac.

Back home after a funeral everybody gathers at the house of the nearest of kin to talk and sip a little spirits to help out til the grief be kinda lifted. And they had some food out there that day. Seemed like everyone who ever owed Miz Adeline a favor tried to pay her back by bringing food. Everybody was talking about Po and how well he was doing. With them fancy clothes and that fancy car and that fancy woman, he musta been doin all right.

Aunt Callie leaned back in the rocking chair, scratched a match on the floor to light her pipe and said, "I have seen them come and I have seen them go. You can't judge a book by looking at the cover. I'm here to tell you!" Nobody said nothing back to Aunt Callie! Not so much because it's impolite to back talk old people, but cause Aunt Callie's been known to put people in their place with little or no ceremony.

Knowing Aunt Callie, that got me to thinking.

Po looked some sad when the family got back from the burying ground, but the young boys especially wouldn't let him have no peace. Out on the porch, all the young unmarried women fell in around Mis Flora, which Po called her "Flukey."

Aunt Callie noticed how all of us young'uns was following Po and Flukey so hard with our minds. She ra'red back and blowed a big puff of smoke from her pipe and said, "Well, Phillip, it seem like you done gone off to the city and struck it rich, huh, son?"

"I wouldn't say that Aunt Callie, but I'm doin all right. Ain't found no cows to tend in the city though."

"What have you found to tend in the city that will afford you a Cadillac car and a fast talking woman? You married to her? Or did you bring her here to make mock of your mother's funeral?"

"No'm Aunt Callie, you know I wouldn't do nothing like that!"

"Then tell me just exactly what you have been doing. You happy enough to tell all these young boys; tell me."

Just about that time Ralph came in from the bedroom and said, "I'm sorry, Aunt Callie, but Po, we need to speak to you in the bedroom."

Po was glad to get out from that session with Aunt Callie.

But what he didn't know was that he'd going from the fat into the fire. I didn't get in the room, but with Skinhead in there, you didn't have to. "WHYN'T YOU COME HOME WHEN WE GOT BURNED OUT? WHYN'T YOU LET SOMEBODY KNOW WHERE YOU'S AT? YOU KNOW'D YOU'S MAMA WAS SICK AND YOU'S HER FAVORITE!"

Ralph: "I'm sorry, Skinhead, but Po, you know Daddy expected more out of you than he did the rest of us! We sure could use an extra hand around here. If we don't give Whitten $500 by the end of the month we stand to lose the 20 acre plot the family place used to stand on."

Po's oldest sister, Miss Jeanine, said, "How dare you to bring that floozy woman to your own mother's funeral!"

"Her name ain't Floozy! And if she good enough for me, she ought to be good enough for you."

The bedroom door popped open and everybody in the house jumped to get like they hadn't been listening. Po, just as cool as a cucumber, walked over to me and said, "Junebug, my friend, I got me some business down in New Orleans. If you want to ride you let the door knob hit you where the good Lord split you! Flukey, Baby, we got to rise and fly!"

"You know me daddy, I wake up in the morning, ready to roll."

"Well Junebug, you crying or flying?"

Everybody looked to see what I's gon do. Aunt Callie broke the quiet by tapping the ashes out of her pipe on the edge of the Prince Albert tobacco tin she used as a spit can and said to one of the young Tatum women standing nearby, "Help me out this rocking chair, baby. I believe I'll go out to the kitchen, get some of that good corn bread and some of that pot liquor off them collard greens." She caned her way back toward to kitchen on her good foot, singing:

Oh, I done done
Oh, I done done
Oh, I done done
I done done what you told me to do.

I said, "All right Mr. Po, I'm ready to go."
All the fellows followed us out to that brand-new powder

blue 51 Cadillac. Four or five of them fought to hold the
door for Flukey, mainly so they could see her prance up to
the car, bend at the middle, rotate those blue stocking knees
into the plush upholstery of the new smelling car.

I cleared a space in the back seat for myself, but before
Po could park hisself behind the steering wheel of that
cadillac car, they said, "Hey, Mr. Po, tell us where you going
to go!"

"That's for me to know and you to find out."

"C'mon Po. Lay one them heavy rhymes on us, man!"

Po thought a bit and said:

My Mama just died
My Dad's a long time gone
I'm out here on the highway all a doggone long
I'm digging like a dog for his very last bone
Living for the City
Trying to make a new home

I'm talking chica chica chica chica chica Chicago
chica chica chica chica chica Chicago
chica chica chica chica chica Chicago
I got to make it on the road again.
So long, y'all.
So long, Home.

Po slammed the door of that Cadillac, dropped it in gear
and gunned it so it cut a dusty gash in Ralph's front yard.

We's half way to Franklinton 'fore I figured out what we's
doing. Flukey had the map out telling him which way to go.
I said, "Excuse me, mam, but Po, highway 51's the best, most
direct route to New Orleans."

"Yes, baby. We know that. But long as we out here in the
country, we thought we'd take the chance to see some of
the sights. Oh Po, Daddy, look! There's a whole herd of
bulls!"

"Ain't no such thing as a herd of bulls, Flukey! Them's
cows! To be so smart about the city, you sure are dumb about
the country!"

I thought about why we's taking them backroads for a

minute and decided since it wasn't none of my business, I'd leave it alone. That Cadillac rocked so smooth on them country roads it wasn't long before I'd drifted off to sleep.

"Hey Junebug, wake up, man. We're in New Orleans."

At that time I's living in this little three room shotgun house down the street from the Dew Drop Inn in New Orleans. Flukey didn't like it 'nair bit. She went with Po that first night to play cards with Tipper Rowe and I didn't see her no more after that.

Four days later, Po came driving up to the hotel where I's working in a different car—a maroon colored Lincoln Continental, fully loaded.

"Come on, Junebug, get your glad rags on. I'm gonna take you to Dookey Chase's restaurant for a high class dinner."

The next day I came home from work and all of Po's stuff was gone. It was a hundred dollar bill on the kitchen table with some printing in one corner. Said, "Keep this for good luck. Po."

It was a good while after that fore I caught up with Po again. But I later come to find that two days before Whitten was to foreclose the mortgage on the old family farm, Ralph and them got a money order from Chicago for $5000 with a telegram from Po saying, "This is for my share of the funeral. I hope things work out fine."

act two

LETTERS FROM JAIL

Chicken in the car and the car can't go.
That's how you spell Chi-ca-go!

I be going around a lot telling stories and since I'm from the country, which most of us are in one way or the other, I tell a lot of country stories. Sometimes ci-ditty people try to hide from the light that shines through the tales I tell by just playing it off—they say, "Oh, that's just another ol country boy talking." But I'm here to tell you I might be a farmer but I ain't no fool!

You don't know what that word "ci-ditty" means do you?

Back home Miz May Ellen Gladstone, now that's Willie Gladstone's mama—she's a Jeter by birth, her people come from down in The Bottom too. They had the place right next to the Tatum family—she's the one that built up the Funeral home Willie runs now. Miz May Ellen is an A-number-one good person. When the Freedom Riders first came to Macomb they stayed at her house. When the Sheriff set up road blocks to keep the director of this national Civil Rights organization from coming to speak at the New Mt. Zion Church, Miz May Ellen sent a hearse to meet him at the airport in New Orleans, put him in a coffin, drove him through the road block straight to Rev. Wright's church.

Right after Samella, Willie's little sister, was born, their daddy, Mr. Granville Gladstone had had a stroke. Miz May Ellen must have been too busy taking care of Mr. Granville, running the funeral home and helping out with The Movement to take good care of those children. Willie's mean as a one-eyed cat, and Samella was all right before she got so "ci-ditty."

The summer before we started high school, Samella went to Chicago. ' came back home with all these fancy clothes which didn't fit-in down home. She even took to sticking her nose up in the air and talking funny. I asked her why she be dressing strange and acting funny. She say, "You are just too, too country, sweetheart, that's how we do it in ci-ditty—I mean *the city!*" Fore long it got to be a saying when anybody got their hips up on their shoulders—got things turned bassackwards and upsidedown—that they was "ci-ditty."

I don't know why Miz May Ellen couldn't see to do better with her own kids cause she sure could see through everybody else. I never will forget the time she called Rev. Dooley out.

When I came back from the Korean war the Freedom Movement was just getting into full swing. My mind was made up and my heart was set. I went home and jumped

right into it. Miz May Ellen was the only one of the so-called
"big time" colored people would have something to do with
me and the Movement. She once took me to a meeting of
the National Business League of Greater Pike County in the
private dining room of the VF&W. I was trying to get them
to come to a meeting to find out about the Supreme Court
school desegregation issue.

Rev. Elmore Dooley, who ran "Dooley's One-Stop Grocery
Store and Grill."—if you stopped there one time, you wasn't
likely to stop no more—he was the first one to his feet.

"Mr. President, Madam Secretary and members in good
standing. As a life long resident of this community, as a
responsible business man, and minister of the Gospel, I feel
it's my bounden duty to say before I go, y'all need to leave
this freedom mess alone! It ain't nothing but trouble and I
ain't having nothing to do with it and if you was smart you'd
leave these shiftless Negroes alone too. If you ain't careful
these crazy white folks will have all of y'all back in the cotton
patch if not dead!"

Miz May Ellen stopped him in his march to the door and
said, "I guess you ought to know a shiftless Negro when you
see one, Rev. Elmore. How much grocery do you sell to
white folks? How many of them thump your collection trays
on Sunday mornings? I don't know who or what you think
you are. Hell, we're all just one step from the cotton patch
anyway!"

That was the Spring of 1957. We never could get us a
school case in Pike County but that fall they did get nine
children to start the white high school in Little Rock, Ar-
kansas. Since I knew you couldn't trust what was in the
newspaper, I figured I'd go on over there to see for myself
what was goin on.

It was October of 1957. I had been in Little Rock for some
months when I got this letter forwarded from home. "July
20, 1957. Dear Mr. Jones: Phillip wants to get in touch with
you. Please let me know where you are so I can put you on
his mail list. Write me at the above address or call me at
CAlumet 2-4210. Sincerely yours, Consuela LeBeaux."

It was two things seemed strange to me: number 1, this

letter looked like it might have something to do with a business or something and I knew the only business Po's likely to be in was monkey business. Number 2, I couldn't figure out why I'd have to get on a "mail list" to write or talk to Po.

I was staying at Mother Mason's Guest House on Elm St. Course I would have stayed at the Hilton but I didn't want everyone to know I was in town.

When my mail caught up with me it'd already been a good while since Miz Consuela's letter had been sent. So I decided to call on the phone and see what was going on.

It turned out that Po had got himself put back in jail. Miz Consuela, the honey dripper, was just trying to help out by finding me since I was the only one he wanted to write to. If you wasn't on their list, the jail house wouldn't let you communicate with him. They had him at the State Penitentiary in Joliet, Illinois. He was doing time for attempted manslaughter and about four other things.

It seems Po had won $1200 in a poker game from this white fellow who had tried to duck out on him. Po had to run the fellow down to get his money. But as the game was in a white neighborhood, when they seen this colored man with a scar on his face and a eight inch switch blade chasing this white man, somebody called the police. Even so, Po probably could have gotten away if he had just taken the money and gone on about his business, but no—he had to hang around giving the man a lecture about how honesty was the best policy, and how it would put a bad light on his people if he didn't pay his debts in a timely way. So because of that he landed in Joliet with a 24 year sentence.

Now I don't want y'all to misunderstand what I'm about to say because I don't believe that it's right what's happening in the jails of this country. You got to understand that something's wrong when over 80% of the people in jail is either Black, Spanish, Indian or some other denomination of poor people, when all together we don't make up 40% of the population. It just ain't right when a man who steals a $20 ham for his family might get three years in jail, while a man who steals $20,000,000 will get a warning and a little fine.

And if they just have to give him some time, they send him to a camp with horseback riding, golf, tennis courts and private rooms in little bungalows they can stay in with their wives and girls friends and whatever.

Now, I ain't in favor of jails and the way they are run but I do think it was a good thing for Po to get that little time when he did. The way he had been going, he might as well a tried to run through hell in a pair of gasoline drawers. If they hadn't put him in jail, they'd had to put him in a pine box.

Po always did like to taste a little bit. But when he got to the city, someone turned him on to dope. By the time he got busted he had begun to mess around with heroin—snorting it and every now and then he pump a little bit. But when they put him in jail he got to reading and studying and practicing on his writing and all kinds of stuff.

You can see the difference in Po by the letters he would write:

June 16, 1957

Dear Brother Junebug,

How are you? Fine I hope. Here I sit behind these four walls of bars. Sad and lonely and all alone I write this empty cell and dream about the times we was fishing on the Bogue Chitto River and wish that I had the wings of a dove and over these prison walls would I fly but since I am not no angel and will be here for a while I wisht that you would send me news of the world out side and books that I can read. PLEASE don't tell my brothers and people where I am.

Your sad friend, Phillip A. Tatum

December 18, 1958

Dear Junebug,

I figured "what the hell!" So I signed up to go to college. Bet you didn't know you could do that in jail? The worse they could do if I fail is kick me out of here. Don't I wish! Well, I had to do something to pass the time. So why not try college?

I figured I'd start off easy so I took this English composition course. It was not as easy as I thought but I came out o.k.

I only made a "C," but that ~~ain't~~ isn't too bad for a fellow dropped out of the ninth grade, is it?

I met this guy in the library named Robert Watson. You might as well say he volunterred to go to jail because he's in here for what he called a "sitting demonstration" at a private club in Springfield. He's a pre-law student. He went and made a sitting demonstration to test the law that says black folks can't go to places like that. He won't even take bail while his case is still in court.

It sounds dumb to me. I'm getting out as quick as I can. What's going on out there? Have people gone crazy?

Your incarcerated friend,

Po

March 20, 1959

Dear Junebug,

I am into chess now. Are you hip to chess? There's this old dude in here that everybody thinks is crazy. Won't tell nobody his name or nothing. He has been here for 37 years and nobody knows his name. They call him Old Dude. Even the guards call him Old Dude.

The only thing Old Dude will do is play chess. He won't do that with just any and everybody either. But he did offer to teach me what he knew about the game. Through that we got to talking. It turns out the Old Dude had first been sent up for 5 years for something they called "criminal syndicalism." I looked it up in the library here and near as I can understand, it's something like crime syndicate. The Old Dude had joined up with this syndicate they call a union they were trying to get at the plant outside of Chicago. Thirteen of them got busted.

After a month or two at Joliet the warden sict one of his lap dogs on the Old Dude to make him rat on his partners. They got in a fight. The Old Dude hit the other guy with the handle of a wrench out the machine shop and called a guard. It took them so long to get that guy to the infirmary that he bled to death.

A month after that happened, they cut the other 12 guys loose but they convicted the Old Dude on a new charge of murder 1.

I'm glad you got me to let my family know what's happening. Ralph and Skinhead both came all the way up here twice to visit me. I told Consuela, "I feel more like a man now that I ain't got nothing to hide." She smiled and said, "You look more like a man to me too, darling." I can't wait to get out of here!

Send me something about these people in Montgomery, Alabama. What do they think they are trying to do? I don't have too much to do with preachers ever since Deacon Johnny Green pulled the covers off Rev. Dr. ABC Golightly. But this King fellow from Montgomery seems to be different. Maybe he's the one who can lead us out the wilderness of North America.

Keep the books coming. After I get thru with whatever you send, I put them in the prison library, so you helping at least a few more besides me . . . maybe.

Your studious friend
P. A. Tatum

November 3, 1963
Dear Junebug,

I got to tell somebody! I'm still gloating about the fact that I did better in this course in "Modern Social Theory" than Babatunde did. Babatunde is just a thesis short of his Masters degree, and the professor said my final paper was "insightful, inovative, very interesting and that it deserves serious consideration." He gave Babatunde an "A" too but he wrote all over the brother's paper about how this point needed "further development" and so forth. I feel like I'm doing all right.

I wrote a critical review of the theoretical differences between W. E. B. DuBois and the White/Wilkins regime of the NAACP. It's really an interesting case study that reveals some of the basic problems that lie at the heart of the Afro-American struggle for freedom, justice and equality in America. If you're interested, let me know. I'll send you a copy of the paper.

Thanks for your help hooking me up with the NAA lawyer for the Old Dude. After a year and a half of correspondence, I got a letter last week from the lawyer. He's willing to try

for clemency for the Old Dude, considering the circum-
stances and some recent rulings on similar cases.

The only problem is, we buried the Old Dude last month.

Yours with undying hope for freedom,

P. Anthony Tatum

P.S. I'm up for parole next week. Wish me luck.

THE DANGER ZONE IS EVERYWHERE

Once, when I's in New Orleans, I heard Mr. Ray Charles.
"The Raelets are international stars! Just in case y'all don't
know what that word 'international' means—it means all
over everywhere! Yes sir! The Raelets are international stars."
(Singing) "The whole world's in an uproar and the danger
zone is everywhere!"

That's what I's trying to tell Po when I went to visit him
the last time 'fore he got out of jail, but he never heard a
word I said. "No, Junebug, now that I'm a college graduate,
I'll get a good job and work my way thru law school. I'm
not fit for real work anyway."

"How you think you going to law school with a felony
conviction rap, Po?"

"They got good lawyers meeting at the bar everyday with
worse records than mine, my brother." I wondered what kind
of bar he was thinking about.

They put Po in a halfway house on the Westside of Chicago till he could find a regular job. It was in a real crowded
part of town. That part of town wasn't much different than
the jail Po had come out of, except the jail was cleaner.
Everybody had they little roosts to go to. It reminded me of
how chickens be stacked in crates on a flatbed truck on the
way to market. You go your roost, you fasten three or four
locks and a chain and there you be—them four walls is
home.

I was working with the Mississippi Freedom Democrats at
the time, and I had jumped at the chance when they needed
somebody to do some organizing work in Chicago. Miz Consuela took to inviting us to her house over on Drexel Boulevard for Sunday dinner. The first time I went I made the

mistake of asking Po how he was coming on his job hunt. "I can't stand these jive time liberals! Things be going just fine till they find out I'm an ex-con, then the stuff gets funny. 'Mr. Tatum, you're overqualified,' 'Mr. Tatum you're under qualified,' Give me a straight up, stomp down redneck any day!"

"You must learn not to be consumed by your own anger, Phillipe."

"If I am consumed by anything, it is my 'legitimate discontent' as your Dr. King might say. I could go out of here this afternoon, after nine years out of circulation and get a stake for either gambling or selling drugs and have $500 or a $1000 of my own to spend by tomorrow nite. Now, with a college degree, I can't even find a straight job that will pay $150 a week. Don't worry. I'm not going back into the life. But you have to recognize that something's wrong with the system that offers a man that kind of choice!"

He grabbed the Sunday Paper and sat in the big chair by the window. He'd read a while, then he would stare out the window watching the children play while junkies went in and out of the empty brown brick building across Drexel Boulevard. Po would cuss the newspaper. Miz Consuela would ask him, "If you find the newspaper so disturbing, why to you continue to read it?"

"Information is an essential requirement of modern life. As Brother Malcolm says, he who manipulates the media manipulates the masses. I have to keep up with what the Devil is saying so I know what not to think!" He turned back to the newspaper in such a way that we knew not to say no more to him.

Finally, the brother got a job. They hired him to be a counselor at the Halfway House, and that picked him up real good. When I pulled out of Chicago on the IC railroad, I felt like my friend Po was doing all right for himself. Me, I was tired of being where you couldn't see the sun go down for all the concrete and steel.

My work took me to a heap of different places. It was a lot of stuff for us Freedom Riders to do in the 60s. The next time I hit Chicago, he'd dug up Miz Consuela's whole back yard. Had some collard greens, I'sh potatoes, tomatoes, squashes, bell peppers, okra and some funny little plants he said was Miz Consuela's teas.

"Po, this garden looks near bout as good as back home."

"Yeah, Junebug, we've got to learn to get back to the land. As long as a people have a piece of land they've got something worth while. Junebug, my man, this is only the beginning. There's land all around here. A vacant lot here, one there. And there's people can't hardly afford to eat. Now there's a likely combination: hungry people and vacant land! All I have to do is put all this land to productive use and I can feed the world!"

Sometime Po and me be talking and I think we're going one way come to find out he's going the other. I thought we was talking about his little backyard garden and he's the new messiah out to feed the whole world.

Still it made my heart feel good. He was almost like the old Po. Had a look in his eye I hadn't seen since before Mr. Jake died. He even started making up rhymes again.

I got a garden in the city
My okra's really pretty
Had no greens that taste so good
Since I was home.
Had to put aside my shopping
Grocery bill it got me rocking
Had to leave that doggone grocery store alone.

Living off my garden, baby
Garden in the city
Living off my garden, baby
Garden in the city

Digga, digga, digga, digga, digga Chicago
Digga, digga, digga, digga, digga Chicago
Digga, digga, digga, digga, digga Chicago
Trying to find a way to make a new home.

Po was running up and down different streets all over the South Side looking at vacant lots. He was still working at the

Halfway House but he had also organized something he called "Development of International Gardens in Chicago."

"DIG in Chicago, you dig it?"

"What do you mean by the 'international' part?"

"All over everywhere! We got the potential to feed half the hungry people in the world right here in Chicago!"

That was the first time I met Johnny Tadlow. He was a fine looking fellow with a black leather jacket, a little crimp brim hat and a gold tooth right here. Kept a big smile on his face so you could see it.

"Brother Junebug, we figure there's an average of 3 lots in every block where some house has been torn down, burned down or just about to fall down, you dig? So if we just take this 6 block area from Drexel to Woodlawn and from 43rd to 45th, that's approximately 12 acres. Now if we convert that to productive land, it'll feed at least 10% of the people in this neighborhood. When we get this neighborhood organized, we're going to move on to next one and the next one. Besides affordable, fresh food for the people, this program will provide jobs for cats like us coming out of the joint, you dig. Now that's what you call reversing the cycle, Brother, dig it!"

"And that's serious, real work that a man can really be productive at, not just copping a slave for some dude that don't care no more about him than Col. Whitten cared for his brother's pet pig."

Well, it worked! By Spring, DIG in Chicago had planted up a bunch of vacant lots. People come in droves from all over to buy those vegetables.

Those were the days! After they'd finish up the day's work they'd meet up somewhere, talk things over and have a nip. They was a fine bunch. Whenever I could, I'd be with them.

There was this one fellow they called Deadeye. Had one eye—he lost the other one in Korea. He had the look of a bulldog. Deadeye: "Before I got to working in the garden, things had got so hard, man, that I didn't have but $1.47 for lunch. I went and sat down in this little greasy spoon joint and this fine young sister came over and I asked her, 'What can I get for $1.47, Baby?'"

"'I ain't your baby, Mister. The only thing you can get in here for a dollar forty-seven cents is hurt feelings. You need more than that to get a wish sandwich.'"

"'A wish sandwich?'"

"'Yes. That's when you get two pieces of bread and a paper napkin and wish you had some meat.'"

"Man that woman offent my mantality! I got up and walked out so fast I tried to take the door off the hinges."

Then there was this other old cat called Hound. He said, "You was lucky you could still afford to buy that much, brother. I was so broke, that I had to borrow eyewater to cry with."

Them guys would carry on! When they weren't laughing and joking, they would be rapping on the problems of the world. When people get a sense of purpose in their lives, it seems like the whole world opens up to them.

Then, it come a day, that next fall, when it seem like the problems of the world blew in on them just as swift and mean as a cold wind off Lake Michigan.

Po: "Here's the situation. Fat Mack, the South Side Numbers Man, brought us a message from the mob. Said we have to start giving them half of what we make at our stores if we want to stay in business."

Tadlow: "Forget that, Man! My grandaddy left Mississippi to get shed of sharecropping!"

Po: "As if that wasn't enough the man downtown has issued building permits for four out of six of our sites on the south side. They've got low income housing slated for these sites. There's somebody big that probably stands to make big money off of it. They plan to bring the bulldoozers in tomorrow."

Hound: "They won't hold off long enough for us to get the harvest in."

Tadlow: "They'll hold off as long as we make them hold off! What we need is action, you dig, action! When y'all get done flapping your lips, meet me down at the battle front."

Deadeye: "Cool it youngblood! Ain't no 'battlefront,' yet. We just got to make a plan for what we can do together! And don't you forget; you still on parole."

Tadlow: "Don't you forget that you got a good bunch of men depending on you for work and people counting on you for food. I ain't no more scared of the Man than I am of the Mob. Besides, it's the principle of the thing. Ain't that what you taught me, Po? Naw, man. Meet me at the battlefront. I'm gone."

Po: "Let him go. He'll be back when he cools out."

They made a plan to meet at the main garden on 43rd St. before day with as many people as they could muster. The next morning, the whole block was full of people. They sang and bragged about how they wasn't "gone let nobody turn them around." They even took over the trucks with the bulldozers on them.

They were feeling real good as the early morning light got bright enough to see into the garden somebody screamed, "What's that out there?" Po hollered, "Don't y'all trample down the product!" as he fought his way through the crowd. There was Johnny. It didn't look like all that blood could have come from the one small round bullet hole in the middle of his forehead.

Po didn't even try to plant a garden the spring of '67. He just went to sitting in the window at Miz Consuela's house staring out the window. Reminded me of how Miz Adeline was after Mr. Jake passed.

Miz Consuela would lite candles in the window and sit with him a while. She'd brew up these herb teas and get him to drink a little. Said it was his medicine. I wished I could have said something to make him laugh. A rhyme, a story. Everytime I'd go somewhere and come back Po look like he was a little worse off.

Sometimes Po be gone. Nobody know where to find him. He lost the job at the Halfway House. He come home hungry and tired. He sleep. He sit, looking out the window. Sometimes Po'd pop up and say something like he's talking to some people we couldn't see.

"A college degree offers little relief from the bondage of blackness in white America. A piece of paper is no passport from the prison of poverty! Malcolm was right. If they won't let you win with the ballot, then you must lay claim to victory with the bullet. . . . Somebody ought to do something about those buildings across the street."

When Po got to talking like that, I seen a kind of cold wildness in his eyes. Reminded me of old A. D. Whitten back home preaching on the Courthouse steps. I didn't have no recollection of Po like that. His eyes used to sparkle and smile, even when he's talking bad about your mama.

Every summer was worse that the one before. Cities burning: Harlem, Watts, Newark, Detroit. Everytime somebody got killed it seemed like a little piece of Po would die too. He'd sit there looking at reports on TV rocking back and forth making something that sounded like an Indian Chant out of "Burn, Baby Burn. Burn, Baby Burn . . ."

It rocked on and rocked on into 1968. That was tough. They killed Dr. King in Memphis, and the whole country went up in flames. They got Kennedy in California. Then they brought the Democrats Convention to Chicago and the whole world was watching.

I was watching the Convention on television when up popped Po Tatum on the local news!

"Why are you trying to take over all these South Side Chicago buildings?"

"There's thousands of people who need places to stay and right now these empty buildings are nothing but shooting galleries for a bunch of junkies."

"But what you're doing is illegal, isn't it?"

"What's happening here now is immoral and destructive to the life of this community. We're trying to liberate these buildings."

"But Mr. Tatum, isn't it true that you're blocking the rightful owners from acquiring permits for rehabilitation?"

"These buildings have been vacant for years. Why do you think these damn landlords just started this stuff when we started this action?"

"Who is this 'we' you refer to? Isn't it true that you represent no real constituency?"

"That's not true. I represent the people."

"Isn't that rather ambiguous and isn't it true, Mr. Tatum, that you were recently released from Joliet State Prison on charges of attempted manslaughter, jail breaking, illegal gambling and a variety of other charges?"

"What the hell has that got to do with anything?"

"We taped this interview earlier today with Mr. Phillip A. Tatum at the site of a building on Drexel Blvd. that he's trying to 'liberate.' We have just learned that Mr. Tatum has occupied the building, he is believed to be armed and is considered extremely dangerous."

"Meanwhile, at the Democratic Convention . . ."

I hit the street flying.
Hell of a storm blowing in off the lake
"Taxi!"
All at once it come as clear as a bell
Po thought he's the only one could tell
All the evil in the world to go to hell
"Taxi!"
Chica, chica, chica, chica, chica, chica, chic—
"El'll take too long . . .
Taxi!
Drexel and 45th. Quick!"
"Loop's blocked off."
   got to go way out the way
   all this mess at the Convention
   tanks in the streets of Chicago
"Faster man, Faster!"
   city streets go flashing by
   city streets no place to die
   who knows which way the wind blows
   who knows which way the wind blows
   who knows which way the wind blows
   in the Windy City.
   Rolling South in a sea of Blues
   rolling South in a sea of Blues
   rolling South in a sea of Blues
   in the Windy City.
"Faster man, faster. Right on 37th. Move it!"

A clap of thunder split the sky

Cop cars screaming around the corner
flashing lights ahead
uh oh. Something's wrong.

"Cops got the street blocked at 40th and Drexel."
"Let me out here.
Keep the change."

Don't run.

Cops.
Blockades.
A sea of Blues.
Strange.

Police frozen.

Guns pulled.

People milling in the street
like a show going on
"Crazy nigger holded up in that building."
"They gon to kill a coon today."
"Let me thru!"
"What's he trying to do?"
"I don't know."
"Let me thru!"

   I couldn't tell what come first, the gun shots, the thunder,
some other kind of explosion.
   It was a many different stories told bout that day. The
newspapers said that Po shot first and the police returned
so much fire that that old building which was in mighty bad
shape anyway just fell down. With all that whirl of thunder
and lightning wasn't many people ready to swear to what
really did happen. There was other stories too; bout Po had
the building rigged with dynamite—there was even one old
man that swore he seen the face of a man in the clouds
when a bolt of lightning hit and danced all around that
building just as the police opened fire.
   It took three days going thru that rubble for they's able
to find the two bodies in there. Both of them was messed

up too bad to be identified for sure. One of them looked like it might have been Po but Consuela swore Po had left the house that morning with a clean red shirt. The body they found had on a green shirt.

Consuela and me took what we believed to be Po's remains to Mississippi in the best coffin we could afford. We buried him out there in The Bottom beside his Ma and Pa.

THE END

epilogue: rap

You can't judge a book by looking at the cover
you may read my letter
but I betcha can't read my mind
If you want to get down, down, down
You got to spend some time
I want to walk with you
I want to talk with you
I want I want I want I want to rap with you
Hey . . . . Hey hey hey

I done told you a story bout by old friend Po
Bout tings he tried to do, places he had to go
bout home boy going out, to get some money
If it wasn't so sad it really might have been funny
told all about the way he tried to make it in the city
told you everything although it really wasn't pretty
told all about the way that he was misunderstood
by his family and his friends thought that he was just a hood
told how the man misunderstood himself
he went to get some knowledge, left the book up on the shelf.
He got the cover of the book but didn't get what it had in it

what should have took a week, he tried to get it in a minute.

When you grow up in the country things are hard and times are tough
take to growing your own food but it never seems enough
think you're too smart for the country and you gotta get away
move up to the city, got to be a better way
So you move to the city, put the country stuff behind
But when you hit the city, it starts messing with your mind.
You get on the straight and narrow and you follow all the rules.
You figure you're the one that's going to outdo all the fools.
You struggle and you scramble just to do the best you can.
You think you're working for a living, find you're working for the man.
People stacked like chickens on the way to meet the slaughter.
They flopping all around the ground like fishes out of water.
A blind man begging on a corner, holding up a sign
It say "No more water, the fire next time!"

jim grimsley

mr. universe

artist's statement

Mr. Universe is a play about castaways that explores the hole in the middle of things. It grew out of my experiences living in New Orleans in the late 1970s and it is concerned with the corners of the world that morality neglects. It is also concerned with obsessions and fetishes related to the definition of genders in our world. I leave these statements vague because I am not altogether comfortable with making any statement about the intent of something as fragile as a play. Meaning is a delicate business. Maybe the clearest statement about *Mr. Universe* is simply a description of the image that began the play: the well-built man enters the stage, confronts the audience, strips off his clothes, displays his perfect body, then paints himself with something that looks like blood. Someone finds him, someone wants to take care of him. Then something happens.

production history

The play was developed through readings in the Alternate ROOTS Writers Workshop at two successive Annual Meetings. Del Hamilton premiered the play at 7Stages in August 1987, and the play was then produced in New Orleans and Los Angeles, prior to an Off-Broadway production at the New Federal Theatre in New York, with Woodie King as producer. *Mr. Universe* won Grimsley the George Oppenheimer/Newsday Award for best new American playwright in 1988. The play was again produced in Atlanta in 1991.

players

VICK: a man in his early forties. For many years he worked as a professional drag queen doing drag shows at a bar on Rampart Street. He has been married and has a son.

JUDY: a man in his early twenties, the illegitimate son of a New Orleans stripper who was raised by his grandmother in rural Alabama. He has only recently moved to New Orleans. For a time he and Vick were lovers.

KATY JUME: a New Orleans native who makes her living as best she can. She has lived in Vick's apartment building for two years.

THE MUSCLE MAN: is a classical bodybuilder with a doll-like face. He is perfectly proportioned and capable of performing a polished routine of physique pose. He is boyish and yet sexual, as if he were a male centerfold come to life.

THE POLICE WOMAN: is a New Orleans cop in full police regalia. She is very tough and butch. The lower French Quarter is her beat.

JUEL LAURIE: is a widow who lives in another of the apartments in Vick's building, which has been her home since her marriage.

THE SAXOPHONE PLAYER: is a musician who inhabits various street corners in the French Quarter and downtown New Orleans.

stage/setting

New Orleans 1979. In particular, the stage must accommodate the following settings:

Scene one: Esplanade Avenue outside Vick's apartment building. The building is very old and falling into decay. The street is typical of that part of New Orleans in late summer—weeds encroaching on whatever shrubbery grows around the building, litter accumulating—particularly liquor bottles, drying patches

of vomit, rotting articles of miscellaneous clothing,
Twinkie wrappers, ominous looking red stairs. The scene
requires only the atmosphere of the street and no
particular objects except one or two large garbage cans.

Scenes two through five: The interior of Vick's apartment.
Two distinct playing areas should be available, one of
which is always the living room, while the other should be
adaptable to use as the kitchen and as Judy's bedroom. A
playing area identifiable as the hallway outside the
apartment would be helpful as well. Vick has never made
a real financial success of his life and his apartment
should reflect his indifference to money. The furnishings
are shabby but not pathetic. There is no television, radio
or stereo to be seen. The walls are plaster, cracked and
flaking. Decorations might reflect Vick's glory days as a
professional drag queen. He is a tidy housekeeper but
Judy is a slob: articles of women's clothing pervade the
apartment, resting wherever Judy dropped them until
Vick picks them up. No single item of furniture is
necessary beyond the portrait of Judy Garland or
alternative; the setting may border on the surreal.
There must be a place for the Saxophone Player to stand
that is distinctly outside the apartment during the latter
scenes; in the first scene he or she may simply be on the
street.

act 1

SCENE ONE

*Esplanade Avenue, a night in late spring. Lights rise on the
Saxophone Player who is rehearsing in the cool night playing
traditional New Orleans jazz.*
*Enter Juel Laurie dragging a bag of garbage. The bag has a hole
in it and she trails garbage behind her. She stops once or twice to
pick up the garbage she has dropped returning it to the bag but
never quite comprehending that the bag has a hole in it. Finally
she reaches the garbage can and puts the bag in it. She walks
away from it a few steps then stands still thinking.*
*Enter the Police Woman who watches the Saxophone Player and
Juel Laurie.*
*Juel Laurie returns to the garbage can, takes out the bag, opens
it. Begins to lay out the garbage neatly around her. The
Saxophone Player lets the music soften and die away. Sits and
begins to polish his horn, clean the mouthpiece, etc. Lights fade
on him. This should coincide with the moment Juel Laurie
finishes arranging the garbage and speaks.*

JUEL LAURIE. I should of brought me some paper so I could do
a list. I hate to throw this stuff away and tomorrow I won't
even remember what it is. Looka this. *(Holds up an old shoe)*
I knew it. I knew. I never meant to throw this out. It ain't
but one shoe but it's a good one. *(Smells it)* Smells just like
Vanice, lord help me. I told him. Vanice, I says, your feet
stink because you never wash from between your toes. I told
him.

Police Woman approaches.

POLICE WOMAN. Excuse me ma'am, what are you doing?
JUEL LAURIE. Oh God, did I do a crime?
POLICE WOMAN. You can't leave all this stuff laying around.
JUEL LAURIE. I was just making a list. Are you going to put me
under suspicion?
POLICE WOMAN. I just want you to clear all this up ma'am.

JUEL LAURIE. This is a good shoe.

POLICE WOMAN. Yes ma'am, you can keep the shoe.

JUEL LAURIE. *(Bagging up the garbage)* You ain't seen Vanice running around here have you? He left the house this morning without no belt on, and his pants so baggy they be all down his legs.

POLICE WOMAN. Is Vanice your husband?

JUEL LAURIE. Lord yes, everybody knows that. Everybody knows Vanice, he's got big feet. Why do you work for the Police? Do you like crime?

POLICE WOMAN. No ma'am.

JUEL LAURIE. Has they been any good crime around here today?

POLICE WOMAN. Found a dead man in a motel over to the Faubourg. Don't know who he is.

JUEL LAURIE. Did he have a belt on?

POLICE WOMAN. Didn't have much of nothing on from what I hear.

JUEL LAURIE. Can't be Vanice then, he ain't never naked. *(Ties the bag closed and puts it in the garbage)* I got to go fry some bologney. You want a piece?

POLICE WOMAN. No ma'am. You don't let no strangers in the house now.

Exit Police Woman. Enter Vick in high drag. He stays out of sight until the Police Woman is gone.

VICK. *(To Juel Laurie)* What did she want with you Mistress Laurie?

JUEL LAURIE. Hey Vick. That's a mighty nice dress you got on, did you go back to work at JuJu's?

VICK. No ma'am, I'm just going out. What did that Police Woman want?

JUEL LAURIE. She got me under suspicion. She found a dead man in a motel, naked as God, over to the Faubourg.

VICK. She don't think you did it?

JUEL LAURIE. She might think I did, and Vanice ain't here to testify. Lord I need him so bad

VICK. Mistress Laurie now I've told you, you got to put him out of your mind, you can't bring him back.

JUEL LAURIE. The Police coming back, you know that, they don't never come just once. She let me have my shoe but she's coming back for me.

VICK. Sweetheart come with me, come on. That's right. We got to get you back in your apartment right now.

JUEL LAURIE. I got to cook my supper.

VICK. Yes ma'am you do.

JUEL LAURIE. Will you be home?

VICK. Judy and me are going out for a little while but we'll be back later, you just knock on the door when the light's on.

JUEL LAURIE. Katy ain't home. I know that. She out walking in a cheap dress, left her kitchen window wide open.

VICK. I know honey, I ain't seen Katy in a few days. But you'll be all right. Just keep the front door closed and come see me and Judy later when we get back.

Enter Judy, also in high drag.

JUDY. What's wrong with her?

VICK. She just got a little confused.

JUDY. Tell me some news.

JUEL LAURIE. Are you still taking up with him *(Indicates Judy)*

VICK. Yes ma'am, Mistress Laurie, and Lord knows I don't know why. *(To Judy)* I'm just walking her back to her apartment, I'll be right back.

JUDY. You better be because I'm not waiting around, not long as it took me to get this garter belt right.

VICK. Oh hush, it won't hurt you to wait two minutes.

JUDY. I know it won't hurt me dear, but what about you, you're aging every second.

VICK. Kiss my ass.

Exit Vick and Juel Laurie.
Saxophone Player has finished his instrument cleaning and stands, begins to play Slow, mournful blues - Judy's Theme, "Your Daddy". Judy struts up and down the stage timing her sashay to the music. Enter Vick, putting on lipstick. Music dies away. Saxophone Player withdraws to his playing area; lights down on Saxophone Player.

VICK. Sweetheart what are you trying to do, make this month's rent?

JUDY. You're just jealous because I have better legs than you do. Don't you think you've put on enough lipstick by now?

VICK. Please don't flap your hand in my face. And who do you think you are teaching me about makeup when I have worked on the professional stage. You can't teach me anything about being a woman, I have done it all.

JUDY. I bet you have. All at JuJu's Hideaway.

VICK. Your Mama never worked any better place honey, not even with real tits.

JUDY. *(Haughty)* I do not want to talk about my Mama if you don't mind.

VICK. Are you ready to go? *(Takes a few steps)*

JUDY. I am not interested in one bar up that street, I am tired of old men and chicken.

VICK. Well I am not going to ruin my good gown walking up and down the waterfront to find you a sailor.

JUDY. Why not?

VICK. You are completely out of your mind; the sailor never sailed who would give you the time of day.

JUDY. But you promised.

VICK. Just exactly when did I promise to walk down to the waterfront and get myself killed?

JUDY. You said you thought it would be fun.

VICK. I said I thought it would be fun if we could fool them boys, but we can't.

JUDY. All we ever do is go to the same old bar and drink the same old drink and talk to the same old men.

VICK. I am not having this discussion with you again.

JUDY. I want to have some fun Vick, please take me down to the river, please please. I'll be such a good girl you won't even know me. We'll just walk down there and walk back, we don't have to stay.

VICK. And you'll pick up some trash not fit to clean toilets and have him laying up in my apartment till I throw his ass out.

JUDY. You're just jealous.

VICK. Sweetheart, when you get your own apartment you can sleep with every bum from here to Lake Charles.

JUDY. Please don't start at me Vick, you know I can't afford my own place, I still got to pay Maison Blanche for my alligator pumps.

VICK. Shut up whining about them shoes. Here comes a friend of mine.

Enter a man whose large muscles are obvious even through his clothes. He walks tentatively as if he is lost in the city. He stops some distance from the drag queens.

JUDY. You never knew anybody like that in your life.

VICK. *(Obviously stricken, not camp)* Did you ever . . . Just look at that!

JUDY. I could peel him like a grape. Do you think he's one of us?

VICK. He's too butch.

JUDY. Well sweetheart, we're not all sissies. Though you'd never know it by the company we keep *(Laughs at his own joke)*

VICK. Don't cackle like a crow, he isn't paying the least attention to you.

JUDY. You mean he isn't paying any attention to you.

VICK. No he isn't. I didn't say he was.

JUDY. What's the matter honey, you falling in love?

VICK. Stop it, don't talk so loud.

JUDY. It's nothing to be embarrassed about dear, you can't help it. It's the Cinderella Complex, it's a common thing for us girls. When you see a man like that you can't help dreaming he's Mister Right.

VICK. Shut up, I'm not dreaming anything.

JUDY. You really are upset aren't you?

VICK. Let's go.

JUDY. No, I think I just want to stand right here for a little while and check out the street life.

VICK. Well you can stand here by yourself.

JUDY. You wouldn't dare leave me here by myself dressed like this.

VICK. Don't bet on it sweetheart.

JUDY. You just wait a minute.

VICK. Life's too short dear. I don't have all night, and neither do you. I've seen you after midnight.

Exit Vick.

JUDY. You come back here bitch.

VICK. *(From offstage)* Why I can almost hear that sweet disco music.

JUDY. Wait a minute. Wait for me, please wait.

SCENE TWO

Black out. Sounds rise: traffic noises, voices, a ship's horn, faint. The lights lower till there is just one patch of light where the Muscle Man is standing. The scene changes. A stage hand drags off the garbage cans. Another clears away any other representation of the apartment building. The Saxophone Player blows a few bars, drinks bourbon from a flask, blows a little more. The Police Woman wanders through, exits. The Saxophone Player descends, circles the Muscle Man, playing. Exits. Traffic noise fades, a pulsing beat begins. The Muscle Man takes off his clothes, slowly stripping to a pair of posing trunks. He simply stands still with his clothes on stage around him. As music grows slowly louder and the lights change he paints himself with streaks of red paint, like blood, as if he is creating wounds. Enter Katy Jume in a tight cocktail dress.

KATY. Told him to get his god damn hands off me. Told him he looked worse than shit in a pot. Touch my titties one more time and I cut his hands off. Make me sick. I don't even want to know who he is or what his name is. Shit ass motherfucker keep his hands off my drink too. Drag your scrawny ass out of here. Leave me money for a drink and get out. Yes sir, I said leave me money for a drink or I'll pull every hair out of your head. I said every one and watch me do it. I don't care who hears me. Don't talk that bullshit to me, I'll snatch the false teeth out of your mouth. Yellow tooth motherfucker. I wish I could embarrass you to death.

Sees the Muscle Man sitting on the grass of the neutral ground.

What are you looking at?

The Muscle Man goes on watching her without moving or speaking.

Get up off the ground staring at me. Answer me when I talk to you. I don't care how good you look, you don't sit on the ground staring at me. I'll beat your head in. I'll be responsible for your death, do you hear me? Get up from there. Get up I said.

The Muscle Man slowly stands.

You got blood all over you.

Enter Judy and Vick. Vick is holding his wig in his hand.

VICK. I'd never believe we'd be on our way home at this time of night.

JUDY. Would you shut the fuck up?

VICK. I don't want to rub salt in the wound but you have just made a complete and total fool of yourself in world record time.

JUDY. If you say one more word I will kill you.

VICK. Never has one queen so completely humiliated herself in public. I doubt Pink Lilly will ever let you back in the door.

JUDY. If I had a gun I'd blow your brains out right here on the street. Not that it would make that much of a mess. What happened tonight is not that big a deal.

VICK. View the wreckage dear. You ran your poor boyfriend right off the planet. You made a shambles of my dress. I smell like dog piss. God only knows what has been on that floor besides me.

They stop near Katy and the Muscle Man.

JUDY. Honey, has he been yours for long or are you just now sinking your teeth in?

KATY. You better back away from me Judy.

JUDY. I beg your pardon, I didn't mean to intrude. We saw this young gentleman earlier didn't we Vick?

VICK. It looks like you've been in a fight.

KATY. I found him sitting on the ground. He won't say nothing. He got blood all over him.

VICK. You poor baby, what happened? *(Pauses for response, gets none)* Did somebody get after you? Did somebody do this to you? *(Pauses; no response)* There's something wrong with him.

JUDY. Not from where I'm standing.

VICK. Shut up Judy. *(To the Muscle Man)* Are you all right? Do
you need some help? *(The Muscle Man does not answer but
makes eye contact with Vick for a beat)* I think maybe we ought
to take him home. Do you want to come home with me?

KATY. He don't act like he knows what you're saying.

VICK. Do you want to come home with me? So I can clean you
up? Don't be scared, you poor thing. I don't think he knows
how to talk.

JUDY. That's fine with me.

VICK. Come on sweetheart, I won't let this mean thing hurt you.
(The Muscle Man moves to Vick's side) You want to come up
for a while, Katy?

KATY. I might as well. I lost my key again.

VICK. Well you can sleep on the couch tonight and call the
landlord tomorrow. Are those his clothes?

KATY. I'll get them.

JUDY. This is wonderful. He looks just like a Ken doll. He can
sleep with me tonight.

VICK. Judy, this man is hurt. Leave him alone.

JUDY. Who named you Florence Nightingale? You can't tell me
what to do.

VICK. You better keep your hands to yourself if you know what's
good for you.

JUDY. You are not going to keep this man all to yourself Vick
darling.

Judy tries to touch the Muscle Man. Vick slaps his hand.

VICK. You listen to me. I am dead serious. You behave.

Judy withdraws, angry.

VICK. *(To Muscle Man)* Come on with me. That's right, come this
way. You coming, Katy?

KATY. I'm right behind you. Lord, these some nasty clothes.

*Exit Vick, Katy and the Muscle Man. Judy remains behind,
furious. Lights dim as he removes his wig. The Saxophone Player
plays softly offstage. Judy smears his makeup with his hands till
it is grotesque. Sashays offstage behind the others.*

SCENE THREE

Vick's apartment. Living room and kitchen. Enter the Muscle Man to the living room, carrying his clothes in his hand. He sits on a low stool or chair under low light and is wearing the posing trunks as before. Enter Judy and Katy into kitchen. Judy is still wearing the dress. They should enter a few moments after the Muscle Man sits. At the end of Vick's speech, lights rise in the kitchen and Katy is heard.

KATY. So I told him I would cut him if he ever showed his face around that restaurant again. I wouldn't even use a meat knife on him, just an old potato knife, and I'd carve him up so good I might as well cook him, there wouldn't be any use to do nothing else with him. Motherfucker turn so white, lord you should have seen it child. His little old cock just wither right away. I told him he rather not ever lay his hands on me nor show me anything so puny. You know I told him.

JUDY. Try this.

KATY. That's got too much bourbon for him.

JUDY. You think so?

KATY. Yeah, he been beat up, you don't want to knock him out. Give that to me and make him another one.

Enter Vick with a basin of water, towels and materials for bandages for cleaning the Muscle Man, even if he must enter during the scene above between Katy and Judy. He makes as many trips as necessary to prepare for his first-aid ministrations. He has washed his face quickly and is wearing either the dress or a dressing gown, somehow maternal. A wig is lying in the living room in a conspicuous place. He bathes the Muscle Man, cleans the wounds and applies bandages.

JUDY. Well how much should I put in?

KATY. Just hold it up and jiggle it a little. Just a little. Yeah, that's right. Now pour something else on it, and you got a drink.

JUDY. Let me see what I can find to mix with it. (Opens cabinet) Look at this mess. We don't ever have nothing fit to eat. Oh, here's some tomato paste!

KATY. You don't want none of that.

JUDY. It would be gummy, wouldn't it. And I guess we don't want any canned baby lima beans and we don't want any cornbread mix, puffy and fluffy and all, and we don't want any presweetened fruitaide and we don't want any instant ice tea or powdered nonfat instant dry milk, *(moves to refrigerator)* no sprouts, god I hate sprouts, no tofu, jello or white minute rice, no we don't want to mix our bourbon with any of that stuff. Did you see this cake? I made it myself.

VICK. *(As he cleans the wounds)* Just hold still now, I'll be real gentle but it might sting a little. That's right, just hold still, that's real good. Nobody's going to hurt you. Vick's going to take good care of you, bandage you up real nice and get you something to eat and put you to bed, and then tomorrow we'll find out who you are and where you live and get you home all safe and sound.

JUDY. Did you say something?

VICK. I was just trying to clean the wounds. He's not hurt so bad. Not as bad as it looked, anyway.

JUDY. Well how nice. I was picturing blood just pouring all over the floor.

Enter Katy into the living room with a drink for Vick and for the Muscle Man. Judy stays in the kitchen long enough to freshen his drink aggressively. Katy gives a drink to the Muscle Man who simply holds it as if he doesn't know what it is.

KATY. That child is about gone tonight.

VICK. Tell me some news sweetheart. Did Judy tell you what happened in the bar tonight? Down in Pink Lilly's Valley? Judy pulled a knife on a married man, with a wife and everything. I didn't even know Judy carried a knife, and me walking the streets with her as pretty as you please.

KATY. I been knowing she carried a knife.

VICK. I tell you what's the truth, I don't know what I'm going to do. She acts crazier every day.

KATY. Her Mama act just like that.

VICK. Don't even mention that bitch to me. Do you know she's back in town and has not even bothered to call? She disappears for months without telling anybody where she is and then comes back without a word. I saw her dancing the other

day at that place on Bourbon Street. I haven't even told Judy
yet.

KATY. Her Mama tell me she don't want no queer boy for no
son, walking around the French Quarters in a wig and a
dress.

VICK. She's just jealous because he's got a better figure than she
does.

KATY. She have got fat. I don't know why people pay her to take
off her clothes. *(Pause)* Judy would have been better off
staying with his Gramama than coming down here anyway.
This place ain't no good for nobody.

Silence.

VICK. I'm beginning to think he's selling drugs out of that bedroom.

KATY. You got to be kidding.

VICK. I don't think he cares what he does any more. Let me tell
you. In the bar tonight you never saw such a flame. The girl
was on. You could not keep her off the tabletops and you
could not keep her skirt down over her knees. She was gone
on something, no telling what.

KATY. Probably two or three things, knowing Judy.

VICK. Well then this man comes up and she is just all over him,
I mean she's got her hands all down in his pockets. This
nice looking man. Then Judy grabs at something and holds
it up, and lord, do you know she had pulled that man's
wedding ring out of his pocket and she was whooping and
waving it around and hooting all over the bar. With that
poor man just standing there.

KATY. You sure it won't a cock ring.

VICK. Lord I hope not, it was mighty little. Anyway, I felt sorry
for him. Then he got mad and went after Judy, tried to tear
off her dress. Judy pulled a knife on him and like to cut his
throat. I had to grab the knife from her. Then the man
knocked me down in the beer and ruined one of my good
gowns. I don't know if that man ever got his ring back. Judy
and me were thrown out of the bar, and we're lucky they
didn't call the cops. Girl was gone with a blade in her hand.

(Pauses and looks at the drinks Katy is holding) Did you bring that drink for me or is it an extra for you?

KATY. On no, it's yours. I was just admiring your buddy here. He sure look good when he clean.

VICK. Yes he does.

KATY. Look on that poor baby's back. You got cut real bad sweet man?

VICK. The cuts aren't all that deep. When they're not bleeding you can hardly see them at all. It's like he fell on glass or something. He's got some bruises too.

KATY. That's going to swell up ugly.

VICK. Yes it is. Who would do something like this to such a pretty baby?

KATY. Lots of folks. I got a boyfriend would do it just so he could laugh about it when he finish. He ain't my main boyfriend but he good.

VICK. I don't think he needs to see a doctor.

KATY. Maybe it was a pack of them little boys that dance in the street when them blue hair ladies throw money. Pack of them mean suckers, them little devils, carrying knives and everything else.

VICK. He don't look like he was cut with a knife.

KATY. You think that's clean enough?

VICK. I need to wash it with peroxide, but I wonder if he'll hold still.

KATY. He looks right calm to me. Peroxide don't hurt.

VICK. Sometimes it does. You think you can be still while I wash your back with some stuff that smells funny?

The Muscle Man simply watches Vick.

VICK. I want you to keep still, do you think you can?

The Muscle Man looks straight ahead.

VICK. That's a good man. That's just what I want.

KATY. I think he must like you.

VICK. Wouldn't that be nice.

KATY. He do look good. He look like this man I knew in Chicago, only this man had great big hands with real big bones.

VICK. His hands aren't so small.

KATY. They ain't big like my man's hands was, when I was in Chicago. Big old knobby fingers. I love them old fingers, old nasty thing.

VICK. Honey you can make anything sound nasty, you ought to be ashamed of yourself.

KATY. I sure don't know why I would bother.

Vick is dressing the Muscle Man in a pair of loose pants.

VICK. Let me help you. Don't listen to this nasty lady who talks so mean, she really ain't mean at all, I been knowing her for a long time.

KATY. Don't you believe it either sweet legs, I cut you as quick as I look at you.

VICK. Why do you want to talk like that to my big baby doll, you know you never cut nobody in your life.

KATY. *(To the Muscle Man)* I will cut you, or your Mama or your little sister, or your wife in front of your eyes, or your boyfriend if you got a boyfriend, or your motherfucking newborn child. *(To Vick)* Look at him! He trip me out.

VICK. He doesn't understand a word you're saying.

KATY. He like a great big doll baby. Stand up doll baby. Stand up.

VICK. Stand up, she won't hurt you.

The Muscle Man stands.

KATY. How come you stand up when this hag tell you to?

VICK. I am not a hag. *(Vick considers putting a shirt on the Muscle Man but decides against it)*

KATY. Hey big boy, why don't you like me? I'm a real girl. This here thing, she ain't even got tits. I got tits. Why don't you come over here to me. *(Pause; no response)* He don't want to come nowhere near me. He a queer is what it is. He a faggot just like you. He don't like to smell no real woman.

VICK. I don't think he's gay.

KATY. Hey girl, just look at him. He got them sweet eyes, he look at you all gooney, just like a faggot. He got big faggot muscles and gooney faggot eyes and he stand on one hip just like a faggot, and he look in the mirror at his body just

like a faggot. Excuse me, I don't mean to make you mad
when I use that word.

VICK. It takes a lot more than that to bother me baby, or else
I'd be right out of business. But like I said, I been spotting
faggots for years and I don't think he is one.

KATY. Wouldn't it be nice if he was.

VICK. What do you care what he is?

KATY. I like to see you with somebody nice. Not like this trash
you got living with you now. This man here would be real
good for you.

VICK. Don't get me started daydreaming Katy.

KATY. But that might be what he came here for. It might be the
angels sent this man for you.

VICK. Stop making fun of me.

KATY. I'm not playing, I'm serious. Ever since I been knowing
you I wanted you to get you some big strong man who treat
you right. This man here look like he might be real good.

VICK. He is sweet-looking isn't he?

KATY. He got sweet eyes, like this man I met in the bar. This
salesman. Fellow with blond hair and big ugly green rings
on his fingers, them kind turns your skin colors. That man
wasn't sweet though. He sold Christmas ornaments, can you
believe that? I told him I thought that was a kid's job to sell
that shit. He have a kid's face too, come up putting his hand
on me, I don't care if he did sell Christmas ornaments.

VICK. What did he do?

KATY. Reach all up in my dress like he know what was there, till
I bout snatch his fingers off. I'm not lying. I like to knock
him down with my whiskey.

VICK. Had you been talking to him or did he reach up your
dress first thing?

KATY. I been talking to him, but that don't mean he can grab
my thigh like it was a chicken leg.

VICK. I didn't say he could, I just wanted to know.

KATY. How would you like it if some fool ass grab on you when
you minding your own self having a conversation? I told him
he better not ever do that to me again. Don't nobody touch
Katy unless she want to be touch. That man got right sweet
then. I told him he act like a kid. Just like my baby brother.

When my baby brother grab my titty I slap him. Then I feel right sorry for him after I told him off so bad, so I ask him to show me his Christmas ornaments. But he say he didn't have his case with him. I ask him where it was and he say in the hotel.

VICK. Did he take you there? Girl you nasty thing, to his hotel?

KATY. I didn't mind, I had me a good time looking at that fool bulbs what he had. Lord I wished I had me some I could wear for Christmas earrings. He never put his hand on my leg again either.

VICK. You mean you went with this man to his hotel room and he already tried to squeeze you in a bar but he didn't even touch you in the room?

KATY. That's what I said. He tried. Maybe he touch me once but that was all. We ought to get something to eat. I want some ice cream. Something sweet.

VICK. We have some cake. Chocolate banana. Miss Thing made it. Betty Crocker in there washing off her makeup.

KATY. I know, I saw it. I didn't know she could cook. I rather have a pizza.

VICK. Pizza's not sweet.

KATY. I rather have a pizza but I want something sweet too. Why do you keep your cake in the refrigerator? Last time I look there it like to knock me out, it smell like you let a dog in it.

VICK. Shut up, don't let this baby hear you talking about me like that.

KATY. I mean it. Or else it had shit from a St. Bernard in it. If it still smell like that in there I won't even mess with no cake.

Heads for the kitchen.

VICK. Save me a piece.

KATY. *(Pauses)* Girl did I tell you I was hired to do me a commercial? Yes ma'am just like that Brooke Shields. On t.v. Don't look at me like I'm crazy, I'm not lying. *(Exits to the kitchen but continues talking)* I'm going to be the Mammarismo Girl. You know what that is? The Mammarismo Exercise Bra? Lord they gave me one and I thought it would pinch me to death. Got these big springs across it. I told them I would take the job but I be damn if I wear one of them ugly things except on the commercial. You ought to get you one, maybe it would develop you some breast.

VICK. I don't want no breast I can't drop in a drawer.

KATY. You mean you don't want a fine set of these here like I have?

VICK. Noo sweetheart, what would I do with them when I'm waiting tables?

KATY. Anyway, I be standing in front of the camera and I have on this big bra and the tops of my boobs is all pooched out, and I pucker my lips and say, 'Mammarismo the Exercise Bra, the Bra with the Squeeze that Pleases.' Can you hear me? 'Mammarismo, the exercise Bra, the Bra with the Squeeze that Pleases.' And I got a scarf around my neck and the wind just blowing and blowing from this big nasty fan they got set up. I believe I'll get me some dark glasses too. I be standing there with nothing on but these dark glasses and a big bra. You never seen anything like it. I will be more fine than fine.

VICK. Don't get that cake on my floor.

KATY. You don't hold no truck with me honey, this floor is already filthy. If you stand still too long the roaches be crawling up your legs.

VICK. When do you do this commercial?

KATY. What commercial? Oh yeah, I don't know. They call sometime tomorrow or the next day. I hope my phone ain't cut off. I make five hundred dollars in one day if you can believe it. And I get my hair done free. They gave me one of them free bras too and I'm going to fasten it to the wall and use it to hold up my bookshelf where I keep my magazines. I read Star Weekly. You ever read that? Girl you can find out everything. I read about this woman had a monkey for a baby because she got the wrong sperm. Some kind of sperm or something. Can you believe that? She was getting artificial disseminated and had a monkey. I say it serve her right. Nobody going to stick a needle in my sweet cake, no no no. I'm not having a monkey for a baby for nobody, I don't care how smart the monkey is. Bad enough having a baby for a baby.

VICK. Do you have a baby?

KATY. I got a little girl, she live with her Gramama. She six. She don't even hardly know me.

VICK. I got a little son.

KATY. What fool do you think you're talking to?

VICK. No, I really do. His name is William Zachry. He lives with his Mama. He's twelve this September.

KATY. You really are serious.

VICK. I was married for about three years. Yes ma'am. Back when I was a real man.

KATY. What did you do with your wife to get that baby?

VICK. What do you think I did with her?

KATY. You mean you did just like a man does?

VICK. Katy sweetheart, I'm not missing any parts. It's not all that complicated.

KATY. But I didn't think people like you could do that stuff with a woman.

VICK. Honey, a monkey could do it if he set his mind to it. If he could get over how funny looking you was.

KATY. Was your wife funny looking?

VICK. No, she was pretty. This blonde hair like you would kill for, and big thick lips and she was pink color all over, like a little lollipop. And my son, lord you should see him, pretty as a girl and sings like one of the angels. They got him in the church choir. One time when I went to see him he sang a solo on, "Near to the Heart of God," all by himself and the old ladies in the Church were looking at him like it was the Rapture. He favors his Momma more than me.

KATY. Did you like her?

VICK. I loved her, I really did. I don't think I was fooling myself. But I liked men too. So we got divorced after she found out.

KATY. How did she find out?

VICK. She caught me in bed with one of her cousins.

KATY. Lord, I believe I would have choked you to death.

VICK. She came at me with a knife. Her Mama tried to call the police but I got out of the house. We're friends now, I send her money and everything. She come to see me when I was doing drag at JuJu's, she thought it was funny.

KATY. What make you like men?

VICK. I don't know. I just do.

KATY. If my men ever tell me they like men better than me I cut they little head off right there. I mean it. I could kill somebody for tricking me like that.

VICK. Why would it be a trick? I won't tricking anybody.

KATY. You must be crazy. You don't think your wife feel trick, sitting there home with that youngun and you out here spending more money on clothes than she does.

VICK. It wasn't like a trick, it was like I didn't know any better.

Judy calls from offstage.

JUDY. Come in here and help me unhook this gown.

KATY. And you carrying on with something like that. Your little child come to see you?

VICK. Sometimes. *(To Judy)* I'll be there in a minute.

KATY. You take him out to the bars with you?

VICK. Fuck off Katy, what do you think?

Vick starts to exit, angry.

KATY. I don't think nothing. Hey Vick *(Vick stops, hearing unaccustomed tenderness in her tone)* Hey Vick I didn't mean nothing by it, I was just asking questions. When my little girl grows up I'll take her out.

VICK. It's not the same thing.

KATY. I know. You got a picture of your little boy?

VICK. Somewhere

KATY. Bring it back with you.

Vick exits.

KATY. I should have known he had a little baby. You know? All this time I been knowing him and he never said nothing about it. Got a little boy twelve years old, and him running around the streets in a dress whooping and hollering and carrying on. *(Laughs)* Vick on a woman, can you imagine it? Vick on a woman just humping away, and got a baby and never said nothing. *(To Muscle Man)* I bet he's a good daddy to his child. I bet he feed that child and write letters to him and talk on the phone, and I bet he say happy birthday to that child and send him Santa Claus at Christmas. Vick would be a good Daddy. If he just didn't have this trash living with him like he got now. Me and Vick, we friends. Yeah. I bet you don't believe it do you? Vick, he likes me, he really do. We been friends a long time, ever since I move downstairs. He look good too, if he didn't put on them women clothes all the time. Don't you think he look good? Come on baby, if you can understand Vick you can understand me. Don't you like Vick? Don't you wish you could stay here with him? I do. I think you ought to. You could be like his little child. He never had anybody real nice like you, he just had these tramps like that Judy. I'm serious. He would take real good care of you. That's what you want, ain't it? Don't look at me like these boys, you don't fool me. You like to wear dresses and strut that stuff on the street, I know. Look here. . .

Katy finds Vick's wig, which has been left on stage, she puts it on the Muscle Man.

Now you look right. You look like who you are.

The Muscle Man removes the wig.

Put it back. You heard me, put that back on your head. Put it on your head I told you. Are you stupid? Can't you hear?

Enter Judy.

JUDY. What are you fussing about in here?
KATY. This man is stupid. He just sits there like he don't know anything, all swoll up like a ape.
JUDY. What is he doing with my wig?
KATY. That's Vick's wig.
JUDY. Well what is he doing with it?
KATY. He had it on his head and then he pull it off.
JUDY. On his head? He put it there? By himself? Wonderful, maybe there's hope. How did he look?
KATY. Like a big Girl Scout.

Judy puts the wig on the Muscle Man.

JUDY. Oooh yes, this is the look of the future. Marilyn Monroe with biceps.
KATY. He need a beauty mark.

JUDY. You just aren't looking in the right place.

The Muscle Man pulls off the wig again. Holds it up in his hand and shakes it as if he does not know what it is.

KATY. He can't make up his mind.

JUDY. Doing drag is a big step in a young man's life, you can't just jump right into it, you have to take it a little at a time. Lucky for him I'm here to provide counseling and guidance.

KATY. You think this boy wants to wear my dresses?

JUDY. Honey, I don't now any self-respecting manchild who would be seen in your dresses.

KATY. My Mama made this dress for me.

JUDY. Maybe she should take up baking.

KATY. You don't talk about my Mama.

JUDY. His shoulders would bust that dress wide open, just look.

KATY. He almost got titties already.

JUDY. Those are not titties, dear. That is called development, pectoral definition. With me it's a definite requirement.

Judy replaces the wig on the Muscle Man. The Muscle Man throws the wig across the room.

JUDY. Now what did you do that for? *(Gets the wig)* This is a perfectly good one hundred percent human hair wig and there is no reason to treat it worse than a dust rag.

KATY. Maybe he don't want it on his head.

JUDY. But he looks so sweet in it. I know! He's mad because he knows the wig doesn't look right unless you're wearing makeup.

KATY. Girl you crazy.

JUDY. Where's some makeup. What you got in your purse?

KATY. Are you serious?

JUDY. Of course I am. We have got to do this boy up right. What do you have?

KATY. *(Looks in her purse)* Here. Here some red lipstick and some eye shadow and some blush.

JUDY. You be like my helper now, you hold that stuff till I ask for it and then you give it to me. I'm going to have my hands full.

KATY. You can cool believe that.

JUDY. Now you just be real calm young fellow. We'll fix you right up, yes sir. Don't worry about a thing. I been turning out pretty girls for years. May I have the blush, sister Katy?
KATY. There it is, take it.
JUDY. You're supposed to slap it in my hand like I was a surgeon.
KATY. Take the god damn mess and stop clowning.

Judy puts blush on the Muscle Man who sits still for it but looks suspicious.

JUDY. Whatever you do don't laugh. Eye shadow.
KATY. What?
JUDY. Give me the eye shadow.

Katy gives Judy the eye shadow. Judy attempts to apply the eye shadow. The Muscle Man draws away from Judy's hands.

JUDY. Look it won't hurt you. See? It's like medicine for your face.

Judy applies the eyeshadow unevenly, hurriedly. The Muscle Man sits still but is becoming angry.

KATY. What do you want to do this to this man for?
JUDY. Lipstick.

Katy gives Judy the lipstick. At the sight of the lipstick emerging from the tube the Muscle Man backs away. Judy follows him with the lipstick.

JUDY. Hold still now, we're almost done.

Judy manages to smear lipstick on his mouth.

JUDY. My God. Throw me the wig. Throw it to me, quick.

Katy throws Judy the wig. Judy puts the wig on the Muscle Man as Vick enters with a tray of food.

VICK. What are you doing?
JUDY. Playing dress up.
VICK. Get that mess off of him.
JUDY. But he looks so cute.
VICK. You heard me, get that away from him and stop teasing him.

JUDY. Well my aren't our maternal instincts just popping out.

The Muscle Man is agitated but does not move, as if the wig has paralyzed him. Vick sets down the tray.

VICK. You can't leave anything alone, can you. You always got to be messing with people. Any fool can see there's something wrong with this man.

JUDY. Don't look like there's anything wrong with him to me.

VICK. Shut the fuck up. You are disgusting to me sometimes.

Vick removes the wig. The Muscle Man begins rubbing his mouth, smearing the lipstick.

VICK. Calm down, calm down, I'll wash it off.

The Muscle Man strips and flexes his arms as if proving his manhood. flexes them again. flexes them one at a time, almost in a frenzy.

VICK. Calm down.

The Muscle Man becomes calm.

JUDY. You make me sick.

VICK. Come over here.

The Muscle Man follows Vick to a window seat.

KATY. I swear this man would do whatever you told him.

JUDY. Why don't you sit down in his lap. Why don't you just crawl all over him since he likes you so much.

VICK. Did it ever occur to you he might be scared? He's been wandering around God knows how long, got beat up, can't talk and lord knows what else. We don't even know who he is.

JUDY. I'm not interested in his identity problems, I just wanted to improve his social life.

VICK. All you know how to do is try to be funny. *(To the Muscle Man)* Don't worry, I won't let them put the wig on you any more.

KATY. I didn't put any wig on anybody, you leave me out of this.

JUDY. This girl is gone on this man, this young woman has lost her mind, looney tunes. She has met the man of her dreams.

VICK. What the fuck do you know about my dreams?

JUDY. Look at how you are behaving, you can't keep your hands off him, you're completely out of control.

VICK. I have not laid a hand on this man except to put on his bandages and wash off his blood. You're just jealous because he likes me and I won't let you play with him like he was a puppy.

JUDY. Here is this handsome young man in our apartment who will do anything she tells him to do and suddenly she is the Mother Superior of Esplanade.

VICK. I wish you knew how sick you sound.

JUDY. What's wrong with the way I sound? This is a gift from God, this doesn't happen every day. Don't be a prude. You can't look a gift horse in the mouth as they say, not when it's a horse like this.

Judy goes toward the Muscle Man.

VICK. Leave him alone.

JUDY. You must be juking.

VICK. If you lay a hand on him I will kick your puny ass.

JUDY. I'm over twenty-one dear and unless I miss my guess so is he.

VICK. I said stay the fuck away from him.

JUDY. Get out of my way

VICK. I'll break your fucking face.

JUDY. The fuck you will.

They come as close to having a physical fight as possible without committing to it. Finally Judy breaks up laughing.

JUDY. This doesn't make any sense.

VICK. You'll think it's real funny when I put your suitcases on the street.

JUDY. Don't start that shit.

VICK. I'm not playing with you, I've had about all I can stand.

JUDY. All you can stand? Bitch, you don't even want to get me started.

VICK. I mean it. You can drag your mealy ass into your bedroom and stuff every feather boa you've got in a shopping bag and get out. Get out. Then see how long it takes you to find somebody else to pay your bills and feed you and drag your drunk ass home from Bourbon Street.

JUDY. I pay my rent god dammit.

VICK. The hell you do. Don't act up for Katy's benefit, I have told her all about you. Strut around here like you're some kind of princess and strew your clothes all over hell, leave your nasty dishes for me to clean up and drag your common-ass boyfriends across my rug, and tell me what you will do and you won't do, hell! I'll pack your shitty dresses myself.

JUDY. I could understand if we were fighting over which one of us is going to get him. But I don't see why at least one of us can't fuck him since he's here.

KATY. You don't have you any babies of your own, do you Judy?

JUDY. What?

KATY. You don't have any children do you? You ain't never took care of nothing but you.

JUDY. What in the fuck are you talking about? I ain't said nothing about a baby. I just want to know what in the hell we brought this man home for if we're going to treat him like a vestal virgin.

VICK. *(Calmer)* He was hurt and we brought him home to clean him up. He's scared and we're not going to bother him. Tomorrow we're going to find out who he is and where he belongs.

JUDY. This is just like what you did to me in the bar. Every time I want to have any fun.

Knock on the door.

KATY. *(Whispers)* If that's for me I ain't here.

JUDY. Well Miss Vain, who would come up here looking for your ass?

KATY. You heard me. You haven't seen me all night.

JUDY. Where are you going?

KATY. To your bathroom to pee and don't you say a word about it.

VICK. What are you whispering for?

Knock on the door.

JUDY. I'm coming, I'm coming, keep your skirt on.

KATY. You do like I said or you'll be sorry.

Exit Katy. Judy opens the door. The Police Woman enters.

JUDY. Excuse me.

POLICE WOMAN. *(Showing her badge)* I'm looking for your down-stairs neighbor Katy Jume.

JUDY. I haven't seen Katy for a while. I guess you already tried her apartment.

POLICE WOMAN. Yes I did. You folks live around here long?

JUDY. I've been here a few months. My roommate has been here several years. Isn't that right?

VICK. Yes.

POLICE WOMAN. How long have you known Katy Jume?

VICK. A couple of years. Is something wrong?

POLICE WOMAN. Does he live here too?

VICK. He's a friend of mine from out of town. He can't talk.

POLICE WOMAN. Can't talk?

VICK. I think it was because of a shock when he was a little boy.

POLICE WOMAN. I don't want to hear all that. You see Katy Jume, you tell her I'm looking for her, and I'm going to find her. You get this man some clothes on.

JUDY. I beg your pardon.

POLICE WOMAN. Don't beg honey.

Exit the Police Woman.

VICK. What was that all about?

JUDY. I don't know but I intend to find out.

Exit Judy and Vick. The Saxophone Player plays softly. The Voices from Outside are heard. The Muscle Man crosses to the wig, lifts it, poses with it in his hand, places it on his head and smiles.

THE VOICES FROM OUTSIDE. You know I heard that yeah Revon-dela do you have any chewing gum in your pocket book lord girl I done tore my panty hose who are you to talk to me like that you shit head mother fucker walk on down to Bourbon Street with your sorry ass think you so fine, so fine I can walk like that, I can string myself all over the sidewalk

like a strumpet, you know what I'm talking about, child go
on out of here, stop looking at that man, he going to come
over here and drag you down in the bushes. He look fine.
He really do.

act 2

SCENE FOUR

*Judy's bedroom. Lights rise on the picture of beautiful actress
Judy Garland or a temporal alternative. Piles of clothes are
everywhere. Enter Katy. Music is playing softly as if from
another room. The sound of water running. Katy pulls off her
dress, drops it on the floor, walks on it, kicks it aside. From her
purse she pulls out a knife, cleans it. The music grows louder.
She dances a sultry dance with the knife. Anoints herself in
perfume. Wraps herself in a feather boa lying on the floor. Enter
Judy.*

JUDY. What are you doing in my bedroom? I been looking all
over the house for you.

KATY. I'm standing here admiring your picture.

JUDY. Where's your dress?

KATY. Over there. I got hot.

JUDY. You know who that was at the door, don't you?

KATY. Yeah, it was the Avon lady bringing me my makeup I
ordered.

JUDY. It was the Police. This hateful acting woman. She was
asking about you. She wanted to know how long you had
been living here and if we had seen you.

KATY. Peoples all over town be curious about me, it don't worry
me at all.

JUDY. Katy why are the Police looking for you?

KATY. Look at these nasty clothes on the floor. You got more
dresses than the Queen of Sheba. Don't you ever clean your
room?

JUDY. Have you been talking to the Police about things you
aren't supposed to talk about?

KATY. If you mean them nasty little drugs of yours, no I have not said anything about them.

JUDY. You better not have if you know what's good for you.

KATY. I shake in my shoes when you talk like that. I really do.

JUDY. Honey if you run to the Police on me there will be bloodshed and hair flying.

KATY. Grow up girl. The cops have a lot bigger asses than yours to worry about.

JUDY. You better be telling me the truth, sweetheart.

KATY. Don't shoot this shit to me. You ain't bought nobody sweetheart. You don't know me that good. You can wave all the shit you want to in my face but I know it ain't mine. Drag me out some of that stuff.

JUDY. Do what?

KATY. You heard what I said. Get it out.

JUDY. You've got a lot of nerve coming in my bedroom and ordering me around.

KATY. As much money as I've made for you, you can spare me a little taste. Come on now, my nerves is all wore out.

Judy finds a metal or wooden chest in which are many baggies and syringes, paraphernalia. Katy reaches for the box. Judy backs away.

JUDY. First you tell me what did the Police Lady want.

KATY. She didn't want nothing man, she was just lonely. Give me that box.

JUDY. Talk to me first.

KATY. She was probably just a dyke who follow me home.

JUDY. When was the last time a dyke follwed you home?

KATY. They follow me around all the time. Give me that baggie.

JUDY. What did the Police Woman want, Katy dear?

KATY. She didn't want nothing, get out of my face.

JUDY. You tell me or you don't even get to smell of this good stuff.

KATY. Girl, you are making it so I just have to pull a knife on you.

Moves toward her purse.

JUDY. *(Reaching for his own knife)* You touch a knife and you'll get more of a fight than you know what to do with.

KATY. Ain't nobody scared of you.

JUDY. Ain't nobody scared of you either baby. Now act like you got some sense. We are in this together. I got a right to know why you're messing with a Police Woman.

KATY. I ain't messing with nobody.

JUDY. All right, you're not messing with her, she's messing with you. She said she wanted to ask you some questions.

KATY. I know what she said. I was with this salesman in his hotel room over in the Fauborg and he had a heart attack. He just fell over dead and I had to go downtown.

JUDY. Where did you go downtown?

KATY. To the Police Farm honey, to big blue heaven. That's right, me myself. Sitting in this grimy room with this big fat belly Police Man in a chair grinding his jaw like he was trying to wear his teeth out. I had to tell them all about this man heart attack why he died. He was just this man I pick up in the bar.

JUDY. He had a heart attack while you were fucking?

KATY. We hadn't even done anything, he just barely got his clothes off. He was kind of old, fluffy ass mother fucker.

JUDY. If you already talked to the Police why do they need to ask you more questions?

KATY. I don't know. They couldn't find any driver license on him and they didn't know who he was. Maybe they have some pictures for me to look at. I think he might have been some kind of murderer. The Police act like they know all about him.

JUDY. You're kidding. Who did he kill?

KATY. A whole bunch of people over in Slidell.

JUDY. God, I've got to start reading the newspaper sometime. *(Starts to give Katy the baggie, then pauses)* Listen, I want you to help me with something.

KATY. What?

JUDY. Help me with that Muscle Man in there.

KATY. What do you want to do to that poor little innocent baby?

JUDY. That baby is not little, sweetheart, and when I get through with him he won't be innocent either.

KATY. If you mess with that man, Vick will kill you dead.

JUDY. Vick can act like some old lady if he wants to, I'm going to put to use what the Good Lord has provided.

KATY. I don't think you understand what I'm trying to tell you. Vick already threw a fit all over you, he will kill you if you mess with that man.

JUDY. I know that. That's why I want you to keep him busy. Get him real upset about the Police. You know Mother Vick, he'll sit right down and forget about everything else.

KATY. You ain't getting me in between all this.

JUDY. Katy honey, I'm your mother. Do what mother tells you. All I need is ten or fifteen minutes.

KATY. What the hell are you going to do in fifteen minutes but scare the poor child to death.

JUDY. You don't worry about him. Once I get him to the bedroom, he'll relax just fine, and so will Vick.

KATY. You are absolutely crazy.

JUDY. I know Vick, honey. He's not a fool. Once he sees me and that man are going to fuck, he'll leave us alone.

KATY. No you don't know Vick, and you don't know that man either one.

JUDY. Stop arguing and do like I said for your sweet sister who gives you candy and takes care of you.

KATY. Why do you have to mess with this? That man and Vick are getting along just fine. You got a new boyfriend every week, you don't need to steal from Vick.

JUDY. That man don't want Vick.

KATY. Sure look like he does to me. I don't know what he want but he sure want something.

JUDY. You're dreaming girl. Face facts. Vick is old news. Now all I want you to do is tell Vick about the Police and get him out of here for a little while, just a little while.

KATY. This ain't right.

JUDY. Don't talk that right shit to me.

KATY. I said this don't feel right. That man already been beat up and you want to get all over him with yourself. I think you better lay back and take a good long look. You hurt that man and Vick will put your bags on the street, and there will go the best set-up your sorry ass has ever had.

JUDY. *(As if he has heard nothing)* I'm counting on you, Katy sister, don't let me down.

KATY. I'm a tell you something. I am up to the roots of my hair with being sister to you. Don't call me that.

JUDY. *(Giving Katy the baggie)* Take your medicine into the bathroom darling, you'll be much calmer about the whole thing when you're loaded.

KATY. You are nothing but trash just like the bitch that brung you into the world.

JUDY. Let's don't talk about Mother.

KATY. You know I saw that sorry ass strumpet the other day, and I thought to myself how lucky you was that you ain't like she is, but I was wrong. You are low as the rug. If I had a child like you I would drown it like it was a dog.

JUDY. You ain't seen Mama, you are a lie. She ain't even in town.

KATY. Oh no honey, she back. She stripping at the Harum Scarum every night, her titties just flopping every which way. Yeah, I saw her. I told her you said hello and Happy Mother's Day.

JUDY. You utter god damn bitch.

KATY. You can't name me nothing I ain't already been named, baby, it just roll right off my back. But let me tell you something. Don't act like that bitch tonight. Just as sure as I'm standing here, you fuck with Vick and this man and you will pay.

Exit Katy. The Saxophone Player plays raucous, almost terrifying strip tease music. Judy picks up his clothes, handling the dresses carefully. On another part of the stage the Muscle Man enters, seating himself cross-legged. Judy continues to clean his room then pauses, standing by the telephone. The Muscle Man pulls the bandages off his back. During the speech that follows he paints himself with blood as before while the Saxophone Player continues to play, softly enough that Judy can be heard.

JUDY. *(Picks up the phone and dials)* Hello. Get me Ruby. Yeah, it's me. Yeah, I'm fine. Yeah look, get Ruby, okay? *(Waits for a long time)* Hello Ruby girl. Why yes darling, it's really me. Well I'm just tickled to hear your voice. You know you are my main woman. That's right. You do have the money?

Good for you. But believe it or not I didn't call about that. I have some news, darling. Yes, it's paradise. I have crystal. Yes ma'am, pure as the driven snow. Well the price is up. I don't quote price on the phone sweet child, what kind of tacky creature do you take me for? Don't worry, I can cut you a deal. I want a favor. Just a little one. Don't ask any questions. In about fifteen minutes I want you to call the Police. The Police. Downtown, that's right. You know Katy Jume? Tell the Police you just saw her coming into this building. Tell them you were walking by here. Well walk by here then, I don't give a fuck. You do what I told you and I'll front you the crystal half price. You don't have to give them your name. Just tell them you saw her coming in here. Don't answer any questions, tell them and hang up. Do it because you love me. Listen to me. Listen. If the Police don't show up looking for the bitch, the whole deal is off. You got me? You can shoot up the desert sands for all I care. All right? Remember, wait fifteen or twenty minutes, like I said. Talk to you later. I'll call you. Yeah, I got the stuff right here. You're just a doll. Don't push your luck, I'll deliver. Night night.

Exit Judy.

SCENE FIVE

Enter Vick into the living room where the Muscle Man is sitting.

VICK. Baby, you've pulled off your bandages, you're bloody all over again.

The Muscle Man stands. Vick takes the bandages, wipes the blood. Enter Katy.

KATY. What's wrong with him now?
VICK. He pulled off the bandages and got the bleeding started again. Get me a towel.

Exit Katy.

VICK. What am I going to do with you? I already got one child in this apartment.

The Muscle Man contemplates Vick carefully then flexes his arms.

VICK. Yes I know, you have nice big muscles.

The Muscle Man continues to flex. Vick begins to touch one of the Muscle Man's biceps, then withdraws.

VICK. Put your arms down. Put them down, that's right. They're real pretty. They really are. But I don't need a show right now. Let me get you cleaned up.

The Muscle Man paces as if disturbed.

VICK. What's wrong?

The Muscle Man will not hold still for Vick or look at him. Enter Katy with a basin, cloth and towels.

KATY. What's wrong with him?
VICK. I don't know. I think he's mad at me. He was showing off his muscles and I wouldn't touch him.
KATY. Why not? Are you crazy?
VICK. I don't know, I just couldn't. I didn't want to think about him like that.
KATY. Like what?
VICK. Like somebody I could touch. Like somebody who might want me to touch him.
KATY. Sound to me like that's what he want.

The Muscle Man allows Vick to touch him now. Vick begins to clean him and put on the bandages again. This continues during the scene that follows. The effect should be that the Muscle Man and Vick are reading each other's minds.

VICK. I don't know what he wants. *(Pause)* Did Judy find you? Did he tell you a Police Woman was here looking for you?
KATY. Yeah, he told me all about it.
VICK. What did she want?
KATY. I don't know.
VICK. What do you mean you don't know.
KATY. Vick, mind your own business. I don't want to talk about it.

A knock at the door different, lighter than the Police Woman.

VICK. Oh lord, they're back. What do you want me to do?

Knocking continues.

KATY. Open the damn door, I don't give a shit.

VICK. You sure?

KATY. You can't act like you ain't at home, they can hear us talking.

Vick opens the door and Juel Laurie enters.

VICK. God knows, Mistress Laurie, you scared us half to death.

JUEL LAURIE. Oh Vick. I climbed them stairs, I ain't got breath. Lord. *(Pause)* You said come up if your light was on.

VICK. Yes ma'am, I sure did.

JUEL LAURIE. Well, bad things is happening out there tonight. I keep hearing Vanice. Like he was in the hall. And the rats is back in the walls. All behind the toilet. Scratching like. I can't get no peace when I go in there. I put out poison but it don't do no good.

VICK. *(To Katy, who has stepped to the doorway)* It's Mistress Laurie from downstairs.

KATY. Hey Juel Laurie.

JUEL LAURIE. Vanice said the Pohlice looking for you girl.

KATY. You can't be listening to what Vanice tell you, he long gone from this world.

JUEL LAURIE. Vanice said how it was all on the news about you.

KATY. What was on the news?

JUEL LAURIE. The news was on when I left. River near up to the levee. Rats so bad you can't hear nothing. I had beans for supper, with ham. They is all off in the walls, you can't shoot em with a gun.

VICK. What was on the news, Mistress Laurie?

JUEL LAURIE. *(To Katy)* It was something I wanted to tell you sweetheart, it might rain. Weatherman said it won't and he ain't never right.

VICK. Juel Laurie, did the Police really come by your apartment or are you just remembering the one you talked to this evening on the street?

JUEL LAURIE. No, it was after that. The Pohlice Woman come by my house while the water was on. Anyway Vanice says the

Pohlice is after Katy Jume from downstairs what has the blue kitchen curtains blowing all out the window from the fan. Says the Pohlice want to put her on the news bigtime. Says Vanice. They fount a dead man in a motel, I was in the kitchen washing my hair. With the water running you can't hear a thing.

VICK. What time did they come?

JUEL LAURIE. Between Twilight Zone and the Avengers.

VICK. That was about the same time the woman was here.

JUEL LAURIE. I don't have no flashlight in my house.

VICK. What do you need a flashlight for, honey?

JUEL LAURIE. You can't see in the dark without no flashlight. That woman in the uniform looking for you, she'll find you too.

KATY. Do you see the future or do you just run your mouth?

VICK. Leave her alone, Katy, she can't help it.

JUEL LAURIE. That woman in the uniform coming to sieze you, child. Take you down to the jail house and lock you in the room with the crazy woman and the dogs. *(Juel Laurie sees the Muscle Man, crosses to him)* Who is this here? Do you live here boy?

VICK. He can't talk, Mistress Laurie.

JUEL LAURIE. He can't?

VICK. No ma'am.

JUEL LAURIE. Why not?

VICK. I don't know.

JUEL LAURIE. What happened to him to get all those bandaids on him?

VICK. I think somebody beat him up.

JUEL LAURIE. Every time I turn around you took up with somebody else. Where is that other boy who used to live here?

VICK. He still does.

Juel Laurie walks around the Muscle Man, inspecting him. After a pause the Muscle Man stands, walks around Juel Laurie, inspecting her.

JUEL LAURIE. Hope you get your eyes full. Looking at somebody. *(To Vick)* How did he get to be shaped all like that?

VICK. I guess he did a lot of exercises.

JUEL LAURIE. He looks like Vanice did when he was in the Navy. I like this man, you art to keep him and get rid of that prissy one.

VICK. Juel Laurie, you got to finish what you started to tell about now.

JUEL LAURIE. What was that?

VICK. The Police Woman coming to see you.

JUEL LAURIE. But I told you everything I know. She's coming back for Katy Jume. She's watching your front door and the lights in your house. She's in the whole neighborhood visiting all your friends. She's coming back for you. She got a surprise.

VICK. I believe I hear Vanice calling you.

JUEL LAURIE. Vanice is in the bathtub reading *True Detective Magazine.*

VICK. I believe he wants you to come home.

JUEL LAURIE. *(To Muscle Man)* Do you have a flashlight I can borrow?

VICK. *(As if she has been speaking to him)* No ma'am. All I got is candles.

JUEL LAURIE. You can't kill rats with no candle. We got a flashlight but the batteries is dead on it. I ain't bought no new ones because we still got toilet paper. Vanice is calling me, ain't he?

VICK. Yes ma'am, he is.

JUEL LAURIE. Katy honey, your kitchen window is open and the curtains is blowing all out of it.

KATY. I don't think it's going to rain right now, Juel Laurie.

JUEL LAURIE. Don't worry sugar, Vanice didn't tell the Police nothing. He was smart. He said he hadn't seen you and didn't know nothing about where you were. You got to treat your neighbors like your kin.

VICK. *(Leading Juel Laurie to the door)* Good night Juel Laurie.

JUEL LAURIE. I believe I'll make some grape koolaid when I get home. Good night Mr. Muscle.

Exit Juel Laurie.

KATY. She said they're watching my house.

VICK. She doesn't know anything.

KATY. I need a clean dress. I ain't been home in three days.

VICK. You lied to me, didn't you? You didn't lose your apartment key. You were just afraid to go home because of the Police.

KATY. I was a fool to come here at all.

VICK. Tell me why the Police want to talk to you.

KATY. I don't know why.

VICK. Tell me the truth, Katy.

KATY. I might have seen something.

VICK. Why don't you play straight with me for five minutes.

KATY. I told you, I might have been someplace where something happened. Someplace where I was tonight. People always be getting killed around here, you can't worry about it. You just got to accept it.

VICK. Did somebody get killed where you were? Answer me.

KATY. Which place? I been a little bit of everywhere tonight, it has been one hellacious day.

VICK. I'm going to ask you one more time. Where were you that the Police want to know about.

KATY. In bed with this two-bit pimp in Gentilly.

VICK. I can't ever tell when you're lying and when you're telling the truth.

KATY. Well this is the truth, honey. I was in bed with this pimp name Wienie Rod, and we was laying up in his trailer in a empty lot in Gentilly, and come a knock on the door. Wienie Rod walk over there in his pajama bottoms and a shotgun blast right through the door and tear his head clean off. By the time I got to him whoever it was with the shotgun had gone and there was Wienie Rod laying in a pool of blood with his head blowed off. I got right out of there. I went off and had me some breakfast.

VICK. You lying whore.

KATY. Who you calling a lie?

VICK. What happened when that salesman took you up to his hotel room?

A beat of silence. Katy watches Vick.

VICK. Would you tell me what happened, please?

Enter Judy.

JUDY. What is this, true confessions time?

KATY. As a matter of fact it was a private conversation. But since you're here you might as well know.

JUDY. Oh, is this about that woman who was here, that darling Police Woman? You already told me about that.

KATY. I know what I told you.

JUDY. So this is an even truer true confession.

VICK. Could you please shut up?

JUDY. Miss girlfriend to miss girlfriend, station to station.

KATY. Judy, I am going to cut up what you don't shut up.

VICK. Don't pay any attention to her.

JUDY. That's right, treat me like the mosquitoes and the flies.

KATY. Girl, you are high.

VICK. Tell me what happened, Katy.

KATY. Nothing happened.

VICK. The Police aren't after you because nothing happened. They want to talk to you about that man, don't they?

KATY What man? I know lots of mens.

VICK. You know what man. That salesman in the bar. The one who grabbed on you, the one who sold Christmas tree bulbs.

KATY. Oh yeah, old sweet bottom. What do the Police want to talk to me about him for? Come on, you been reading my mind, do it some more.

VICK. You said you went with him to the Fauborg.

KATY. That's right, I did.

VICK. The Police told Juel Laurie . . . *(Hesitates, visibly decides to change the subject)* Fuck it, forget I asked you anything.

KATY. No baby, you don't get off that easy. You want to act so concern, go ahead. Tell me what you think happened with that man.

VICK. *(After a pause)* I think he's dead.

KATY. I can't hear you.

VICK. He's dead. He died.

KATY. Well lord help me. How did he get dead?

VICK. I don't know.

KATY. You lie. You think I killed him.

JUDY. Vick's been watching too many police shows on TV.

KATY. *(To Vick)* You really think I could kill somebody?

VICK. I don't know what I think.

KATY. You another lie. You think I could kill somebody, don't you?

VICK. Yes.

JUDY. Well Katy girl I guess now you know who your friends are.

Katy laughs in such a way that it becomes plain Vick is right.

KATY. You should have seen that man, Judy, he was a trip. Greasy fucker. Think he can have me easy. Took me up to his hotel room and serve me cheap vodka on crush ice. Talk nasty in my ear about what he want to do, and then take my clothes off with his fat hands, and then show me a picture of his wife. Can you believe that? I don't know why. He was just drunk and one minute he was all over me and the next minute he was feeling bad and want to show me his wife, this nice looking woman with good hair and smiling all kind of a nice smile. And him laying there on that hotel bed with the sheet pulled up over his fat belly, and him looking all ugly with his teeth yellow from cigarettes. Waiting for me. I told him to put his pictures away and he did, and I thought it would be all right, but then he start to touch me and kiss on me and tell me how she didn't treat him right, and all about how she can't even cook breakfast in the morning without breaking the yolk on the egg, when he so fat he don't need to eat another egg forever in his whole life. I got mad. I don't know why. I couldn't stand to look at him and I couldn't stand for him to touch me and I tried to get away but he was grabbing onto me, and I just got madder and madder.

JUDY. You told me he had a heart attack.

KATY. That's right, he did. I attack his heart myself. That was all last night. I got out of there and I been wandering around ever since.

VICK. Katy.

KATY. Don't say nothing. Because I'm not sorry. No sir, not one little bit. To tell you the truth I don't feel nothing at all.

VICK. But why?

KATY. I told you I don't know. It's done now and I can't take it back. It felt good to stick a knife up between his ribs. Men always sticking something in me, I wondered how it felt.

Enter Juel Laurie onto another part of the stage as if she is passing by in the hall outside.

JUEL LAURIE. Vanice. Vanice honey, are you out here? Vanice, supper is ready and I can't find you nowhere, I been looking all day.

JUDY. There she goes again.

JUEL LAURIE. I cooked a ham like you like. With the can cherries on it. You can make you some good sandwiches, Vanice baby. And we got baby lima beans and hot rolls. Vanice you got to change your socks, they all clean. Vanice, where are you, please answer me.

KATY. I hate it when she hollers like that.

VICK. She's upset tonight.

JUDY. That man been dead long enough she ought to know it by now.

JUEL LAURIE. Vanice, the Saxophone Man is down by the no parking anytime. We can go down and listen to him. He got the big gold horn, he'll play like you want. Where are you baby? I miss you. I ain't seen you all day.

KATY. Please go make her shut up.

VICK. She'll calm down in a minute, just sit still honey.

JUEL LAURIE. If you don't come back soon I'll be gone. That's right. Vanice, the Pohlice looking for me, they think I killed somebody. The Pohlice came talking to me wanting to know where you were. You're the only one who can save me, they gone back after the big guns and the dogs. I need you so bad. You know it? You ain't no good. Do you hear me? You ain't no good for leaving me.

Exit Juel Laurie, mumbling. For a time there is silence in the apartment, Judy wanders to the window sipping bourbon, smoking a cigarette if the actor smokes. Katy paces. The Muscle Man goes to Vick, who checks his bandages.

VICK. This is driving me crazy, I can't stand it. Give me the key to your apartment.

KATY. What for?

VICK. I'm going to get you a dress. Then I'm going to check the back door to see if there's anybody watching the court-yard. The Police might not even know to watch there.

KATY. You must be crazy.

VICK. I can't just wait here.

KATY. You start helping me and they'll lock you up right along with me.

VICK. Sweetheart, they will never know. You are not going to sit here waiting for them to arrest you because you killed some fat mother fucker from out of town. Give me your key.

KATY. Hell, I'll go down there.

VICK. No you won't. You're going to wait right here till I get back. Don't argue with me.

KATY. The key's in my purse.

JUDY. *(Gleeful that Vick is leaving)* Your purse is still in my room, Katy sweetheart. I'll go get it.

Exit Judy.

VICK. I'm sick to my stomach all of a sudden. *(Goes to window)* All you can smell is rain rot and garbage.

KATY. Can you see the Police?

VICK. Not from here. I can see the Saxophone Man though, right where Juel Laurie said.

Enter Judy with Katy's purse and dress.

JUDY. *(Giving Katy the purse)* Here you are.

Katy searches for the key.

VICK. *(To Muscle Man)* I'll only be gone for a minute, I'll be right back.

JUDY. He looks tired, poor baby. Why don't I put him to bed in your room while you're gone? Then you can sleep with me tonight.

VICK. Are you serious?

JUDY. Vick, I am not a monster. I don't want to hurt this man any more than you do.

VICK. Well.

JUDY. Vick, please let me do something nice. I'll tuck him in real pretty and by the time you get Katy all fixed up, he'll be asleep for the night.

VICK. That sounds real sweet. All right. *(Gets the key from Katy)* I'll be right back. Is there anything else you want?

KATY. Bring me my red cocktail dress you gave me for my birthday.

VICK. How am I going to see that dress in the dark?

KATY. It glows, honey. You'll find it.

Vick moves toward the exit. The Muscle Man follows.

VICK. No, you can't come with me. I'll be back in a little bit.

KATY. That's sweet. He don't want you to go.

VICK. I'll be back in a minute. You let them put you to bed, all right?

JUDY. Aunt Katy and Aunt Judy will fix you right up.

KATY. *(To Vick)* Don't let no spook get you. I thought I saw old man Vanice myself the other day.

Exit Vick.

JUDY. *(To Katy)* Poor baby. You need to calm down. *(Approaches her)* Come on sweetheart, let me take you back to my room.

KATY. Get the fuck away from me. I can't stand you when you try to act nice.

JUDY. But I just want to give you a little something to settle your nerves. Killing people is hard on a girl, you probably worked up quite an appetite.

KATY. You are sick.

JUDY. You mean you don't want any more of my candy?

KATY. You know better than that.

JUDY. Well I tell you what. You go get you some. You know where it is. And take you a little bit for the road, you probably need it.

KATY. Are you serious?

JUDY. Of course.

KATY. You're going to let me in that box without hanging all over my shoulder?

JUDY. Katy dear, you are my friend. Friends trust each other. Besides, I promised Vick I would put this poor man to bed.

KATY. Oh, I get it now—

JUDY. No no no, you've got it all wrong. I'm going to do exactly like I said, I'm going to put this man to bed and I'm not going to bother him one little bit.

KATY. You must think I'm a fool.

JUDY. I'm telling you the truth. I did a lot of thinking about what you said. I don't want to end up like my Mother, keeping company with trash for the rest of my life. She threw away everything that ever did her any good. I don't want to do that. Vick is good to me and I'm going to start being good to him. So don't worry. I wouldn't hurt this man for all the muscles in the world. I'm going to take him into Vick's room and put him to bed and turn out the lights and leave him alone. I might even sing him a lullaby.

KATY. *(Wanting to believe him)* I hope for your sake you're telling the truth.

JUDY. I am. You can believe it. Now go on back to my room and look in my box.

Exit Katy.

JUDY. *(Calling after her)* Now don't take everything I got.

Judy turns to the Muscle Man walks slowly around him, a wide circle. The Saxophone Player plays Judy's Theme, low.

JUDY. You think she really killed somebody? Do you? Come on, answer me. I know you can talk. Do you think Katy looks like a killer? She looks really hot in that slip, don't she? Yeah, you like that stuff. I can tell. The Police are coming; did you figure that out yet? They'll probably drag you and her off both, don't you think? I mean, Katy killed this man. And you look suspicious too.

The Muscle Man moves toward the door. Judy intercepts him.

JUDY. Where do you think you're going? Vick's not out there. Vick's not coming back. The Police will be in Katy's apartment any minute, just hundreds and hundreds of them. He won't be coming back for a long time. He'd probably go downtown with Miss Katy anyway. He's so good. You can count on Vick, yes sir. Vick will take good care of Miss Katy. And you and me will stay right here.

Judy approaches the Muscle Man slowly. The Muscle Man withdraws.

JUDY. You can understand me, can't you? Yes you can. Don't run

away. I just want to put you to bed. I can make you feel real
good. Make you relax. I want to take you back to Vick's room
and put you to bed. And maybe get to know you a little.

*Judy continues to approach throughout. The Muscle Man
continues to retreat. Judy is surprisingly anxious that he should
believe Judy is sincere.*

JUDY. Why are you afraid of me? Why do you let that bitch Vick
put his hands on you but you won't let me?

*Judy manages to corner the Muscle Man. The Muscle Man
pushes him violently away.*

JUDY. If you would just let me try I could be okay. There's
nobody here but you and me. You know? You don't have to
pretend any more. This is what you came here for, isn't it?

*Judy and the Muscle Man are some distance apart. The Muscle
Man peels off his shirt in slow motion. Strips to his posing
trunks. Judy freezes, watching. The Muscle Man poses as the
light changes. Eerie music playing as if they are in some strange
dimension. The Muscle Man does a smooth, polished posing
routine, both standing and kneeling poses. He does the double
biceps. Spreads his lats. Shows off pectoral striation, thigh
flexion, curved triceps and flaring deltoids. Judy watches for a
long time and then approaches. The Muscle Man pushes Judy
away contemptuously and continues to pose. Judy approaches
again and is pushed away again.*

JUDY. I've done this before, I'm sick of it. You can't just stand
there, you can't just wait. You have to come to me. You have
to want me too. *(Any anger here dissolves and becomes pleading)*
If you just try. Please. I can be okay, I really can. Please. Let
me touch you, just once.

*Approaches the Muscle Man who coolly slaps him and pushes
him away. Judy goes off, anger building till he cannot contain
it. He destroys the apartment, completely wild, ripping papers
and magazines, old clothes, throwing things, breaking things,
absolutely out of control. The Muscle Man stands serenely, as if
he had expected this reaction.*

JUDY. *(When he is finally calm)* Somebody is making all this up. You are, aren't you? You're making all this up while I'm standing here. Look at me. Look at me god damn you. *(Pulls a knife.)*

Enter Katy. She stands at the side of the stage, watching. Judy does not notice her.

JUDY. Look at me. I'm here. I'm pretty. I am pretty. You can't just stand there, I'll kill you. Do you hear me? Answer me, I know you can talk. I'll kill you.

KATY. Judy girl, put that knife away.

JUDY. Fuck you. Fuck you and fuck him too. I am pretty, I am, I am. I'm as pretty as he ever was. But you can't tell him that, oh no. He's so holy. He can't even see you. Oh god. I can't do nothing with him, I can't even touch him. I could never reach him if I live forever.

KATY. Baby you're just high.

JUDY. No, it's him. You know what I mean. It's just him, it's just me and this man and we're stuck here, forever and ever and ever, oh god damn everything.

Judy rushes the Muscle Man a final time. In the struggle that follows Judy is stabbed with his own knife. The movement ends in an embrace and Judy, in dying, slides toward the floor, tearing away the Muscle Man's bandages. Silence. The Muscle Man kneels over Judy. Touches the wound, tries to move the body. When it will not move he backs away. Katy walks slowly toward Judy, watches the Muscle Man, kneels, hesitates, picks up the knife, grips the knife as if she had killed Judy. She and the Muscle Man watch each other. Enter Vick with red cocktail dress and red shoes.

VICK. Katy, some Police cars just pulled up out front, Juel Laurie is going to let us know what they do. *(Stops)* What is Judy doing down there? *(Kneels)* Judy. Judy what's wrong?

KATY. She's dead.

Vick simply looks at Judy. Finds the Muscle Man's bandages in Judy's hands. Picks them up. Looks from the Muscle Man to Katy.

VICK. What happened? *(Waits; no answer)* Katy, tell me what happened.

KATY. *(Lifting the knife)* This. This happened.

Enter Juel Laurie without knocking.

JUEL LAURIE. They're here sweeties. They got you surrounded, better come out with your hands up.

KATY. Where are they?

JUEL LAURIE. Down under the big crack in the plaster with the water stain like Jesus face, Vanice is on the landing keeping watch.

KATY. Are they coming up here?

JUEL LAURIE. Vanice says not yet. Don't worry. He won't sing out loud, they won't see him. Vanice can be real quiet when he wants to. I told you they would come back. Katy Jumc is here and they know it, they say they got a call. They see through walls and open windows without their hands. Better hide, better transport you away on one of them beams, honey, the Police have got your name and your number. *(Sees Judy)* Who is this?

KATY. Judy. Vick's roommate.

JUEL LAURIE. What happened to him?

KATY. *(Looking at the Muscle Man, who also watches her)* I killed him.

JUEL LAURIE. What did you do that for?

KATY. I just did.

JUEL LAURIE. He got a knife hole on his rib. Vick, get up from him like that.

KATY. Leave him alone, Juel Laurie.

JUEL LAURIE. Now the Police will drag you off for sure.

KATY. They would have anyway. And I'm too tired to care.

JUEL LAURIE. *(Looking suddenly surprised, turning to the Muscle Man)* He was on this man, won't he?

KATY. What do you mean?

JUEL LAURIE. He was on this man. That's what it was. Don't shake your head at me, I know. *(Moves closer to the Muscle Man)* You should be ashamed of yourself.

Vick stands, looks at the bandages, drops the bandages and gets the dress.

VICK. *(To Katy)* Here's your dress.

Vick helps Katy put on the dress.

VICK. They'll be up here in a minute.

KATY. I know.

VICK. They did say somebody called. *(Looks at Judy)* I wonder who it was?

KATY. It don't matter now.

VICK. Poor baby. He didn't have anybody. Anybody at all.

KATY. He had you.

JUEL LAURIE. There's a dead boy on the floor.

VICK. There sure is, honey. *(To Katy)* I brought you a pair of pumps too. It was hard to find the right pair in the dark.

KATY. How do I look?

VICK. You need to fix your hair. Juel Laurie, run to my bathroom and find me a brush or a comb.

JUEL LAURIE. Vanice says the Pohlice could be here any second.

VICK. I know, and Katy's not quite ready yet. Find me a brush like I asked you to. She's got a long night ahead of her and I want her to look just right.

Exit Juel Laurie.

KATY. Will you call my Mama? Tell her I'll talk to her when I can? *(Almost breaks down)* Tell her I ain't no bad girl, please tell her.

VICK. I'll tell her.

Enter Juel Laurie with hair brush.

JUEL LAURIE. It was on the back of the toilet with a hair net on it.

VICK. *(Brushing Katy's hair)* Thank you ma'am. Do you hear anything?

JUEL LAURIE. *(Goes to the door)* Vanice says no. They're still right down there shooting the shit, right where the landlord bordered up the window.

The Muscle Man comes closer to them. Stops.

JUEL LAURIE. You got blood on you.

VICK. He can't help it, Juel Laurie.

KATY. You need to take care of him.

VICK. I will in a minute.

KATY. No. I mean you need to take care of him from now on.

VICK. He'll be gone as soon as I find out who he is.

KATY. He ain't nobody. He just walking around in the world. I know him from the minute I saw him. You want to stay here with Vick, don't you big man? You want to stay right here and let Vick take good care of you?

VICK. Hush, Katy.

JUEL LAURIE. The Pohlice got their hands on their guns. They say they answering a call. They pulling down their belts like the cowboys.

KATY. I know what I'm talking about. You're going to stay right here, ain't that right? Ain't that what you came for?

VICK. He can't understand you.

KATY. He can understand me just fine.

VICK. You got such nice hair.

KATY. I feel good now. I feel real good. I feel like I'm sitting out on the levee watching the river.

VICK. I thought I heard a ship horn a little while ago.

KATY. You know it didn't even feel like I was doing anything to that man in the motel. I just thought he was a fool.

VICK. Hush.

KATY. Will they make me meet his wife?

VICK. I don't think so.

KATY. She look so sweet in her picture.

JUEL LAURIE. They on the stairs now, coming up.

VICK. It's all right. Katy's about ready.

KATY. Go see my baby girl. You'll do that for me, won't you? And tell stories about her Mama.

VICK. Yes baby, I will.

KATY. I love my baby girl. I really do.

VICK. I know.

JUEL LAURIE. They knocking on my door now, but I'm not there, and Vanice don't let nobody in when he's alone. They're knocking but he don't care. (*Laughs, as if she sees it*) That's right. Turn away. Nobody home.

VICK. They'll tear this place to pieces.

KATY. Yes ma'am, they will.

Voices and footsteps outside.

VICK. I wonder where I put this man's clothes. I guess I'll have to dress him and bring him down to the station.

KATY. They're in the bathroom.

VICK. I better go see.

Exit Vick. Katy crosses to face the Muscle Man.

JUEL LAURIE. You look good Katy Jume. The Pohlice going to want to eat you up.

KATY. *(To the Muscle Man)* You owe me for this mother fucker.

JUEL LAURIE. I had me a fine red dress like that one time. From Maison Blanche.

Knock on the door.

But I couldn't find no clutch that would go. Worried me to death.

Knock on the door.

Somebody ought to open that. The Pohlice is here.

KATY. I will. Even though this is not my home.

Lights fade as she goes to the door; light lingers on the Muscle Man who kneels at Judy's side. He touches the wound and smears blood on himself as before. When Vick enters, the Muscle Man stands and faces Vick. Lights continue to fade as Vick inspects the blood, sets down the clothes.

VICK. You've got blood on you again. What am I going to do with you?

Street noise rises. Vick and the Muscle Man face each other as lights fade to black. Last of all the sound of the Saxophone Player blowing Judy's Theme from the street outside.

linda parris-bailey

dark cowgirls and prairie queens

artist's statement

Dark Cowgirls and Prairie Queens was developed in response to a community need; the need to hear stories that validate and strengthen us. Each year African American theater companies that are community based are innundated with February requests,both from within and beyond the African American community itself. As a good friend is fond of saying "All Gods children work in February!" Of course our history doesn't suddenly dissappear at the beginning of March as some would have us believe, but one responds to the need as it is expressed. As we began to consider what would be the subject of that "Little something for our Black History Month program", we began to search for the least-told stories of our past. This gave us a *wide range* of options.

As the artistic director of the company and one of the writers, I was especially interested in finding material that would not simply rehash the same stories. In my search for new materials, I came across a book that I'd been given some time before called *The Black West* by William Lorenz Katz. As I leafed through the book, I met the eyes of a Black woman who started a conversation with me that lasted for the next two years. When I brought the idea for "Dark Cowgirls" to the company, for the first time in weeks we all agreed, we all were excited, and we all were ready to work.

"Dark Cowgirls", conceived and written by myself, was developed in the company. The original cast researched, reworked, reviewed, improvised, criticized, and put its stamp on each section. Subsequent cast members have embellished it, reshaped it and made it live. Our audiences have shared it with us and have added to its rich wealth of information by giving us new bits of material, making it grow and change and expand. It is difficult to commit this work to the print form. Each time we perform it, we learn some new facet of the history of these women, some new tale that needs to live with us. Ten years later, it continues to evolve. We thank you all for the contributions you have made and dedicate this first publication of *Dark Cowgirls and Prairie Queens* to all those who have travelled this journey with us, and all those who have stepped beyond.

production history

Dark Cowgirls and Prairie Queens has been performed at many important venues throughout its ten year history. It has been present at endings, such as the funeral of The Free Southern Theatre in New Orleans, Louisiana, and beginnings such as The First National Black Theater Festival in Winston Salem, North Carolina. *Dark Cowgirls* has roots at the Alternate ROOTS Festival in Atlanta, Georgia and has lived in communities from Mississippi to California, and from Massachusetts to Florida. It has been performed for women (at the Women in Theater Festival in Boston and The Foot of the Mountain in Minneapolis) and men (the Black cowboys of northern Alabama and northern California). *Dark Cowgirls* owes its longevity to the many small stubborn sponsors who believe that it is important to tell stories of empowerment and to celebrate the forgotten lives of Black women. Carpetbag Theatre continues to tour *Dark Cowgirls and Prairie Queens.*

original cast

Linda Parris-Bailey

Jermaine Hendrix

Jeff Cody

Linda Hill

Adora Dupree

subsequent cast

Sharlene Ross

Victor Cranford

Raphael Clemmons

Bert Tanner

Vida Werner

Sylvia Rupert

Belinda Hicks

Margaret Ann Miller

characters

DARK COWMAN I: (Jeff Cody) James, Mexican Soldier

DARK COWGIRL I: (Linda Parris-Bailey) Martha/Mama, Edmonia Lewis, Hannah, Washer Woman I, Emily Morgan West, Madame Lazarine

DARK COWGIRL II: (Adora Dupree) Black "Stagecoach" Mary, Anne, Hannah's Daughter I, Mary Alexander, Big Matilda, Soldadera I, Mammy Pleasants, Woman on the Porch I

DARK COWGIRL III: (Linda Upton Hill) Woman in the Camp, Biddy Mason, Washer Woman II, Soldadera II, Julia Boulette, Sarah, Woman on the Porch II

DARK COWMAN II: (Bert Tanner) Bob, Cowman in Debt, Mr. Langston, Man at the Exposition, Hannah's Son, Chuck Wagon Man, Turner, 49'er, Man on the Porch

act 1

Slow fade up - dusk colors: Five characters enter as if settling down for the evening camp gathering. They carry personal belongings and are singing "Home in Tennessee". Cowman I speaks as song ends.

OPENING SONG

Home in Tennessee
Well, ain't no use to sit and cry
Sail away lady now sail away
You'll be an angel by and by
Sail away lady now sail away

Chorus
Don't you rock 'em Daddy-o
Don't you rock 'em Daddy-o
Don't you rock 'em Daddy-o
Don't you rock 'em Daddy-o

Come little children go with me
Sail away lady now sail away
We'll go down to Galilee
Sail away lady now sail away

Chorus
I got a home in Tennessee
Sail away lady now sail away
See my man and he sees me
Sail away lady now sail away
Chorus

COWMAN I. Colonel Fant thought a whole lot of my mama, so when she asked him. . .
MARTHA. Colonel, why'nt you give my James a job workin' that cattle down there on the Santa Rosa?
COWMAN I. . . . he said, "All right Martha," that wuz mama's

name. So Colonel Fant loaded me on a wagon with some more Goliad men, you know,

MAMA. That's men from Goliad, Texas

COWMAN I. . . . and carried me out to his ranch. Colonel Fant had a contract with the government to furnish beef for the Indian territory, so he hired 'bout a hundred Negroes and Mexicans every year to drive his herds up the trail to Ardmore, Oklahoma or work the cattle. I started to work for Colonel Fant when I wuz eighteen year old.

MAMA. You wuz 17!

COWMAN I. They us'ta call us Colonel Fant's Dark Cowboys. I come home from the trail one day, thought I'd tease Mama. . . *(to Martha)* 'Hey Mama. How's my Dark Cowgirl doin'?

MAMA. Boy, I'll dark your eye!. . .

COWMAN I. She near 'bout knocked me down. Mama didn't like bein' called a Dark Cowgirl. Wuzn't nothing wrong with bein' called no Dark Cowgirl. Hell, Negro women been driving wagons 'cross the country for years—cookin' and launderin' on the trails and in the new towns springing up headed west. Hard women. Some fightin' women too. Women like Black Mary of Montana. Now Black Mary wuzn't shy with a weapon. Folks say Mary wuzn't satisfied with just a handgun. She'd tote a pistol and a shotgun too. Mary had a taste for big black cigars and hard liquor. She started out as a nurse for some Ursaline Nuns. I guess that's where she got that thirst from. Well anyway, she musta' got tired of that cause she left the nuns and started hauling freight by wagon. She wuz the restless type cause she stopped doin' that and started driving a stage coach. Folks say she had a restaurant too! When she got to be seventy years old she opened up a laundry in Cascade, Montana. Now Montana wuz kinda wild in those days.

COWMAN II. Hey ladies. This here saloon is now open for business.

ALL. Unison yell

Buffalo Gals
Buffalo Gals won't you come out tonight,

Come out tonight, come out tonight
Buffalo Gals won't you come out tonight,
And dance by the light of the moon.
And dance by the light of the moon.

I danced with the dolly with the hole in her stocking,
Knees keep'a knocking, toes keep' a rockin'
Danced with the dolly with the hole in her stocking,
Danced by the light of the moon.

Buffalo Gals won't you come out tonight,
Come out tonight, come out tonight
Buffalo Gals won't you come out tonight,
And dance by the light of the moon.
And dance by the light of the moon.

By the light, by the light, by the light of the moon,
By the light, by the light, by the light of the moon,
By the light, by the light, by the light of the moon,
We danced by the light of the moon.

COWMAN I.   Well, I saw Mary in a saloon in Cascade, one time,
and what a sight she wuz. Mary stood six foot tall. She musta'
been close to eighty year old. She wuz sittin' at the bar
downin' straight shots a' whiskey when a young fella come
past in a nice clean shirt. Look like he'd just stepped out a'
Mary's laundry. Well Mary, she downed another shot and
squared off against that young fella. Everybody wuz expect-
ing to see a real gun-fight, *(Mary tosses gun to bartender)* but
she just grabbed that fella by his collar and knocked him
down with her fist and said. . .

MARY.   His laundry bill is paid. *(She downs another drink and goes
to sit down. . . hears laughter)* What y'all laughin' at? You think
'cause Miss Mary is gittin' up in age she can't take care of
her own business? You think I been runnin' a laundry all
my life? You young folks don't know. Out here you either
do or be done to, and I ain't never been one to be done
to. Why I useta haul freight for a lot of folks. I'll tell you
what made me give up hauling freight. It wuz a blizzard and
a pack of hongry wolves. That's what did it. I wuz drivin' a
team of hosses from Cascade to Fort Benton when snow

started comin' down like duck feathers on a slaughter farm. The trail started gettin' sluggish straight off slick too! Wheels wuz slippin' where they shoulda' been stickin' and stickin' where they shoulda' been slippin'. Hosses seemed like they wanted to pull in two different directions. I wuz drivin' as hard as I could, tryin' to get to Fort Benton befo' we froze to death on the trail. Almost wished I wuz back with them Ursaline Nuns.

(Sits down and lights a cigar) Woulda' been too if it hadn't been for that Bishop! Ol' Bishop fired me for a shoot-out I had with a fella. Unh unh, I like working for me. Wuzn't nobody tellin' me what to do. Heck wuzn't nobody tellin' me nothin' at all out there. Just me and them hosses on that trail. Least ways that's what I thought till I heard that long high howl come to me over the snow. The hosses started gettin' skittish, right off. Can't nothin' smell danger like a good hoss, I say. Well, they took to backin' up and goin' sideways, just pushin' each other from side to side. I held 'em just as hard as I knew how and I talked a blue streak to them animals, cuz they couldn't see in all that wind and snow. Whoa there boy, steady now steady. That's a good hoss, good hoss, easy now. Easy now. . . all of a sudden it got real quiet. Even the wind and the snow seemed to stop for a minute. It wuz so still that I stopped the hosses and I stood up in the wagon to listen. Somethin' told me to get ready to do battle. Just as I wuz reaching down to get my shotgun, a pack of wolves come up on the hosses just a snarlin' and barkin' and snappin'. Well, the hosses reared back, the wagon turned ovah, my shotgun went flyin' that way and I flew the other. *(Falls back in chair)* I musta hit my head on a rock when I fell—cuz when I woke up it wuz all quiet. My hosses wuz gone , my pistol wuz broke, and my whole load wuz dumped out on the prairie. I wuz having trouble feeling my hands and feet it wuz so cold. So I went ovah to the wagon and got some wood and dry matches and started me a fire. Just about the time I started gettin' warm I heard that howling again. I went lookin' for my shotgun but it musta been covered by the snow. Then the wolves come up. I saw

those beady eyes on the outer edge of the fire. Now I know I got trouble. I grabbed me a stick out of the fire and started wavin' it at those big gray dogs. They stood they ground, and I stood mine—no closer, no further away. Well, we stayed like that all night long. If I moved, they moved, and if they moved I moved. I guess we wuz tryin' to see who wuz gonna give up first. The sun finally come up the next mornin'. . .Them wolves wuz sleep on the ground. I took what I could carry on my back, which wuz a considerable amount, off'a that wagon and headed for Fort Benton. I found a couple of them hosses 'bout twelve miles up the trail, so I didn't have to walk the whole way. When I finally made it to Fort Benton, I holed up there 'til spring. Warm weather come, I went back and got my wagon and quit. Some folks thought I shoulda give up hauling freight befo' that, but I liked the trail. Tried my hand at the restaurant business for a while, but I didn't cotton to feedin' folk. I missed the feel of being on the open prairie. The trail wuz freedom to me. So I took to driving a stage coach and hauling mail. Now that wuz a life. I won't tell you it wuzn't hard, and cold too. I recollect drivin' up north sometimes and it'd be so cold my eyelids would 'most freeze shut. But I felt so free. *(Instrumental music begins—"Free")* I didn't have to answer to nobody and I didn't depend on nobody neither. I ain't gonna tell you how I know, but I know what it feels like not to be free. Now I'm a big woman. I ain't scared of much. I ain't afraid of takin' no whippin'. I ain't afraid of giving one neither. Why, I whipped some horses when I had to and I whipped some men too. I ain't a woman to take much off a' nobody. That's why I'm free. That's why I'll stay free.

Mary sings.

Free
Free. I'm free
Ridin' the range
and roamin' the plains

Free. I'm free
Blazin' the trail
That's freedom to me.

(Singing continues under narration) I'll be free. . . .

COWMAN I. She always wuz real particular 'bout her freedom.

MARTHA. Some folks say her mama and daddy were slaves down in Tennessee where she wuz born, but you know how folks talk.

COWMAN II. Course you never could tell where women like Mary come from or where they wuz gonna wind up for that matter.

COWMAN I. Some women just got a spirit that makes 'em do things that other folks wouldn't even dream of.

MARTHA. Raisin' all kind of cain, heading off to places that they'd barely heard of much less ever seen.

COWGIRL III. Seems like folks wuz always heading someplace. Just all kinds of folks.

COWMAN I. Why I wuz on a train one day headed for Ohio when I come across one a the most unusual little Prairie Queens I done ever seen. The first time I seen her she wuzn't much more than a little girl. Now you could tell right off she wuz two kinds a' folks mixed together. She wuz the color of dark coffee with fresh cream. Looked like one a them Indians from over there in that place called India that I seen in the picture book. Well sir, she wuz quite a little rascal. Mama usta say that there wuz some women that wuzn't meant to raise nothin' but hell. She said she could tell right off from the time they wuz babies. They come into the world with they fist balled up and they just keep tryin' to wrench something from the world from then on. The only good thing 'bout them is they usually give something back to the world too. You could tell that this little Black Chippewa wuz one a them women. Her name wuz Edmonia Lewis. The Chippewa called her Wildfire. Little Wildfire wuz living in the Reverend's house in Oberlin with some other young girls from the school. It wuz Christmas time and most of the girls had gone home. Anyhow, Edmonia invited a couple a girls up to her room for a taste a hot wine 'fore they all set out on a sleighride with some local boys. Edmonia musta figured that the hot wine would liven things up just a bit. Like I said, some folks just born to raise hell. So Edmonia decided that maybe a little potion in the wine might liven things up that much more. See this stuff wuz supposed to make folks feel a little more affectionate towards one another, if you know what I mean. So anyway, by the time those girls got 'bout halfway through with they little ride, they wuz just as sick as they could be. They rushed back home and went straight to the doc. The doc say they'd been poisoned! Well you know what happened then; everybody in town started lookin' for Edmonia. *(Enter Edmonia. Anne follows chasing her)* They accused her of poisoning those girls and wanted to lock her up or hang her or both. She wuz in some kind of trouble now. White folks wuz out to hang her and Black folks wuz afraid to help her cause the white folks had been good 'bout helpin' the runaway slaves. Edmonia wuz between a rock and a hard place all right, and she sure got squeezed! Some white folks come and whipped her pretty bad. A black lawyer in Oberlin decided he wuz gonna defend her. The story goes he wuz half Indian too, so I guess he felt like she wuz kin.

Edmonia and Anne are together. Anne is attending to Edmonia.

ANNE. You're in big trouble young lady.

EDMONIA. Trouble ain't no stranger to me. I know him too well.

ANNE. Do you know that you're gonna have to leave Oberlin? White folks will not tolerate the poisoning of its young womanhood.

EDMONIA. I didn't try to poison anybody.

ANNE. That ain't even important now. They think you did and when they send somebody in here to talk to you about it, you'd be wise to act like you're real, real sorry 'bout what you "didn't do."

Enter Mr. Langston.

LANGSTON. Edmonia Lewis?

EDMONIA. *(Startled)* Who are you?

ANNE. He's you attorney. *(Exits)*

LANGSTON. We've got a lot of work to do before you go to trial.

EDMONIA. Trial! For what?

LANGSTON. They have charged you with attempted murder.

EDMONIA. I didn't try to murder anybody. I just wanted those girls to loosen up a little and have a good time! It wuz just a joke.

LANGSTON. Whites have a very poor sense of humor when it comes to 'murdering niggers' and 'red-skinned savages.' Unfortunately they see you as both.

EDMONIA. Is that how you see me Mr. Lawyer? A murdering savage?

LANGSTON. My name is Langston. Mr. Langston.

EDMONIA. Well, Mr. Langston, you think maybe they'll hang me for trying to murder those girls? Or do you think maybe they'll be so impressed by my fine colored lawyer that they'll let the poor little savage go?

LANGSTON. Oh, I can get an acquittal and it won't be because of my appearance. It won't even be because you didn't try to poison those girls. The fact is, they can't prove that you did poison them.

EDMONIA. That never stopped them before.

LANGSTON. Well, it will this time.

EDMONIA. Well, let's get it over with. I want to leave here as soon as I can. Folks talk as if colored people have it easy here, education, freedom. Every time they hit me, I said "Thank God I'm free."

Pause.

I'm goin' back to my mother's people. I'll weave baskets and bead moccasins like they do.

LANGSTON. That's freedom.

EDMONIA. What do you know about it? You think you're free 'cause you're a big time colored lawyer working in the white man's court?

LANGSTON. No, I think I'm free because I'm doing what I choose to do. Because I'm making a contribution to my people, to you. Do you think you'll be free sitting on a blanket beading moccasins and selling them to white mercantile stores? Think woman. If you're gonna be free, what are you gonna choose to do?

EDMONIA. (*Confused*) I'll go to California and live with my brother. I can do laundry.

LANGSTON. Just what the world needs another 'nigger' washer woman.

EDMONIA. You forgot the savage part didn't you! Just get me outta here. I don't need a colored lawyer to tell me what to do or anybody else.

LANGSTON. You need me to get you outta here. You need me to be free. You need somebody to show you that to be free you must choose to do what you want to do. Edmonia, what would you choose to do if you were free?

EDMONIA. I'd choose to be what I am. I'd take some clay and I'd push it and mold it until it wuz something beautiful. I'd take a hammer and a chisel and carve marble or stone until it looked like my people. I'd make figures of men and women who wouldn't be afraid to do whatever needed doing to make all people free. Great black heroes who couldn't be bound by anyone or anything.

LANGSTON. And what if I told you that Negro artists only do portraits of the sons and daughters of prominent white families, if they are good enough. What if I told you that you would never be a successful artist, turning out busts of what white folks don't want to know about, and that's brave Negro men and women.

EDMONIA. Then I'd say that I'll just have to be the first.

LANGSTON. I believe you just might. See you in court young lady. *(Exit)*

EDMONIA. Mr. Langston. *(Exit)*

COWMAN I. They let Edmonia go all right. She went off to Boston and studied that sculpturin' with a man name a' Brackett. I seen some a that sculpture that she done once. It wuz at the Philadelphia Exposition of 18 and 76. I wuz at this exposition and there it wuz in between these two great big ol' statues. "The Death of Cleopatra" that wuz the name of it you know.

COWMAN II. "The Death of Cleopatra" I tell you I ain't never seen something so pretty, everybody wuz standing around admiring it when she got there . You could tell by lookin' at her that she wuz real pleased by the way folks wuz admirin' what she'd done.

DARK COWGIRL II. It wuz just like she said it wuz gonna be. She made a statue of her people that wuz beautiful.

COWMAN I. Kind of made you feel beautiful too! I can't remember anything doin' that to me before. You could just feel the spirit a' the folks she wuz sculptin' right inside you every time you looked at her statues. John Brown, Colonel Robert Gould Shaw, the Old Arrow Maker too.

COWMAN I. Yes sir, she made us think about those great heroes. Course there wuz a lot of heroes that didn't have no statue made after them, but they sure shoulda. Women who come west to get away from slavery, willing to die fore they let themselves be hauled back into slavery. I wuz in San Bernadino after a cattle drive and heard 'bout a woman name a' Biddy Mason. She wuz a slave from Mississippi come to California with her master on a Mormon wagon train. Mormon trains even had their own songs!

Come, Come Ye Saints
Come, come ye Saints, no toil or labor fear;
But with joy, wend your way.
Though hard to you, this journey may appear;
Grace shall be as your day.

Tis better far for us to strive, our useless
Cares from us to drive.
Do this and joy your hearts will swell
All is well! All is well!

We'll find the place, which God for us prepared;
Far away in the west.
Where none shall come to hurt or make afraid
There the saints will be blessed.

We'll make the air with music ring,
Shout praises to our God and King.
Above the rest these words we'll tell,
All is well, All is well!

Narration resumes as second verse begins—Music softens.

COWMAN I. Now Biddy Mason wuz a sure enough dark cowgirl. The story goes that she walked from Mississippi to California behind 300 wagons. Her job wuz to keep the cattle together on the trail west. Bein' a slave, she didn't have much choice in the matter. I sure wouldn't a wanted to walk behind 300 wagons and a couple of hundred head a cattle! But Biddy wuz one a those women that you had to outright kill to stop her. She made it to California. They say she didn't loose a single steer. She didn't loose her master either, try as she might! Now let me tell you a little something about California in those days. There wuz laws that said there wuzn't no slavery in California, but they had some other laws that said masters could come get they slaves outta California if they wanted to. Or they could stay in California with they slaves as long as they waned to. Well, this created quite a problem. You see slaves and freed men were workin' close to each other and the word wuz passing between them pretty quick 'bout the freedom law in California. Those slaves that wanted to be free bad enough wuz fighting their masters in the street for their freedom. Some white folks wuz even goin' to court to help these slaves get their freedom from the masters. Like I said, word of these things wuz goin' 'round pretty fast. Well, one day Biddy's master, Master Smith, decided he wuz goin' back east to Texas. Well, Biddy had been thinkin' real hard about bein' free and when she heard this, she knew she wuzn't goin' to Texas.

Biddy speaks as narration ends.

BIDDY. I ain't goin' to Texas. Massa say it ain't gonna be no different in Texas than it wuz in Mississippi. "I'm gonna treat you all the same," he say. And I say "Yassu massa, I knows that's right", *(To companions)* and that's exactly why I ain't goin'! I'll fight him in the streets like a man if I have to. Hannah, you remember that slave name a' Frank? He took his master on in the middle of town. Right there in front a' everybody. One a' them white lawyers took him to the court house and got his freedom for him. That's how I'm gonna get freedom. I'll back massa down in the street and wrestle our freedom from him. Find us a white lawyer and get us some feedom papers. Then we'll take those papers and work for anybody paying a good wage. *(Pause)* Then I'll buy me some land. I'm gonna buy me some rich land and build me a farm, with a big house. Can't you see it Hannah? That big 2 story house with the white clapboard siding.

HANNAH. Ooh yes, and the green shutters.

BIDDY. And the long low picket fence. You see those roses growin' up the trellis on either side of the porch? Them's Premroses. And over there that's my garden. Got that good Southern exposures. Got some beans and greens. And that okra, that's red okra. Be as tall as a man 'fore it's through growin'.

HANNAH. And corn too! Wait a minute. Who's that out there workin' in your field? Lord she got some white folks workin' in her field.

All laugh.

BIDDY. Gonna have every kind of animal God put on this good earth.

COWMAN II. Every kind, Aunt Biddy?

BIDDY. Every kind 'cept a bull and a cow. I don't care if I ever see another steer in life. Me and my girls done ate more cow dust between Mississippi and California. That man can't hardly believe he's gonna walk us back east behind another 300 head of cattle.

COWGIRL I. Aunt Biddy I've got a good cow song for you. *(Begins call and response song)*

COWMAN II. *(Interrupting)* You mean we supposed to be so happy we want to sing?

HANNAH. Now just hold on. Ain't nobody ever said slaves sang 'cause they wuz happy. Man told me once that slaves sing most when they the most unhappy. Now this the most unhappy time we done ever seen so I guess we better sing and sing loud!

Feed My Cow
Well, did you feed my cow?
Yes mam.
Can you tell me how?
Yes mam.

What did you feed her?
Corn and hay.

What did you feed her?
Corn and hay.

Did you milk her good?
Yes mam.
Did you milk her like you should?
Yes mam.

How did you milk her?
Squish, squish, squish.
How did you milk her?
Squish, squish, squish.

Did the cow get sick?
Yes mam.
Was she covered with the ticks?
Yes mam.

How did she die?
Umph, umph, umph.
How did she die?
Umph, umph, umph.

Did the buzzards come?
Yes mam.
Did the buzzards come?
Yes mam.

How did they come?
Floop, floop, floop.
How did they come?
Floop, floop, floop.

"Run" tops end of last response of "Feed".

Run Chilun' Run
Run chilun' run

The paddyroller's gone get you
Run chilun' run
It's almost day.

Run chilun' run
The paddyroller's gone get you
Run chilun' run
It's almost day.

BIDDY. Dear God, I ain't goin' back. *(The outburst disrupts the singing)* We been living here for three years. Living almost. . . almost like free folks. A slave in California got a chance to be free, but massa won't stay here, he won't leave us here and I ain't goin' to be no slave in Texas. I gotta find me somebody knows something 'bout the law. Where I'm gonna find me a lawyer? . . . that white woman that's always helping the freedmen. I know she'd help me. She'll help me.

Ad-libs: Trying to stop Biddy, Biddy tries to break away from the women who try to keep her from running away. As she breaks free, the scene changes to the interior of the jail.

BIDDY. You know being in jail ain't so bad. We ain't got nothing to cook or clean or nothing. Kind of like when the rich white folks take a vacation. Ain't you goin' to say nothing?

COWMAN II. Ain't nothing to say.

HANNAH. How long we got to be in this tiny little room? I can't hardly breathe with all of us in here. Lord Biddy, there's eleven children in here!

BIDDY. Hannah you got a stop acting like this around these children. Now, they gonna act strong as long as we act strong. You go to complaining they gonna start crying and whining all day everyday.

HANNAH. They got a right. This ain't no closer to freedom, it's further away. I don't care what you say.

BIDDY. Look here Hannah. These children gotta learn to understand that freedom got to be won no matter what is cost you, and they need to be learning from their mamas!

HANNAH. You only got three children here. I got seven and one more comin' any day. You think I want freedom less than you? You think I want less for my seven children than you want for your three! I want freedom 10 times more. These last children wuz born right here in freedom and the rest been here long enough to know what freedom feels like even if they wuzn't really free. But you asking me not to think about what could happen to all of us. Ain't many slave women been allowed to keep that many children with them when the massa moves on. Lots of massas sell the young ones and use the money to pay for supplies or men big enough to work the trail. I got my children with me now. Suppose they only let some of us free? That white woman what bring us the food told me that if they too young to understand 'bout the slavery law, then the judge set them free, but the rest of us, she don't know. You want me to cut myself in two and send one half to slavery and the other stay here in freedom? Don't tell me this ain't so bad. Maybe slavery ain't so bad compared to loosing half your family. Yesterday that white woman told me that there's a law says that we can't talk in the courtroom. She said that colored wuzn't allowed to talk in the courtroom, slave or free. What we gonna do in a courtroom we can't even talk?

BIDDY. Now Hannah, you know anybody can keep me from talking when there's something I got a say? How many times massa done whupped me for saying what wuz on my mind when he didn't want to know? *(All laugh)*

HANNAH. This ain't nothing to laugh about. . .

BIDDY. This ain't nothing to cry 'bout neither. This ain't hard Hannah, don't make it so. If we wuz back down Mississippi we wouldn't have no chance to make it to freedom by sitting on our backsides in no jail cell. We'd be taking our lives in our hands, hiding in bushes and following the drinking gourd, with dogs hunting us and paddyrollers dragging us back to slavery, them that would go. Them that wouldn't be dead. That's what I'd be, dead. 'Cause once I got started to freedom wouldn't nobody get me to turn back, not even you Hannah. Now you start thinkin' on how lucky you are to be out of harms way in this here jail. Be thankful that we here. Ain't no law say a black woman can be free in Mississippi or Texas neither. There is one here in California. So you stop that whining right now or I'm gonna smack your face. You like my sister and I love you, but I'm gonna knock you down if you don't stop, sister or no.

HANNAH. I'm sorry Biddy, you right. I just can't stand being in here worrying not having no work to keep my mind off a' trouble. I can't stop thinking 'bout what's gonna happen if that judge gives us back to massa Robert.

BIDDY. Don't think about it Hannah. Why don't you go over and practice letters with Moses. That'll keep your mind of massa. . . Just hold on Hannah.

Go Down Ole Hannah
Won't you go down ole Hannah
Well, well, well *(echo: well, well well)*
Say won't you go down ole Hannah
Oh Well, well, well.

You should'a been on that river
Well, well, well—in eighteen an' ten
They wuz driving the women
Like they drove the men *(echo: Like they drove the men)*

Say won't you go down ole Hannah
Don't you ride no more.

BIDDY. I ain't gonna tell you that I know 'bout the law. I think the law'll be whatever you folks say it's gonna be. No, I don't know nothing 'bout the law, and you don't know nothing 'bout slavery. I guess that's why I'm here. Slave all my life, got three daughters that are slaves. All my life I wanted to be free. I'd heard 'bout slaves running away and goin' north, but I never did get my chance to go. Two of my babies come close together and I couldn't run when they come to take us. I heard tell of a woman who tried to go north to freedom with a little baby, but she got caught. They tried to take her and the baby back to her massa. They beat her so bad nobody could hardly recognize her. Well, when they finished whooping her, they gave her baby back to her, and she took a stone and bashed the child's skull. She tried to kill herself too, but the marshal stopped her. She said she would never raise another child in slavery. When massa Smith told me we wuz goin' to Texas, I felt that woman inside of me. I took a knife and tried to cut my Maggie's throat but I couldn't do it. God knows I tried, but I couldn't. She is here today because my hand wuzn't strong. No, you don't know 'bout slavery. Every slave in this country wants to be free more than anything on earth. And everyone of us is working for it in one way or another. Some of us never get a chance in life to be free, but we works for it anyway. Then some of us be in these free states and still be slaves. No sir, I don't understand your law, and you don't understand slavery. There's a man I heard 'bout name of Dred Scott been trying to get his freedom in the courthouse for ten years now. They say he tried to buy his freedom, his family's too, but his master cheat him and steal the money he saved. He live in a free state. Don't the white man have no law for the colored that he got to obey? I want to be free. I been working all my life to be free, now is the time. I done heard some folks talking about it being a waste of time to have niggas in the courtroom. Most of them so lazy they couldn't even make it on their own. Massa should let a few of them go just to save time. Let me tell you, ain't nobody lazy 'bout freedom, no matter how they go 'bout getting it. If you told me I had to walk through hell to get freedom I'd do it straight away. I ain't goin' to Texas. Ain't no way on God's earth to make me live in slavery again. I figure every man, woman, and child gets one chance to do what they gotta do in life. This is my chance. And if you don't let me do what I gotta do, then you better keep me and my girls in the jail house, 'cause I'll find my courage somewhere and take all of us to the Maker some kind of way. Now, you done let me talk and I done told you 'bout slavery. Now all you got to do is tell me 'bout your law. Ten years is a long time to wait for the law, and I won't be a slave for ten more years while you trying to make up your mind.

COWMAN I. Well massa Smith went to Texas all right, but he wuz minus fourteen slaves.

ALL. *(Outcry of Victory)*

Ain't Gonna Let Nobody Turn Me Around
Ain't gonna let nobody turn me around
Turn me around
Turn me around

Ain't gonna let nobody turn me around
Keep on walking
Keep on talking
Walking to the freedom land.

Repeat three times. Hum a fourth time under the narration.

COWMAN I. Biddy traveled on up to Los Angeles by and by and did what she said she wuz gonna do. She bought up a whole bunch of land and give some to folks to build up some churches. She started up some schools and nursing homes. She even helped folks that got caught in the big flood. And she never forgot that time she spent in jail neither. She use to tote food up to those poor hungry devils up there in the jail house right regular. Biddy got right well to do. Don't nobody know what happened to Hannah. Guess she just got herself on another wagon again and headed someplace else. Now me, I'm just a cowboy traveling over this country meeting folks making friends and some enemies too, I suppose. Never got me a family of my own, not that I know'd about anyways. After I took to the trail I never had a real home again. Even Mama moved on by and by. Packed up one day and headed west again. Mama couldn't read nor write so it wuz kind of hard to keep in touch. But every now and then she'd run across another Goliad man and give him a message for me. I suppose there must be a whole mess of messages from Mama that I never got. But I did get one and I know'd it wuz from Mama because a fella told me it wuz from a colored woman called herself a Dark Cowgirl. The message wuz real short too. It said. . .

MARTHA.
Home In Tennessee
Don't you rock 'em Daddy-o
Don't you rock 'em Daddy-o

Don't you rock 'em Daddy-o
Don't you rock 'em Daddy-o

Come little children go with me
Sail away lady now sail away
See my man and he sees me
Sail away lady now sail away

Chorus

Repeat from first verse as cast exits.

act 2

---

*As the lights come up a man and woman are at the chuck
wagon. The man is singing. He has prepared a meal. The other
women are at their washing across the front of the stage. They
join singing on the chorus.*

Promised Land
On Jordan's stormy banks I stand
And cast a wistful eye
To Canaan's fair and happy land
Where my possessions lie.
Chorus

I am bound for the promised land
I'm bound for the promised land
Oh who will come and go with me
I am bound for the promised land.

There generous fruits that never fail
On trees immortal grow
There rocks and hills and brooks and vales
With milk and honey flow.
Chorus

COWMAN I. Lots of folks thought the west wuz the promised land. Seems like every year some fella would bring colored folks west, promising them land and feedom just like the two went together like a horse and buggy. There were whole towns full of nothing but black folk. Nice towns where black folk owned everything, newspaper presses, stores and schools. There were even folk talking 'bout goin' to New York and getting a boat back to Africa. Well, freedom wuz the dream and everybody wuz trying to make that dream come true anyway they could. And it wuzn't only colored folks looking to that dream. There were colored, Chinese, Indian and white all looking for freedom in one way or another. Out there in California there were some pretty towns where all these folks wuz living together. I heard tell 'bout this place where everybody went down to the creek to do their laundry.

MARY A. *(Loud and off key)* Steal away, steal away, steal away to Jesus. Steal away, steal away home. I ain't got long to stay here. *(Narration comes up. Song continues under narration)* My Lord he calls us, etc. . . . .

COWMAN I. ..Colored, White and Chinese. Well now, see there wuz this one colored woman who loved to sing. She use to be a slave so all she knew wuz some old slavery songs. Well, this white fella who lived 'cross the creek use to hate to hear that woman singing them old slave songs, so he took her to court.

COWGIRL I. Here ye, hear ye, the second circuit court of California is now in session, Judge Huey P. Long presiding. All rise.

COWMAN I. ..trying to make her stop singing. Well the judge said, "I'm sorry mister there ain't no law against singing but I know how sad those slave songs can be. So what we'll do is get her some singing lessons, teach her some new songs." He said, "by the way what type songs do you like?" Well when the man said opera . . .

MARY A. OPERA!

COWMAN I. . . .that woman liked to fainted dead away. But don't you know, she started singing opera that very next week.

MARY A. *(Sung to the popular tune of the Habenera from Georges Bizet's "Carmen")*

La la la—la, la la la—la, la la la-a-a-a la la la la—. *(Last note held under narration)*

COWMAN I. . . . combining opera songs with the slave songs. . .

MARY A. La la la—la, la la la—you've, got to ste-eal away to Jesus.

ALL. La, la la la—la, la la la—you've, got to ste-eal away to Jesus. La, la la la—la, la la la—you've, got to ste-eal away sweet home.

Grandios Exit repeating song.

COWMAN I. I wuz real surprised there wuzn't a law against singin', especially that kind. They wuz a law against most everything black folks could do. That's been so long as I can remember. Didn't matter where you went from Texas to California to New York. Just 'bout all over the country I'm tellin' yah. And it seem like it wuz wanting to get worse after the war. It seems to me that folks starting out after fighting for so long do one a two things. They either just give up and die inside or they get up and fight like hell. Yup, win or lose, fighting does funny things to folks. I remember long ago hearing 'bout a woman named Emily Morgan West. They called her "The Yellow Rose of Texas."

Song: "The Yellow Rose of Texas" - sung as a ballad.

The Yellow Rose of Texas
There's a Yellow Rose in Texas, that I am goin' to see.
No other fella knows her, no fella only me.
She cried so when I left her, it like to broke my heart.
And if I ever find her we never more shall part.
Chorus

She's the sweetest rose of color, this fella ever knew.
Her eyes are bright as diamonds, they sparkle like the
   dew.
You may talk about your Dearest May and sing of Rosa
   Lee.
But the Yellow Rose of Texas, beats the bells of Tennessee.

Optional.

Where the Rio Grande is flowing and the starry skies are
   bright.

She walks along the river in the quiet summer night.
She thinks if I remember, when we parted long ago.
I promised to come back again and not to leave her so.

COWMAN I. Emily wuz a slave woman come out of New York.
Colonel James Morgan brought Emily to his town of New
Washington. Colonel Morgan wuz just starting to build up
the town so he brought some highlanders and free Blacks
from Bermuda in too. Well this wuz all goin' on at the same
time that Santa Anna wuz fighting with Sam Houston and
the boys over the Texas territory. Now Colonel Morgan wuz
a real American patriot so he figured it wuz his duty to go
off and fight with Houston. Santa Anna wuz riding into New
Washington burning, looting, and killing. It just so happens
that Emily wuz out on the docks loading supplies there in
New Washington when all this wuz goin' on. Now Santa
Anna wuz quite a ladies man, and when he caught sight of
that pretty Yellow Rose he just had to have her.

Cowman I becomes a Mexican soldier. Enter soldaderas.

MEXICAN SOLDIERS AND SOLDADERAS. Al Ataque!!
YELLOW ROSE. *(Soldaderas fight with Emily and bind her)* Take your
hands off me, I can't run away you fellas will see to that.
SOLD. II. Abajo las manos.
YELLOW ROSE. You're women! I've been captured by Senorita
Soldiers.
SOLD I. Soldaderas, si.
YELLOW ROSE. Soldaderas? Is that what you call a female soldier?
(To Sold. I) (Pause) Do you speak English? *(To Sold. II)* Do
you?
SOLD. II. Si, un poco.
YELLOW ROSE. Soldadera, does that mean soldier? Fighter?
SOLD II. Si we fight beside our men. We fight for the land. We
survive.
YELLOW ROSE. Well what do you want with me?
SOLD. I. ¿Que dijo ella?
SOLD II. Ella dijo ¿Que quieren de me?
SOLD I. El emperador quiere que seas su querida.
YELLOW ROSE. Can you tell me in English?
SOLD II. Si, the emperador wants you for his woman.

YELLOW ROSE. I'm supposed to be one of you soldaderas?

SOLD II. No, no una Soldadera. No, not a Soldadera. His WOMAN!

YELLOW ROSE. His woman?

SOLD II. Si, the emperador had to leave his new bride on the other side of the river. He sees you and wants you to take her place, for a while. *(Emily tries to escape but is grappled down by the soldaderas)*

YELLOW ROSE. No! I won't do it! I won't be used that way by anybody!

SOLD II. If you want to survive you will be used anyway the emperador wants to use you! *(Emily tries to escape as Turner and soldier enter)*

MEX. SOLD. *(Breaking up Melee)* ¡Basta¡ si le hacen dano, Santa Anna las va a maertae. ¡Vayanse!

TURNER. Emily, stop that! *(Unties her)* You're gonna get us both killed. This ain't the way to deal with these people. I been talking to ole Santa Anna and he offered me all kind of money and things to tell him where Sam Houston is. Lord it sure is tempting.

YELLOW ROSE. There is not one thing tempting 'bout what he's offering me.

TURNER. I don't know Emily. Hell, he's the Emperor of Mexico, and if he win this here war, he'll be the Emperor of Texas too! It's their land, Emily. They're just trying to hold on to it.

YELLOW ROSE. Emperor or no, he can't steal people and turn them into his women. This doesn't have anything to do with land. This has to do with one man trying to have one woman! I'm not gonna be that kind of servant for nobody. I'm telling you Turner I won't be used.

TURNER. Santa Anna may be a thieving rascal but we just might be better off being used by the Mexicans than we would be with the Texans.

YELLOW ROSE. In what way?

TURNER. Folks are saying that if we were an independent territory that the first thing that the white folks would do would be to make all the indentured servants in the territory slaves again.

YELLOW ROSE. I don't know if there's any difference between

being a Texas slave or a Mexican indentured servant for ninety-nine years. Colonel Morgan got around the anti-slavery laws and you can't convince me that Santa Anna is my Moses. That man is a conniving scoundrel and I won't consort with him! I know the difference between being a man's house servant and being a man's concubine.

TURNER. Well being a man and not being sought after for my personal favors, I could just be tempted to tell ole Santa Anna where Sam Houston wuz, if I knew. No I guess not. My trade is printing not being a traitor nor a spy

YELLOW ROSE. What did you say Turner? We can get out of here. I know where he is. Santa Anna wants to know where Sam Houston's camp is. Well, I'm sure that Houston could use the same information 'bout Santa Anna, and we could get that information to him. Listen to me now. You agree to locate Houston's troops for a party of Santa Anna's soldiers. You tell him that you'll lead that party right into Houston's camp. You lead them in the opposite direction. When you have their confidence, you break away and you ride like the devil to Houston's camp and tell them all 'bout Santa Anna's plan. In the mean time I'll keep Santa Anna busy!

TURNER. How am I gonna do that? I don't know where they are.

YELLOW ROSE. I do. Turner you're a good horseman, you can do it. Will you?

TURNER. Can and will are two different things.

YELLOW ROSE. Come on Turner.

All exit except Cowman I.

COWMAN I. Well ole Turner did what Emily asked him to do. He got that information right out there to Sam Houston. Left those Mexican soldiers in the dust! After they won the battle, Houston's men were looking every which way for ole Santa Anna. Seems he slipped away in all the confusion. Since New Washington wuz pretty much destroyed by the Mexican soldiers. Some folks didn't have no place to go and just wandered around until somebody found them. I suppose Emily weren't no different.

TURNER. Emily . . . where you goin'?

YELLOW ROSE. I'm just walking.

TURNER. Slow down Emily. I'm tired of talking to your back girl. Now, where you goin'?

YELLOW ROSE. Maybe I can walk to New York.

TURNER. Don't be foolish girl. Once Colonel Morgan starts rebuilding New Washington he'll be looking for all his servants. You'll be among the first.

YELLOW ROSE. I didn't lose anything back there. It wuzn't my home. I've only been in Texas for a year. Just a place to sleep and work.

TURNER. For somebody who has no loyalties to a place you sure made a big effort to stop Santa Anna. It would have been a lot easier for you had you run when you had the chance. But you decided to stay and talk me into being a spy. Now you want to run away when you finally got a real chance at freedom.

YELLOW ROSE. What are you talking 'bout?

TURNER. You did a great thing today. Now you trying to run away like you ashamed of what you did.

YELLOW ROSE. Maybe I should be. What good did it do me? I'm still an indentured servant—will be of ninety-eight more years. You, you're a free man. I can understand why you . . .

TURNER. You don't understand nothing! We all have to use whatever we got to get free. I learned how to print so that I could get my freedom. I know how important newspapers and documents are so I made myself valuable to them. It's because I do what I do that I am not the property of any man and it's because you've done what you've done that you are goin' to be free. Now we'll go tell Colonel Morgan and Sam Houston everything that you did today. They'll be grateful; they'll be very grateful. And if you make them grateful enough they'll give you your freedom. Do you understand what I'm telling you? Now let's go back to camp. Oh, I been holding something for you. I told him I'd give it to you as soon as I found you.

The Yellow Rose of Texas

Oh, now I'm goin' to find her for my heart is full of woe. And we'll sing the song together, that we'd sung so long ago.

We'll play the banjo gaily, and we'll sing the songs of yore.
And the Yellow Rose of Texas shall be mine for ever more.
Chorus

COWMAN I. They say the words to that song about the Yellow
Rose wuz written down in a love letter by one of Emily's
admirers. Sometimes there's a fine line between good and
evil. Sometimes you got to do a little sinning to do a lot of
good. I've never been one to judge somebody, but it seems
to me that it didn't make no difference to Sam Houston
what kind of woman Emily wuz when he wuz standing up
on the hill talking 'bout he hope that she keep Santa Anna
occupied all night. See it's all in the way you look at folks.

Fools of '49 *instrumental in background.*

Some might think that Biddy Mason wuz a great saint and
Julia Boulette wuz a great sinner. Julia Boulette, now there's
a woman for you. That wuz a woman for a whole lot of folks.
You know, back during the gold rush a forty-nine, mining
camps were springing up where ever somebody found a little
yellow sparkling on the ground.

Enter Mining people singing Fools of '49.

Fools of '49
When gold wuz found in '48 the people thought it wuz
    gas,
And some were fool enough to think the rocks were only
    brass.
But they were soon satisfied and started off to mine.
They bought a ship came round the horn in the fall
    of '49.

When they thought of what they had been told;
When they started after gold,
That they never in this world would make a find.

*Accompaniment continues changing to a low down Blues for
Matilda.*

COWMAN I. . . .and most of those miners were men. Now , when
you got a whole lot of money there's a certain kind of

woman that just naturally starts to show up. Yeah, I remember a little saying they had 'bout that . . .

COWMAN II. First came the men who worked in the mine.

LADIES. Next came the ladies who lived on the line.

COWMAN I. . . .Oh, now there wuz some women I'll never forget. Iodoform Kate, Madame Lazarene and Big Matilda. *(Music changes)* Now that wuz a biiiig woman. Use to carry these little pieces of paper round that said. . . .

MATILDA. Big Matilda. 300 pounds of Black Passion! Hours: All hours, Rates: 50 cents each or 3 for a dollar.

Music ends.

COWMAN I. I never said another bad word 'bout a fat woman after that one! But the most beautiful woman to grace the west wuz Julia Boulette. They called her Queen of the Comstock, and when she pranced through town with diamonds and furs everywhere, with that team of white horses, you knew exactly why they called her that. Some of those line women wuz real ambitious and they tried to be like Miss Julia. She usually handled them pretty well, that is usually.

JULIA. *(A knock is heard)* Come in. Just make yourself comfortable. I'll bring us some refreshments.

WOMAN. Why thank you, don't mind if I do.

JULIA. *(Seeing her for the first time)* Can I help you?

WOMAN. I figure maybe we could help each other.

JULIA. Who are you and what do you want?

WOMAN. Who I am ain't important. What I want could be real important. See you and me, we's in the same business. You got a nice little situation here and I thought I might buy into it.

JULIA. What do you mean?

WOMAN. Well with some of the money I earned, I bought me a little claim. It didn't make me rich, exactly, but I figured maybe if I put up oh 'bout five-hundred dollars and you put up a little we could earn one hell of a lot more money than we're making now.

JULIA. You're not serious.

WOMAN. Serious as the clap!

JULIA. With your exquisite manners and eau d' Burrow perfume you couldn't pay me enough to go in with the likes of you.

WOMAN. You must be pretty well off to refuse my money. Tell you what I'll do, I'll double it. Does that help you any? We could be quite a team.

JULIA. The only thing that I'd team you up with would be one of my horses!

WOMAN. I'm serious. I just got this little bit of cash and I'm trying to make it a big bit.

JULIA. You my dear are a common mining camp whore. You women of the line will never learn, will you? Now you're attractive. You might clean up pretty well if we could get you into a bath.

WOMAN. Oh, now that's real kind of you to say. So you think you're more than a line woman cause you got diamonds and furs? *(She remove Julia's jewels)* Now, you're just like the rest of us, and if you died today all anybody would say 'bout you wuz that you wuz an ordinary, Comstock, mining camp whore!

JULIA. I'm the queen of the Comstock!

WOMAN. A colored whore who means nothing to nobody.

JULIA. If I were to die today there'd be so many men devastated by my death, they'd have to close the mines. I'm respected around here. People love me because I care for them.

WOMAN. They can get that kind of care anywhere on the line for ten cents.

JULIA. I've got breeding and good taste. My father was a senator in New Orleans.

WOMAN. I've heard that. I've also heard that your fella dumped you here on the line with nothing in your pocket and nothing on your back.

JULIA. That's a damn lie!

WOMAN. Damn lie? Well tell me the truth Miss Boil—lette. Tell me what you'd say on your tombstone if you was gonna die today.

JULIA. I'd write "here lies Julia BOU-lette, daughter of a Louisiana Senator and his Creole mistress. She made her fortune by providing fine entertainment for the gentlemen of Comstock and is remembered for her great contribution to the city. She was a member of the Volunteer Fire Unit Number

9, and was always ready to answer the alarm. She gave freely of her time and money to the citizens of the town. She was loved and respected by all."

WOMAN. There won't be anyone who'll care 'bout you one way or another. There won't be a marker on your grave.

JULIA. They'll hang my portrait in town hall, and build a huge crib over my grave. The entire Engine Company Number 9 will carry my body to the grave-site raised high over their heads. Oh yes, this town loves Julia Boulette.

WOMAN. Now I'll tell you how it's gonna be. They gonna hang your picture in the Bucket of Blood so all the patrons can drink to their favorite whore. All the good you ever did they'll say someone else did 'cause everyone will only remember you as a common whore. And when they get to thinking that maybe you wasn't so bad, maybe you did do some good, they'll probably decide that you musta been a white whore so they'll be able to say, "She had her faults, but she did a lot for the community."

JULIA. You're still a d . . ., a liar. I don't need your money. Get out of here.

WOMAN. One last thing. Let me tell you how you're gonna die. Some common fella is gonna come into this room and take off his common clothes, and take out his common gun and cut you down and out of mind. See, honey, you and me we in the same business and no matter what you do they gonna treat us both the same. You can't do enough good to be more than a colored line woman to the folks who gonna tell the story.

COWMAN I. Yup, Julia sure loved diamonds and furs. Matter of fact it wuz just that love that killed her. They found her laying dead on her bed one morning, all her furs and diamonds gone. When they buried her, the whole Engine Company Number Nine, all dressed up in uniform, followed that casket all the way to the grave. Some of the women folk didn't like that at all, but shucks, they couldn't stop those men from givin' a fine burial to the Queen of the Comstock.

Song: Julia-ette Boulette *the music under the narration. After the camp people line up for the funeral procession, they sing.*

Julia-ette Boulette

Julia-ette
echo: Julia-ette
Boulette
echo: Boulette
Queen of the line
On the old Comstock Mine
She died 'fore her time *(Hold)*
echo: Killed in her prime.

Refrain repeats as all exit.

COWMAN I. Well, now, I been 'round a whole lotta women folks. Jewels and rebels, big-round-jolly ones and little biddies. But some women wuz just a puzzle. Had so many sides and ragged edges that couldn't nobody figure where they fit in. Good and evil mixed up together like hemp rope. Couldn't tell which side they wuz on. Mammy Pleasants wuz like that. She had more sides to her than a cat-o-nine tails. She got real rich and well to do and poor and outcast in the same lifetime. Back in April of '52 Mammy Pleasants came up to San Francisco on the Oregon—up from New Orleans. Folks say when she got to town she had forty-thousand dollars in her pocket. Seems she'd been married to a plantation man from down Cuba, big abolitionist fella. He musta left her lots of money when he died. They say she kept right on working for to free the slaves after her husband passed. She'd give money for supplies for slaves goin' to freedom. Even rode that underground railroad herself. She wuz so strong in her working for the freedom cause, that she gave thirty-thousand dollars to John Brown. Well sir, it got so she wuz starting to be real familiar to those slave catchers and she had to stop fooling around in the South. That's when she come West. She started out as a cook. But Mammy never did do nothing just like everybody else. So when Mammy cooked that's all she did! She didn't wash no dishes, she didn't do no housework—just cooking. To hear her tell it she wuz a world famous what you call chef. And for that she got somewheres 'bout five hundred dollars a week. Mammy had her own way of doing things all right. She bought up a bunch of houses out there in San Francisco. She had a little business that brought together young ladies of breeding with old men of money. Now they tell me that Mammy had a little finishing school for these ladies right there in her home. Not all of these young girls wuz as appreciative as Mammy would of liked them to be.

MAMMY. Mr. Winston came to call, where were you?

SARAH. I was out. Is he gone?

MAMMY. Yes, he's gone and this will be the last time that you will be out when he comes to call.

SARAH. Don't threaten me Mammy. I'm not one of those superstitious fools that you push around at will. I don't believe in Voodoo.

MAMMY. Oh, and what do you believe in?

SARAH. I believe in my God given right to do as I wish.

MAMMY. Apparently you haven't noticed that certain men have taken the God given rights of our brothers and sisters away.

SARAH. Not the abolitionist speech again.

MAMMY. Don't you dare make light of slavery As a gentleman's wife you'll never feel the lash. You'll never have your family sold away from you. Why there are women half your age still being molested by their masters over and over again.

SARAH. I've heard about our poor colored sisters since I was a child. You don't seem to have any trouble discussing their freedom, what about my freedom? I'm 20-years-old Mammy and you haven't allowed me to make one decision for myself. You choose my clothing, my friends, my interests; I believe that you've even selected Mr. Winston as my mate.

MAMMY. Mr. Winston is a fine man. He has money and position. Think of what an important ally he'll be.

SARAH. You have haven't you? Mr. Winston is to be my husband.

MAMMY. He's kind and loving—extravagant with women. Truly he is the best of the lot.

SARAH. You like him so very much, why don't you marry him?

She tries to exit.

MAMMY. Where do you think you're going?

SARAH. To my room.

MAMMY. You'll stay right here until this is settled.

SARAH. It is settled. I won't be married off to Mr. Winston. I'm leaving tomorrow.

MAMMY. The hell you say! You're going to stay right here and marry Mr. Winston, or anybody else I tell you to. After you're married we'll be allies. You're a leader Sarah just as I am. Sometimes I look at you and I see myself forty years ago. You are more a part of me than my own daughter. There is so much that we can accomplish together.

SARAH. Mammy I am not you. I'm my own spirit. I'm not an image of you. I want my own life not one you've concocted for me. You're a great woman, but you can't recreate yourself in me. I'm Sarah.

MAMMY. Sarah I don't want to recreate myself. I want someone to carry on. You were born with a gift just as I was. You aren't going to throw it away because of adolescent desire.

SARAH. You know about. . . .

MAMMY. I know what's in you heart; believe me I do. I can feel it. But you have a larger purpose. The people who hold power over us are not going to respond to the colored people's pleas for freedom out of a sense of justice. They respond to power, and that is something that people like you and I have inside. What I am trying to give you is money to use as a tool of that power.

SARAH. Mammy, you're eating away at whatever I am and filling the empty spaces with what you want me to be. You are smothering me to death.

MAMMY. No Sarah, you won't die. You'll go on stronger than before, more determined than ever to do what's right. What is being replaced in you is selfishness and doubt. Sarah it's not all sacrifice you know. There is no greater feeling in this world than to save another life, to know that you have made a difference. Love and gratitude from many can be just as satisfying as love from one. Those of us who lead must be willing to give up at least as much as those who would be lead by us. The question we must ask is have we gained something for our people as we've gained something for ourselves.

SARAH. And is the reverse true Mammy? Can we do something for others without first doing it for ourselves? What we do for others has to come from a deep personal concern.

MAMMY. And what about the overriding concerns of people who don't have food or clothing—people who are bound by masters, beaten and killed?

SARAH. Mammy I can't save the whole world.

MAMMY. You will try.

SARAH. Dear God Mammy will you ever let up?

MAMMY. Never.

COWMAN I. And she didn't either. Sarah went on and married that fella, and old as he was they had them some children. And Mammy stayed with them too. They tell me she gave that girl a terrible time. Took over her kids, bossed her around, poor girl didn't have no kind of hand in the doings in her own house. Well don't you know, when that old man finally did pass on, that young girl threw Mammy out on her . . . threw her out in the street. Folks say Mammy just hid away in one of her houses after that. Seemed like kind of a waste to me. She was a woman of so many talents. I guess you had to be to make it out here. Being a cowboy or a cowgirl for that matter ain't an easy life.

Motherless Child

Sometimes I feel like a motherless child.
Sometimes I feel like a motherless child.
Sometimes I feel like a motherless child.
A long way from home, a long way from home.

Narration comes up. Verse is hummed once under narration.

I guess nobody really came out here looking for it to be easy. That ain't what it's all 'bout now is it? I mean life being easy that is. Nope, we was just looking for it to be fair, that's all, just fair. Seemed like you could stand being poor or tired or hungry if you knew that it wasn't gonna be like that always; if you had the same chance as the next fella or girl. Oh well, maybe someday. Yes sir, I done known some women in my time. Women you just couldn't help but love. Young and old. Women that built up the whole territory. Women who went out looking for freedom. They found out that they had to make freedom wherever they went, and they wasn't afraid to do it. Some women made freedom with their hands like Edmonia Lewis, some with a horse and wagon like Biddy. They stretched they arms out and spread what they had as far as it would go. Now you take mama. She couldn't do a whole lot to help herself but if it hadn't of been for her I'd still be back in Goliad breaking my back and never ever having a taste of freedom. She taught me a lot. She taught me how to tell a good lie! *(He laughs)* Course now I never tell no tales that couldn't have been true. The things that I told you happened. Might not have happened just that way, but from what I know to be true, they sure could have. See, Mama had a lot of sayings. She'd say . . .

MARTHA. Never believe more than half of what you already know. What folks tell you 'bout themselves is only what they want you to know, and what somebody tells you 'bout somebody else is only what they think they know, and somebody else told them that. And somebody else told them that. If you got two mouths, you got two different stories.

COWMAN I. And she didn't trust nothing that wuz written down. She'd say . . .

MARTHA. All that stuff what they put on paper is just more of the same lies they be tellin' you with they mouth and they act like 'cause it's written down, it's gospel like in the Bible.

COWMAN I. I guess Mama wuz suspicious 'cause she couldn't read or maybe it wuz because she used to be a slave, and she say after she got her freedom papers wuzn't a thing different. Mama said . . .

MARTHA. All them laws the white folks make for the colored they gonna take back, that is if we let them. That's why you got to keep the spirit of every brave black man and women that you ever meet right up here in the front of your head. 'Cause when you ain't got no more strength left, all you got to do is reach right up here in the front of your head and pull a little of they strength out and you use it.

COWMAN I. I wuz a young fella then and thought that wuz crazy talk, and I told Mama so. She tried to knock me down again. Well now that I'm older I know better. She always told me to believe the best 'bout folks. You know, sometimes I ask myself what makes you remember some folks that ain't got nothing and forget 'bout those that seem to have everything. I think 'bout some of the people that I remember and the thing that sticks out like a sore thumb is the way they makes things change for themselves. Mama told me . . .

MARTHA. Folks come West looking for freedom, folks go North

looking for freedom. Someday it gonna turn all around and Black folks be going back South again looking for freedom. Be calling Georgia the land of Zion.

COWMAN I. I don't know 'bout all that, but I know that it's people that change things. Not land, not north, south, east or west, but people! Well Mama always said . . .

MARTHA. Don't try and mix preaching with telling lies, 'cause somebody might think that you got some new kind of gospel.

COWMAN I. I guess I better get back on the trail and get those cattle where they supposed to be instead of where they is. You all just keep on trying to wrench something good from this world, and give us back all the good you can. I guess Mama's up in heaven someplace with the rest of the saints, guiding that boat to glory saying. "Don't you rock 'em daddy-o."

Voices come in under the narration singing "Don't you rock 'em daddy-o," etc. from Home in Tennessee.

COWMAN I. We love yah Mama, and we'll take care of things down here. We'll make sure that someday won't nobody need to go to glory to find the promised land.

Song: Home in Tennessee *starts with the third verse, then continues until all have exited on the last wagon train.*

Home in Tennessee *(Third verse)*
Only thing that we did wrong,
Sail away lady now sail away.
Stayed in the wilderness much too long,
Sail away lady now sail away.
Chorus

Repeat from first verse

Chorus
When I get my new house done
Sail away lady now sail away
Give the other one to my son
Sail away lady now sail away
Chorus

rebecca ranson

blood on blood

artist's statement

Blood on Blood was written as a response to a Bruce Spring-
steen song which haunted me. The play ended up being an
exploration of options for people who might not have many.
Most of my work is about choices and most of it presents
people whose stories are not often told, people caught in a
struggle with a tiny intimate system that is the result of the
larger social system in which they live. I am moved and
angered by injustice and want to give empowerment to the
voices who are not understood. I write what moves me.

production history

Originally produced by Seven Stages, Atlanta, Georgia, under the direction of Del Hamilton, in 1987. The original
cast was (Maria) Kim Castle, (Joe) Mack Anthony, (Frankie)
Kelly Hill. Monica Gross directed a production in 1990 that
was part of the London Fringe Festival and won an award
there for best script. Gross's production also played a run
at the Cubiculo in New York City in 1990.

pretty sleeping people

Frankie and Maria are sleeping in the bed. Frankie is against Maria's back with his arm draped around her. Joe enters, studies them.

JOE. Hey Frankie, boy. It's your brother. It's Joey. I'm looking at you pretty sleeping babies. Your eyes are all closed and you're breathing so soft.

FRANKIE. *(softly)* Joe is here.

MARIA. What?

JOE. It's me, honey.

MARIA. Joey. Ah, shit.

JOE. You two were like a picture. When I first came in, I thought how pretty you looked—people I love—my wife and my big brother and they're snuggled up soft together. Frankie, haven't I always been the one to save you when you got in trouble?

FRANKIE. Yeah.

JOE. You pushed it to the absolute limit this time. I don't reckon even you could go any farther than sleeping with my wife.

MARIA. Joey.

JOE. Shut up, honey. This is between me and Frankie.

FRANKIE. Let me tell you what happened.

JOE. Tell me, Frankie. Tell me one of those good stories you always tell. You never done nothing that didn't come with a good story behind it, did you?

FRANKIE. The truth is that things got all twisted up. I was down at the bar just drinking a few with the boys. Gene and Sandy were there. You can ask them if you don't believe me and we were putting away a bottle of Jack and all of us were horny as hell. You know, Gene's old lady threw him out and all so the conversation naturally got around to pussy and how none of us had any and there wasn't one damn woman in the bar. I got tired of all the talk and thought I'd come by here and see what the two of you were up to. See, I forgot you were gonna be out of town tonight. When I got here

Maria was already in bed and I guess I was so drunk I lay down beside her and just passed out. I know it looks bad but it's not what you're thinking.

JOE. How many times have you plain out lied to me?

FRANKIE. You're my brother. I don't tell you lies. Ask Maria.

JOE. I ain't asking Maria nothing. I'm talking to you.

FRANKIE. Well, I'm telling you the truth.

JOE. There wasn't the first word of truth in anything you said. You don't believe that bullshit story any more than I do.

FRANKIE. I don't think you want to do this, Joe.

JOE. You're wrong, Frankie. I been waiting to do this.

FRANKIE. Look, can I get up out of this bed?

JOE. No. No, you can't get up yet. You sit right there beside Maria and tell me the goddamned truth for once in your life. I'm gonna save you but I'm not gonna make it easy. What kind of clothes you got on?

FRANKIE. I'm in bed. I'm not wearing clothes.

JOE. I never once seen you take your clothes off before you passed out.

FRANKIE. Maria must have waked up and done it.

JOE. She must have.

FRANKIE. It ain't no big thing. She's done that before.

JOE. That's right.

FRANKIE. You're trying to make a big deal out of nothing.

JOE. That could be true.

FRANKIE. It is true.

JOE. You had enough of this bullshit now, Frankie?

FRANKIE. How many times I gotta tell you the same damn thing? It's just one of those things that happens to me. I get a little drunk and pass out.

JOE. I done picked you up out of every hole in town. I guess I ought to know what you do by now.

FRANKIE. Well, see that's all there was to it.

JOE. What was it you said you was drinking?

FRANKIE. Same thing. Jack, what I always drink.

JOE. I don't smell no liquor.

FRANKIE. It's wore off.

JOE. You ain't been drinking tonight.

FRANKIE. Joey, I want to tell you something, little brother. You would be a hell of a lot better off if you stopped pumping out those questions. I'm trying to do something that would be the best for all of us. This time Frankie is trying to save us.

JOE. What is it you're saving us from?

FRANKIE. The truth. Let's just say I had a little too much and ended up here by mistake.

JOE. Now why would we want to say that when we know it's a lie?

FRANKIE. Let's just say it won't happen a second time.

JOE. Wouldn't that be piling one lie on top of another?

FRANKIE. No, Jocy. I swear it would be the truth.

JOE. I was waiting down the road in my car. You know that empty lot with the big tree, that magnolia tree. Well I pulled in there and just watched to see if you would pass by and you did. I tried to get a good look at your face but you was looking the other way. I thought about pulling out right behind you, stopping you before you ever got to the door. I couldn't do it. I started up the car and I couldn't even move my hand to put it in gear. I just sat there the longest time with the car running. I let these pictures of the two of you come in my head and I was thinking what you might be doing and was you saying stuff about not doing this to Joey or was you not even saying my name . . .

FRANKIE. Let's don't do this.

JOE. We got to.

FRANKIE. Can't no good come from it.

JOE. When in the name of God has that ever made any difference to you?

FRANKIE. This time. Now.

JOE. Because of her?

FRANKIE. I guess so but it's more than that. Where can we go from here?

JOE. I got some ideas about that.

FRANKIE. They better be some good ones.

JOE. They are. I sit in my car studying on it. First, you have to tell me the truth.

FRANKIE. I think you know it.

JOE. I want to hear the words said. Say it. Say all of it.

FRANKIE. I don't want to do this.

JOE. For once, what you want don't matter worth shit to me.

FRANKIE. Okay. Okay. I come over here tonight because I knew you would be gone. It started a long time ago, Joey, a real long time ago. I been holding back for ten years or more.

JOE. More, I'd say.

FRANKIE. More. It seems like it would have gone away, that I wouldn't have lasted so long wanting what couldn't happen.

JOE. Was it worth the wait?

FRANKIE. No. Can you understand that? No.

MARIA. What the hell do you mean?

FRANKIE. I've wanted you so long I'm just about crazy from it.

JOE. Why didn't you take her before this, Frankie?

FRANKIE. She's your wife. I'm your brother. I didn't want to do this to any of us.

JOE. I been thinking what would of made it easier.

FRANKIE. Did you know all this time and you never said anything?

JOE. I didn't know what to say, Frankie. I couldn't say go ahead and I didn't know the first damn thing about stopping you. You know I knew. Nobody could be in the room with the two of you without knowing it for certain.

FRANKIE. Why didn't you tell me you knew?

JOE. Because I didn't want it to happen. Was this the first time?

MARIA. No.

FRANKIE. It was the first time we were alone in the house and in a bed and

MARIA. the first time I ever let Frankie come inside me.

JOE. My place. I'm the only man who has ever been in that place before
I got to do that sacred act with Maria
I was the one who put myself in her
the one who broke through to that secret place
We done it perfect
We done it the right way
We got married first
We went away and I took her blood as I entered her secret place
I was the one who made her a woman
I was the only person who would ever know what it felt like to be inside Maria.

FRANKIE. The more we talk the worse it'll get. That's why I wanted us to lie and all of us act like we believed it. The truth in this case is gonna be a whole lot worse than lies.

JOE. I would have known anyway. I'm the only person who ever touched that place in her.

secret places

Maria is twelve. Joe is thirteen.

MARIA. You're a yellow chickenshit, Joey. That's what you are.

JOE. Ain't

MARIA. Are. I was gonna show you some secret stuff. All you have to do is take out your weenie.

JOE. I told you I ain't gonna do it and stop saying that word. You don't even know what it means.

MARIA. I know all about it. It's how people have sex. They have sex with their weenies. Josephine did it with Bobby and she told me all about it.

JOE. You shouldn't be telling me about what Josephine did.

MARIA. Why? She said it was fun. She said Bobby squirted some stuff in her and it felt real good. She said it was stinking stuff though.

JOE. Shut up right now. Just shut up. Josephine is gonna grow up to be bad and she shouldn't be telling you that stuff.

MARIA. She's not gonna be bad. She likes it. She told me . . .

JOE. Don't tell me anything else she said.

MARIA. I was gonna surprise you. Now you gone and spoiled it.

JOE. You're too young, Maria.

MARIA. I'm not. Well, you talk like you were old, like you were twenty or something.

JOE. Boys get older faster.

MARIA. My Mama says boys don't ever grow up.
I think she says that cause of how Daddy is
Daddy drinks all the time and then when he drinks too much, he starts crying like a little baby and Mama has to get his clothes off and Mama has to put him to bed
Mama says that besides us kids, she's got one more baby

> She don't say that to Daddy's face
> He would slap her
> He tells her how a man has got to let loose sometime
> I don't like him when he drinks like that
> He don't act like my Daddy then
> I bet Frankie would take his weenie out.

JOE. Promise me you won't ask him.

MARIA. I will if I want to. You can't stop me.

JOE. Please don't do that, Maria. What would you do if I took mine out?

MARIA. Put it in a secret place that I know about.

JOE. Where?

MARIA. Inside me.

JOE. You have to get married before you do that.

MARIA. Josephine isn't married to Bobby and she did it.

JOE. She should wait. That's what girls are supposed to do.

MARIA. Why?

JOE. We want to turn out to be good. The preacher says if you don't act good, God ain't gonna take you in heaven.

MARIA. Mama says there wouldn't be anybody in heaven if that was true.

JOE. The Bible says that girls are only supposed to lay down with one boy and they have to marry him first.

MARIA. I don't think my Bible says that.

JOE. It does.

MARIA. I was gonna let you be the first person to ever touch my secret place.

JOE. I want you to let me do that.

MARIA. Josephine says that Bobby's weenie got real fat and turned red.

JOE. Don't tell me any more about it.

broken dreams

JOE. I taught Maria everything I knew about loving. The way I thought it would be is that she would always be beside me and I would always be beside her and we'd get old together, real old and we'd still be holding hands and we'd talk about the forty or fifty or sixty years we spent together. I had it planned out, how good it would be.

MARIA. Well, damn, Joe, it hasn't been that far away from that. Except we haven't lived long enough to look back over that many years yet.

JOE. Don't you see that Frankie has been between us all the time, honey? I never got all of you.

MARIA. Yes, you did. You got all of me.

JOE. Frankie was always there.

MARIA. You put him there. I didn't do it.

JOE. Was I gonna turn my back on him?

MARIA. Yes. Sometimes you could have made me the most important.

JOE. Frankie needed me.

MARIA. So did I.

JOE. When did you need me and I wasn't there?

MARIA. The worst time was when I lost our baby.

JOE. Don't go bringing that up.

MARIA. You asked me. I didn't go just bringing it up out of nowhere. I was answering you.

JOE. That's the one thing I don't want to talk about.

MARIA. Well, I do and I got just as much right to talk about what I want as you do. Both of you was crazy as hell that day. I was so mad. I'd just cleaned up the whole house for Christmas and you knocked over the damn Christmas tree and broke every one of those ornaments I had been collecting.

FRANKIE. We didn't break them all, Maria.

MARIA. You broke every god damned one that I liked. And you even broke the baby Jesus in the manger scene. There I am cleaning up your mess and the two of you go talking about getting in the truck and finding some mistletoe.

FRANKIE. We was gonna hang it all over the house and kiss you back into a good mood.

JOE. We was gonna hang it everywhere all over town and people would all be kissing each other. It was gonna be our present to everybody. You know we wasn't trying to do anything but have a good time, honey. Maybe we got a little crazy but we're men. Once in a god damn while we're supposed to be able to let go and have fun.

MARIA. Not like that.

JOE. You're talking like we tried to do something wrong.

MARIA. You were drunk out of your minds.

JOE. We was celebrating the holidays.

MARIA. There ain't nothing you can say to make it right.

JOE. I ain't trying to make it right. I'm just saying how it was.

MARIA. How it was is you fools went and got in the truck. You couldn't hardly walk to the damn truck and I had to go running after you and you wouldn't let me drive. You didn't need no woman driving you around—you was men and you stuck me in the middle of you and you both had your rifles loaded laying across our laps. Frankie was the worst drunk and you let him drive.

JOE. I didn't let him drive. It was his truck.

MARIA. We was making most of the payments.

JOE. It was still his.

MARIA. And he was driving HIS truck about ninety miles an hour.

FRANKIE. I wasn't doing ninety.

MARIA. How would you know?

FRANKIE. They clocked me at eighty.

MARIA. Okay, eighty then. Too damn fast. And Joey was shooting out the window at the mistletoe in the top of those trees and you only picked up about half of it. And then it was blowing right back out because Frankie was driving so fast. I was crying.

FRANKIE. You was cussing us.

MARIA. I was crying too. Neither one of you paid me a bit of attention. I was three months pregnant and screaming and neither one of you paid me any mind. When that cop got after us, you just speeded up. You was tough. You was gonna outrun him.

FRANKIE. They woulda put us in jail for Christmas.

MARIA. Well, damn. That woulda been a lot worse than the hospital.

FRANKIE. We wasn't planning to have a wreck.

MARIA. But you did and I ended up flying into some tree and knowing I had heard the gun go off and Joey was yelling and I didn't know who had been shot. It coulda been me for all I knew. I don't remember nothing after that except

I woke up in the ambulance and wanted you and they told me that you had gone in another ambulance with Frankie and he'd been shot in the head. Any time it come to a choice between us, you picked Frankie.

JOE. *(Angry)* They said you wasn't hurt bad they didn't think.

MARIA. I was so scared of blood
It was coming all down my legs
and that man in the ambulance made me pull off my pants
so he could look and see what was happening
What would of been our baby was right there
a little ball of blood and white stuff
I was looking at it
and wanting it to get back inside me so I could take care of it
That man said there weren't no way you could put it back
He took it away and put it in a plastic bag
Poor little baby was gone because some damn drunks wanted to have a good time.
I think God knew we wasn't supposed to have no children. When they got through scraping out what was left of our baby boy, where were you?

JOE. You know where I was. I was watching them take a bullet out of Frankie's head.

MARIA. We should have just all three died in that wreck. I kept wishing we had. You brought Frankie over here for me to take care of. You didn't ask me was it okay or nothing. You just said we was doing it, and you put him in our bed.

JOE. We didn't have no other bed. Where else was I gonna put him?

MARIA. Why wouldn't you talk to me about it?

JOE. What was I gonna say?

MARIA. Something. You could have said something. You could have said you was sorry.

FRANKIE. You knew we was sorry.

MARIA. You could have said it. I was gonna leave you then, Joey. I told myself, that you and Frankie was enough for each other and you didn't need any woman around you. I told both of you that you got to talk about things that happen. You can't just act like I never was pregnant and nothing happened at all.

JOE. We thought it was better if we didn't say stuff about it because you was so tore up over it and all.

MARIA. It didn't stop you from wanting to make another baby.

JOE. You know I wanted us to have kids.

MARIA. You wouldn't even say that. What you did say was pure meanness.

bad seeds and barren ground

JOE. Looks like to me by now you would of got us a family started.

MARIA. I had us one started two years ago.

JOE. I'm talking about since then.

MARIA. Something isn't working right.

JOE. What isn't?

MARIA. I don't know, Joey.

JOE. It couldn't be anything you're doing, could it?

MARIA. Like what?

JOE. I been thinking that it just might be something you're doing.

MARIA. Meaning what?

JOE. I expect you could figure out what I mean if it's something you're doing.

MARIA. Could you speak plain? I don't have an idea what you got on your mind.

JOE. It's just that getting pregnant isn't all that hard a thing to do I wouldn't think.

MARIA. You think I'm taking something, don't you?

JOE. I guess you'd be the only one who would know that.

MARIA. You have got to be kidding.

JOE. I'm asking you what's going on.

MARIA. Not one damn thing is going on.

JOE. Then where are our kids?

MARIA. I don't know. You want me to go to a doctor and ask him. I wonder if maybe somehow I'm messed up inside from that wreck.

JOE. I've heard a woman can hold off the seeds if she don't want a baby.

MARIA. Who told you that?

JOE. Frankie.

MARIA. I shoulda guessed. Frankie is an expert on what women can and can't do. I never heard no such thing as that.

JOE. Frankie says it's a strong power in the mind, that a woman can will herself through her mind not to get pregnant.

MARIA. You think I'm doing that?

JOE. You could be.

MARIA. Joey, I want a baby. Most of the time I feel like we got a pretty good chance of raising a kid decent.

JOE. What you mean "most" of the time?

MARIA. You couldn't say with all the things Frankie is always doing that our house would be the best place for a little baby.

JOE. I don't see how Frankie has got anything to do with a baby.

MARIA. You wouldn't want a baby seeing the kinds of things he does.

JOE. It wouldn't hurt a kid.

MARIA. The hell you say. It hurt you and me and Frankie bad to see the stuff we seen in our homes. I'm not letting a kid see that.

JOE. That's why you're not pregnant. You do have your mind power set against it.

ain't no place to go but home

Joe and Maria are in bed watching TV. It's late and they're snuggled close, about ready for sleep.

JOE. You want to watch the rest of this?

MARIA. I do but I can't keep awake can you? We need us a VCR tape machine so we could get it on that and watch it tomorrow.

JOE. Maybe we'll get us one.

MARIA. I'm so sleepy I can't think about it now.

Tires squeal.

JOE. Sounds like we got company.

MARIA. Tell him to go drink somewhere else.

FRANKIE. *(Off)* Joe, Joey, Ace, hey, what's going on in there?

JOE. We're getting ready to screw. Don't come in.

MARIA. *(Punches Joe)* We're not.

JOE. You told me to get rid of him.

FRANKIE. Well, hold up a minute. I got to talk to you.

JOE. Not now, little brother. In the morning.

FRANKIE. Just hold up a minute. I got something to show you. *(Enters with a giant bottle of Chartreuse)* Can you believe this? I had to buy it for us. We got to see how this stuff tastes.

MARIA. It's an awful color. What is it?

FRANKIE. I don't know, something I-talians drink. I thought we should try it.

JOE. Why? I ain't no I-talian.

FRANKIE. We don't do nothing that's different and I thought we should. Tonight specially.

MARIA. Why tonight Frankie?

FRANKIE. It just seems like a good night. We got this big bottle of green stuff and none of us knows what it tastes like.

MARIA. I reckon I could have one drink to get me off to sleep.

JOE. You said you was sleepy.

MARIA. I was. *(Maria hops out of bed in her baby doll pajamas)* Now I ain't.

FRANKIE. Look at her. Ain't she just a sight?

MARIA. I'm sposed to look sexy.

FRANKIE. You always look that, don't she Joe?

JOE. I was about to get me some before you come in on us.

FRANKIE. You can get it later, can't you?

JOE. I can get it any time I want it. *(Maria exits)* Where you going?

MARIA. *(Off)* To pee and get us some glasses. Who wants ice?

JOE. Me.

FRANKIE. Me too.

MARIA. Since you men ain't got no feet, I'll bring it to you.

FRANKIE. La-te-dah. We appreciate it so much.

JOE. I thought you was going out with that new girl down to the plant.

FRANKIE. I am out with her.

JOE. Where's she at?

FRANKIE. The motel.

JOE. What's she doing there?

FRANKIE. Watching a movie on TV.

JOE. You just up and left?

FRANKIE. Not exactly.

JOE. Well, exactly what did you do?

FRANKIE. You wouldn't believe it, Joey. We get to the motel and Betty says she wants a drink so I fix her a big one and then she turns on the TV and plops down on the bed. I told her we could have watched TV anywhere, that we didn't need to rent a motel to do it. She got her nose stuck in the air, then said how she wasn't used to being treated that way so I acted like my feelings was tore up and she come snuggling up to me, asking me to put it to her and I told her how I had to have me another drink cause I was upset. Then I poured what was left of Jack down the drain, told her I run completely out and I'd just go to the liquor store and get me some more. She was laying back on the bed watching TV 'fore I got out the door. She don't talk or nothing, just kinda makes these noises. You know what I mean?

JOE. No.

FRANKIE. You know. I'd say something and she'd go oh, hnnn and giggle. Then it'd be up to me to say something else. I thought we wasn't never gonna get through eating dinner.

JOE. She don't have no car at the motel does she?

FRANKIE. No. And I ain't paid the bill.

JOE. You're going back, ain't you?

FRANKIE. After I get me a drink.

MARIA. What did I miss?

JOE. Frankie left that new girl from the plant at the motel.

MARIA. You didn't do it.

FRANKIE. She don't talk, Maria. She just makes little noises.

MARIA. What kind of noises?

FRANKIE. Well, you say something regular like Chevrolet got the best engine made and she says, ewww, ewwww and laughs.

You shoulda seen her eating her dinner. She made noises over every bite she took like uhmmmpf, whew. I couldn't tell did she like her steak or not. I asked her what did she like to do and she laughed so hard she like to a choked. I was just trying to make conversation.

JOE. You don't show a woman no respect.

FRANKIE. How am I gonna respect noises like them?

MARIA. Uh, well, ew, uh, oh well. . . . .

FRANKIE. That's it. How did you know Maria?

MARIA. She's sitting next to me on the line now. That's what she does all day long, that and wiggle around in her chair. I want some of that stuff if we're gonna get kept up half the night.

FRANKIE. That's right. Gimme those glasses. *(Opens bottle)*

MARIA. God this stuff is horrible.

FRANKIE. Got any Jack we can cut it with?

JOE. Right here.

FRANKIE. Man at the state store said it would make you start to sing if you drunk enough of it.

JOE. I bet this is the first bottle of this shit he ever sold.

FRANKIE. Jack helps. Try it.

MARIA. You always think Jack helps, Frankie.

FRANKIE. He always does.

MARIA. So, did I miss all to stories about Betty?

JOE. Frankie talking about leaving her at the hotel without them ever doing nothing.

FRANKIE. If the right woman comes along, I won't have to leave her in no motel.

MARIA. You would so. You don't never want to answer to nobody. Frankie does what Frankie wants to do.

FRANKIE. This is a celebration.

JOE. What the hell we celebrating?

FRANKIE. It don't have to be a birthday or Christmas or something. We can just celebrate. I don't want to be doing the same thing every day for the rest of my life. I want to celebrate something.

JOE. Okay. We're fucking celebrating.

MARIA. We need some music.

FRANKIE. I'll sing for you.

MARIA. You can't sing worth shit.

FRANKIE. I don't care.

They do a whole routine of songs from high school, etc. have a wonderful time, dance.

MARIA. I could have done that, honey. I could have been a country singer.

JOE. Do you wish you were doing that?

MARIA. No, Joey. I couldn't really have done it. I'm just talking.

JOE. You and Frankie are always saying you wish you could do something you're not doing.

MARIA. It's a game. I can talk to myself and say what if I decided to buy a sailing boat and go somewhere or what if I dye my hair red and wear a long dress and wear a diamond necklace. It's a pretend game.

FRANKIE. With me, it's not pretend. I want to do all that stuff.

JOE. Wear a long dress and diamonds?

FRANKIE. Yeah.

JOE. And act like a queen?

FRANKIE. I'd just like to be in somebody else's skin. Wear some other clothes. Be somebody besides me for a change.

JOE. That green stuff is gone to your head.

MARIA. I'm so sleepy. Frankie, where you staying tonight?

JOE. Don't you think you better go get Betty?

FRANKIE. Nah, she's probably already asleep.

MARIA. Just give me room enough to breathe. Good-night, Joey, baby *(Kisses him)*.

JOE. Night, babydoll.

FRANKIE. Don't I get one of those?

MARIA. *(Kisses Frankie lightly)* I'm sorry you wasn't in love with Betty.

FRANKIE. I got you and Joey.

JOE. Everybody has to shut their trap up now. We're gonna end up being late for work again.

FRANKIE. I hate going to that place anyhow.

MARIA. Shhhh. I'm trying to get me some sleep.

FRANKIE. Shhhhh. Shhhhh.

MARIA. Oh, Frankie.
FRANKIE. Shhhhhhh.

Everything gets quiet. The lights go soft. Frankie sits on the edge of the bed looking at Maria and Joe who have snuggled up close. He is drinking and smoking. This would be a good place for a song. He lies down on the other side of Maria, touches her somewhere, sleeps.

ties that bind

FRANKIE. I tell you one thing I really need a drink.
JOE. I thought you would. I brought you a bottle.
FRANKIE. You done that knowing what you might be seeing when you got here?
JOE. I done it because I knew what I'd be seeing. I thought we all might need it. I'll get us a glass.
MARIA. I'll do that, Joe.
JOE. No. You two stay right where you are. I'll get the glasses.

Joe exits.

FRANKIE. Get up and get your clothes on fast.

Frankie pulls jeans on. Maria puts on a skirt and underpants.

MARIA. *(Whispering)* Maybe you should just get out of here.
FRANKIE. I don't think I want to leave you here with him. Joe's not acting right.
MARIA. Well, hell, Frankie.
FRANKIE. Shit, you know what I mean.

Joe enters.

JOE. Ya'll going somewhere?
FRANKIE. We was just putting clothes on.
JOE. That's enough clothes.
MARIA. I just want to get a blouse.
JOE. No. You aren't showing anything we haven't already seen.

MARIA. That doesn't mean I want to sit around with you looking at my titties.

JOE. You look pretty.

MARIA. I don't feel pretty.

JOE. She is pretty though, isn't she Frankie?

FRANKIE. Yeah.

MARIA. Shouldn't we have a big fight or something? It doesn't seem like we'd just sit here after the things that have happened.

JOE. What we're gonna do now is have a drink and talk.

MARIA. We gonna talk about the weather or what?

JOE. Aren't you getting kinda big-mouthed for somebody just slept with my brother.

MARIA. Well, Joey, what do you want me to say?

JOE. Nothing right now. I don't want you to open your mouth. You knew this would happen, didn't you? You been in love with Frankie.

MARIA. You love Frankie just as much as I do.

JOE. Frankie is my blood.

MARIA. That's right.

JOE. Well, it's different if you're blood kin.

MARIA. You ain't telling me nothing I haven't seen between the two of you.

JOE. I ain't trying to. I'm just telling you that Frankie has always been part of me.

MARIA. And I'm telling you that I tried to be. Frankie always gets all your attention.

JOE. Frankie has stood by me.

MARIA. So have I but I couldn't never compete with Frankie.

JOE. Frankie got beat up for me and Mama.

MARIA. I know that.

JOE. Frankie is the one always gets the short end of the rope.

MARIA. He always had you holding on to it so big deal. Big god damn deal.

FRANKIE. Either you got to let me out of this room or shut up.

JOE. You ain't going nowhere.

FRANKIE. Okay, Joey.

MARIA. See, look at you. You two start talking like I wasn't even in the room.

JOE. Shut up, Maria.

MARIA. I will not.

dancing with maria

MARIA. *(In a robe)* Where we going to?

JOE. Can't tell.

MARIA. Now how in hell am I gonna know what to wear?

JOE. Put you a slip on and hold your horses.

MARIA. Am I getting a new dress?

JOE. I don't guess you'll find that out if you don't do like I asked. Put on that black slip I give you for Christmas.

Maria puts on black panties, bra and slip.

MARIA. I didn't see no packages around the house.

JOE. Do you think I'd be bringing anything I didn't want you to see into this house?

MARIA. Well, what am I waiting for if nothing is here?

JOE. It might come some other way.

MARIA. What way?

JOE. Frankie.

MARIA. Joey, I thought we was gonna spend my birthday with just the two of us.

JOE. It woulda hurt Frankie's feelings. Besides the best part of your present was his idea.

MARIA. We don't ever do anything without him.

JOE. *(Hugging her)* Yes, we do. We do some good stuff without Frankie.

MARIA. I don't mean that. Oh, baby . . .

JOE. Shhhh. Just give me a grown woman's kiss. I want to see how you feel now you're older.

Joe kisses her. Maria resists then gives in totally. Frankie enters with three big packages and two big cards.

FRANKIE. If I'm interrupting something, please keep going and I'll watch.

(Sings) Happy birthday to you *(Joe joins singing)*.

MARIA. Ya'll shouldn't have. What's in them?

FRANKIE. You got to open them in a certain order. This one first.

Shoe box with high-heeled red shoes with lots of thin straps.

MARIA. They're the prettiest shoes I've ever seen.

JOE. Put them on, honey. See if they fit.

MARIA. They fit perfect.

FRANKIE. Ain't she tough? This one next.

Dress box with a red, red dress like Dolly Parton or Loretta Lynn would wear.

MARIA. On, no, oh, no. I can't believe it. This can't be mine.

JOE. It's yours. You better believe it. Put it on.

FRANKIE. You put it on her, Joe. Maria'll be like a princess and we'll dress her. You'll be like a princess and we'll dress you.

MARIA. I can put it on.

FRANKIE. You can do a lot of things.

Adjusts it and zips it, takes the brush from Joe and brushes her hair.

MARIA. I feel stupid.

FRANKIE. Give her the next box to open so she'll have something to do.

Has a black shawl in it.

JOE. Honey, you look so beautiful.

MARIA. I feel like some movie star or something.

FRANKIE. You are our movie star. Open the cards.

MARIA. This is airplane tickets. To Nashville.

JOE. That's right.

MARIA. Are we going to Nashville tonight?

JOE. In about an hour and a half.

MARIA. I can't believe it.

JOE. This part was Frankie's idea. We got them clothes and then Frankie says well, where in hell can she wear that dress around here and we got to thinking and we decided wasn't nowhere near here good enough for that dress and that's how come we thought about Nashville. Open up the other card.

Has tickets to the Grand Ole Opry.

MARIA. The Opry.

JOE. We going to the Grand Ole Opry tonight. Hot damn.

MARIA. Well, shit, I ought to a turned thirty a long time ago.

FRANKIE. Me and Joe wanted to make this a birthday you couldn't ever forget.

MARIA. Joey, I'm scared to get on a airplane.

FRANKIE. *(Produces bottle)* Here's your courage.

MARIA. Lord, I just can't believe this. *(Kisses Joe)* Joey, how do I look?

FRANKIE. Good enough to eat, honey. Like the best dessert there ever was.

JOE. Give Frankie a big kiss. Most of this was his idea.

MARIA. *(Tearing up)* Thank you, Frankie.

FRANKIE. Any time, M'am.

MARIA. Ah, shit, all this is about to make me cry.

FRANKIE. I bought a camera. The first pictures ought to be here.

JOE. You took half a roll of nothing but that kiss. You're gonna run out of film before we get to the airport.

FRANKIE. I bought a five pack.

MARIA. It makes me feel like a movie star or a model or something with you taking all those pictures.

FRANKIE. That's just the way I want you to feel. *(They look at pictures and react)*

MARIA. I only had two swallows out of that bottle and I'm just as high as a kite.

JOE. Let's go board that big silver bird and fly away to country heaven. We only got forty-five minutes to get to the airport.

MARIA. I guess I'm as ready as I'll ever get.

FRANKIE. Joe, take one of me with Maria.

JOE. Get next to each other. You look like you don't even know each other. *(Frankie and Maria stand side by side but not touching.)* You two are so ugly you might break this camera.

MARIA. I just thought of something bad.

JOE. What?

MARIA. What if it have to sit by myself on the airplane?

JOE. We got three seats together. You'll have me on one side

and Frankie on the other and we won't let nothing happen
to you.
FRANKIE. That's right. You're gonna have love coming at you
from both sides.

nashville

JOE. Nashville.
> I *never* seen Maria that happy.
> Me and Frankie wanted Maria to feel like the *most* beautiful
> woman in the world.
> That red dress.
> One minute Maria looked like she would cry
> the next minute she was *laughing* like crazy.
> Frankie is the *best* brother a man could have.
> There Frankie was looking in *love* with Maria.
> I wasn't no fool. I could see the *love* between them.
> High on *love*.
> I kept seeing Maria and Frankie *looking at each other.*
FRANKIE. Nashville.
> I *never* wanted Maria so bad.
> That red dress. That red dress.
> I couldn't keep quiet.
> It was the *best* idea Joey and me ever had.
> That night we was pure fools.
> *Feeling* high as a kite.
> I knew that Joe could see that I wanted to make *love* to Maria.
MARIA. Nashville.
> I *never* had such a good time.
> We were on that plane and Frankie had his arm just touch-
> ing me
> and Joey kept leaning over me to talk
> and I felt like the *most* important person in the world.
> That red dress.
> I was *laughing* and crying
> Frankie was so excited he was yelling

Joe and I kept having to tell him to talk quieter
It was the *best feeling*, having Frankie and Joey there.
We was all in *love* with each other and ourselves that night.
Between us there was this *feeling*.
I was hoping Joey wouldn't see me *looking at Frankie*.

Don't make much of a case for holding back, does it?
JOE. I guess not.

coming home

FRANKIE. Joe.
JOE. God damn, I don't believe it.
FRANKIE. It's me. Believe it.
JOE. You've worried the hell out of me and Maria.
FRANKIE. I didn't mean to do that.
JOE. Maria isn't here.
FRANKIE. I was hoping she still went to the grocery store on
    Tuesday night.
JOE. She's made herself sick worrying about you.
FRANKIE. You can tell her I'm okay.
JOE. You can tell her yourself.

Long silence.

JOE. So where were you?
FRANKIE. Drinking.
JOE. For three weeks?
FRANKIE. Most of it.

Silence.

FRANKIE. I beat a man up. I think I was trying to kill him. I got
    to hating him just because of the way he looked at me. There
    he was, sitting with this woman and she was hanging on him
    and rubbing his neck and loving up on him. He was laugh-
    ing at me like I was some piece of shit on a sidewalk or
    something so I went after his head.

Silence.

FRANKIE. I guess you don't want to hear about it.

Silence.

FRANKIE. Ain't you even gonna talk to me?
JOE. You want some Jack?
FRANKIE. I ain't drinking right now.
JOE. You still got the truck?
FRANKIE. Yeah. Yeah. She's doing great.
JOE. Maria and I bought us a new one.
FRANKIE. Chevrolet?
JOE. What you think?
FRANKIE. I didn't mean to leave you in a bind.
JOE. It wasn't the first time, Frankie.
FRANKIE. Yeah, I know but. . . .

Silence.

JOE. You got a place to stay?
FRANKIE. Yeah, I got some ideas.
JOE. You can stay here a few days. You lost your job.
FRANKIE. I figured on that.
JOE. Yeah.

Silence.

FRANKIE. I'm sorry, Joe.

Silence.

FRANKIE. Did you hear me?
JOE. Yeah.
FRANKIE. I went all the way to Mexico. We ought to go out there. You and me and Maria could tear Mexico up. I'm telling you. They ain't seen nothing like us. It's cheap, Joey. We could live a long time on the money we make. They got roads there with nobody driving on them.

Silence.

FRANKIE. I didn't think you'd freeze me out. I've done a lot of bad things to you.

JOE. Just one, Frankie.

Maria enters.

JOE. I'm glad you're back, Frankie. I'm glad you're safe.

FRANKIE. You shouldn't be glad after the stuff I've done.

JOE. You're my blood. You're a part of me. You know every bit of my life from the day I was born. Things will work out, Frankie. You'll see.

FRANKIE. I'll be good from now on, Joe. I will be. *(They embrace)*

limits of love (new version)

JOE. When we was kids, Daddy give Frankie this big dump truck
 one of them kind with the back that you hand crank.
 You could fill it up with stuff, then grab the hand crank and dump it out.
 Both me and Frankie thought it was cool.
 We had got us some M&M's in a big bag so we put them in the back.
 We was making us some food stations around the house, little piles of candy we was gonna eat later.

Then Daddy come home.
 He was feeling mean.
 Me and Frankie told him about our food supplies but he was drinking too much and he wasn't listening to us.
 He stepped on a pile of them M&M's and it went all over him, how Frankie was wasting food.
 Daddy slapped Frankie up side the head
 took the truck and put it on top of the refrigerator.
 Soon as Daddy lay down on the bed
 Frankie got him a chair, got the truck down, got him a hammer and tore shit out of the truck
 broke off the hand crank, the wheels, everything.
 It was a lot of noise.
 Daddy come to see what was happening.
 He picked Frankie up in one hand and what was left of the

truck with the other and knocked them together hard as he
could.
Hurt Frankie bad.

When Daddy was drunk, me and Mama got out of the way.
Frankie, he'd go turn up the TV louder
or whistle real loud
something to work Daddy's nerves.
He'd keep it up til Daddy would come after him
beat the hell out of him.

Frankie would push everything too far.
When it was a stopping place, he'd go one step more.
He didn't learn nothing about limits.

What happened that night when you got back from over-
seas?
FRANKIE. I got drunk as hell.
JOE. Before that. Before I got home.
MARIA. I picked Frankie up at the airport.
JOE. Look, we've gone too far not to say the truth. I just want
to know before we come to the end of this night.
MARIA. You were working a double shift. I had to pick up
Frankie by myself.

letting go

MARIA. Frankie, I'm over here.
FRANKIE. Hey, little darlin, where's Joey?
MARIA. He's working a double shift. He'll be home when we get
there. We just got your telegram yesterday and it was hard
for Joey to change his schedule. Are you hurt? Are you okay?
God, have we ever missed you.
FRANKIE. It's so damn good to see your face. Your letters was
about the only thing that kept me alive.
MARIA. I wrote you almost every day.
FRANKIE. I would get four or five at once. If I could I would get

a couple shots of bourbon and go somewhere quiet and I'd read them out loud and I'd imagine your voice and your face . . .

MARIA. Joey would have wrote you more but it takes him so long to just do a few words. I like to write even if I ain't got a thing to say.

FRANKIE. You love me. You're in love with me.

MARIA. Course I love you.

FRANKIE. I mean you really love me.

MARIA. I think we ought to be getting home.

FRANKIE. I've got to talk about it.

MARIA. Frankie don't.

FRANKIE. I have to. I thought about everything about you over there. I'd try to think what it would be like to have you in the bed beside me or I'd think about how you smell.

MARIA. It's just not right for us to talk like this.

FRANKIE. I don't give a good god damn what's right or wrong. I'm alive, Maria, and a whole lot of people are dead. Put your arms around me. Kiss me. Help me to know that I'm alive and here and you, you, are here with me.

MARIA. Frankie, I want you so bad. I've wanted you so bad forever. Press up against me. I can feel how hot you are and how you're reaching to the deepest part of me. Put your hand on my breast. Please, touch my nipples.

The sounds of the airplanes whining increase as Frankie and Maria really kiss for the first time. Mostly the only noises they make are sounds with words like baby and some moans, etc. It is obvious that they have gone too far to stop the loving. Think the words here might be recorded.

FRANKIE. Shit, I've never felt anything like this.

MARIA. I almost feel like you're inside me.

FRANKIE. I feel like I am too.

MARIA. You're so sweet, so sweet.

FRANKIE. Oh, baby.

MARIA. *(laughs)* I'm gonna come.

FRANKIE. Oh, yeah, come to me, baby.

MARIA. Well, I am, I can't help it.

FRANKIE. Neither can I.

MARIA. Shit, oh god, oh god.

FRANKIE. Jesus, oh god, oh no.

MARIA. Yes.

FRANKIE. Yes.

They collapse in laughter, then grow silent, holding each other,
still as death for several minutes. The laughter rises up again.

MARIA. We didn't do that, did we?

FRANKIE. We did.

MARIA. Joey might be home by now. We got to go, Frankie.

FRANKIE. This is gonna be tough on Joey.

MARIA. No, it ain't. Don't you never dare breathe one word
about this.

FRANKIE. We have to.

MARIA. Joey is just about the best person who ever lived and
nothing has changed, Frankie. I always did love you and I
always will. Get yourself together for your brother. This was
our first time and our last time together.

FRANKIE. No.

dead ends

JOE. You stood right there in the airport and made love?

MARIA. Yes.

JOE. You would never have done that with me.

MARIA. We weren't desperate. We had a home and bed.

JOE. But would you ever have done that with me?

MARIA. I can't compare.

JOE. I'm asking you to answer me.

MARIA. I'm telling you that I can't answer. You and I have always
been able to get to each other and it was always right to do
what we did. It's totally different with Frankie. Not having
makes you want worse.

JOE. Did you make love with me thinking about Frankie?

MARIA. We're going too far.

JOE. This is our last chance to talk.

MARIA. Why?

JOE. Because we're at a dead end. There is nowhere we can go from here.

MARIA. What do you mean by that?

JOE. I brought my gun. *(Pulls out of pocket)*

MARIA. To do what with?

JOE. I was gonna just walk in the room and shoot you but when I saw you, I couldn't do that. I thought we should say the truth first.

There is a long silence.

FRANKIE. Is the gun loaded?

JOE. You can't kill anything without bullets.

FRANKIE. Don't kill Maria.

JOE. We're stuck, Frankie, all of us. We're at the end of one road and we can't turn around and go back and there's nothing in front of us.

FRANKIE. I'm the one who is in the way.

JOE. Or is it me who is?

MARIA. I think it could be me.

JOE. It's all of us. I've thought about it and thought about it. I've been looking for a way we could get free. It looks like to me that dying is the only way to get there. What I think is that each of us should be the one to pull the trigger on ourself. This is why the truth is so important. We have to say it all. We have to say every truth, no matter how hard it is to say and then we'll die in some kind of honest way so if there's a god or anything, even though we haven't been doing right, we will have said it and we'll be in a more pure state.

MARIA. I'm not killing myself. One of you will have to do it. And I'll say every truth I can know to you, Joey, if that helps you but I don't want a close place to any god who would pass judgement on me for having feelings. Maybe it is a terrible thing that I love Frankie but you know, Frankie can walk in the room and I can feel myself waking up all over, like my blood beats a little stronger or something.

I don't feel that way when you walk in the room, Joey. With you it's this kind of steady thing—like you was a little heater or fan humming right next to me all the time.

I've loved you both since we were all little kids. Now that Frankie and I have climbed in the bed together and lay on top of each other, you think we have to die.

What for, Joey?

What in the hell is the big difference between wanting Frankie and finally having him?

You wouldn't sleep with me until we got married cause you had this thing about us being so perfect acting or something. I slept with you a hundred times or more before we had that ceremony.

Okay, so maybe it ain't possible for the three of us to live without making some rules but it won't change a feeling in me. It makes me mad as hell to have to die because of love.

Far as I'm concerned, I never got much in this life so far.

I didn't go to no college.

I don't have no big house or fine job.

Nobody comes around and asks me what I think about nothing.

All I've got is the two of you and that stupid job at the plant and a few days off and enough money to buy a drink or a hotdog.

I lied to you about the thing with children.

Unless I knew I could give a baby more than what we have, I wasn't gonna have one.

Used to be, I thought love might be enough but look at us. We've got love. I even think my Mama and Daddy loved me but so what?

I didn't get enough of anything to want to go out and fight.

You could shoot me now and what would be the difference? Maybe about ten people would cry a little bit and then some person who don't have a job would get mine and that's about it.

I don't stand for anything.

I wonder sometimes if that got me in this mess I'm in.

What made me love Frankie was that thing in him that made him want more.

You almost always messed it up though, Frankie.

FRANKIE. Always did.

The best times I ever had was thinking one of those jobs or

one of those ideas I had was going somewhere and was gonna take me with it.

For a while I thought if I could have you, Maria, that you would help me get somewhere else but then the truth is that I'm a drunk and I never worked hard and Joe always took care of me.

Most of what I've done is dream but I've done that as good as you can do it.

I don't think anybody should kill anybody, Joe. I think we all ought to pack up and head in three directions and put as much distance between us as we can.

We just need to start over.

JOE. Now that's a dream for sure.

We don't own enough to get one car out of town and we sure can't get three going.

Besides, where would we go? And how would I know what to eat for breakfast if Maria wasn't here to tell me and who would I drink with if it wasn't you

And all I would do is think about both of you all the time. See, this whole thing is different for me. I had exactly what I wanted. I had Maria for my wife and my brother for my best friend. I didn't want to do anything big. I liked the way things were. I don't even hate my job. It don't matter that much to me. I even thought I would just let this night go, not say a word about it but I figured I'd get mean, always suspecting it was going on.

MARIA. I don't know about the two of you but if I'm gonna get shot, I'd just as soon not have to think about it for a long time. You'll have to shoot me in the back because I don't want to look at you when you do it. Joey, you're gonna be the one who has to do it.

You'd think I'd at least fight for my own stupid life, wouldn't you?

Shoot me a whole bunch of times so I'll die fast. Okay?

JOE. Sure.

MARIA. Where do you want me? How about over here?

FRANKIE. Maria, quit egging him on.

MARIA. Why? Maybe this is all there is to it. Pick a place to stand. He shoots. It's over.

JOE. Don't you want to say anything to us?
MARIA. Yeah. To you, Joey. You're one sonofabitch for not leaving us any choices. Now for god's sake, go ahead and do it.

tying the love knot

MARIA. Me and Joey is getting married.
FRANKIE. Yeah, that's what Joe told me.
MARIA. I think it's the right thing to do.
FRANKIE. Then you ought to go ahead and do it.
MARIA. I guess we knew since we were little that we would do it.
FRANKIE. Joe's been saying for a year or two he was gonna ask you soon as you both got through high school.
MARIA. Joey is different from me. He thinks about things way ahead of time and figures what he wants.
FRANKIE. You want to marry him, don't you?
MARIA. I guess I do.
FRANKIE. You haven't been dating him all these years for nothing.
MARIA. It don't really seem like dating to me. You were always with us. It was just like family, like we were this little family or something and it was natural that we would all do everything together. Now I feel funny. Joe asked me last night and give me this ring and now it looks like everything changed overnight.
FRANKIE. You're growing up.
MARIA. I guess I am. I wish you were marrying somebody too.
FRANKIE. I ain't planning on marrying.
MARIA. If you was me, would you marry Joey?
FRANKIE. He's my brother. I don't want to talk about it.
MARIA. Frankie, sometimes I wish it was you and me.
FRANKIE. It would kill him if he ever heard you say that.
MARIA. I love both of you.
FRANKIE. I got to be leaving this kind of talk.
MARIA. Please talk to me Frankie.
FRANKIE. I can't.
MARIA. Please.

FRANKIE. Let me do one thing right, will you?

MARIA. You love me too. I can tell it.

FRANKIE. You're like my sister.

MARIA. When you drink too much you tell me you want me.

FRANKIE. It's liquor talking.

MARIA. It's you. It's your heart.

FRANKIE. Shut your mouth up. I'm not doing this to Joe. He ain't never had nothing but you and me and he's gonna have all of you.

MARIA. But you love me Frankie.

FRANKIE. I'll get over it.

jo carson

a preacher with
a horse to ride

artist's statement

Preacher has been a classic writer's nightmare. Katherine Ann Porter worked on *Ship of Fools* for twenty years. I have a ten-year-plus leg up on her with *Preacher.*

It began in 1982 or 83 with a call from a friend who was a librarian at the Appalachian Archives at the University of Kentucky at Lexington. She said some papers had just come in and I should drive the five-and-a-half hours to Lexington to look at them. (I take tips from librarians seriously.) She had the papers of the man I fictionalized in the play as Hershel Lilly. Not only was the Dreiser story there, but a worthy adversary too.

So I began extensive research, talking to people who remembered the events; looking at more archives and newspapers from the time, all that and before long I knew a mess of history. Then I tried to write it. Every little tiny bit of it. I didn't get a play out of the work until enough time had passed that I had forgotten some of the history and could finally see which stories I wanted to tell.

I was driving home to Tennessee from Los Angeles (I had been there for the premier production of *Daytrips* by the Los Angeles Theatre Center) and there were vast stretches of I-40 during which I had nothing better to do than think about what was stashed in boxes under my desk at home. Poor old *Preacher.* I saw two options: I could make a novel and keep it all, or I could cut it and make a play. I opted for a play for no better reason than that *Daytrips* was still running in LA.

With that decision, I cut a third of the characters and half the work. I cut the reason why I called it *A Preacher with a Horse to Ride* (my favorite scene), and Molly Jackson didn't show up with her preacher speech until much later. I emerged from this surgery—it took a while—with some bones for a play, no more, but I knew what it was about then in a way I never had before. Every writing teacher who reads this is going to say "Ah, yes, a theme!" True. It is a play about good intentions. There are terrible things that happen in it—betrayal, murder—but there is not a character who is acting out of anything but the very best intentions.

I've learned some very specific, very helpful things out of the work. So it was time spent, not time lost.

1. I can't write history in plays. I can be—to a certain extent—true to history, but I can't be factual. Art is selective and I have to be capable of seeing and making choices. A theme helps.

2. I have to cut whatever part I love the best. I can see the rest of the work better then. It might go back in, but it probably won't, and I have to be willing to lose it.

3. (This is just practical.) No more large-cast plays if I want people to consider producing them.

I've written two other plays (and stories and essays) since I began work on *Preacher,* and all my work has benefited from the experience of this one. *Preacher* has been an education in itself and I am glad I didn't give up on it. I am pleased with it now.

production history

1984 - I received a small fellowship from the Center for Appalachian Studies and Services to search for photographs from the era and of the Dreiser Committee's trip to Kentucky to go with the script I had.

1985 - The Road Company of Johnson City, Tennessee, did a public reading of the play with the photographs projected as part of the fellowship obligations. The play was incomprehensible.

1986 - minor revisions.

1988 - Southern Appalachian Playwright's Conference, Mars

Hill, North Carolina, did a reading of the play. It was no less incomprehensible. I think maybe I should give it up.

1988 - An informal reading at ROOTS annual meeting. People grasped what I was trying to do but the play didn't work any better.

1989 - I re-wrote the play, massive revisions, major cuts.

1990 - The Road Company and Virginia Polytechnical Institute did a workshop/production. College students got to work on a play in process. It was still changing two nights before opening.

1991 - I re-wrote the play again, massive re-structuring, more cuts.

1993 - Cleveland Playhouse in Cleveland, Ohio, did a workshop of the play. It flew better than I dared hope.

1993 - minor re-writes, some additions.

1993 - Cleveland Playhouse applied to The Fund for New American Plays. *Preacher* won a Roger L. Stevens award.

the incidents that make up the play

The incidents that make up the play are based on real events, but great liberty has been taken with time, sequence, and place to make a drama. The Dreiser Committee's trip to Kentucky was in 1931.

Many of the characters hold positions held by real people but any resemblance to any person living or dead is accidental. I have used what I can find of some characters, including Molly Jackson, Theodore Dreiser, John Dos Passos, and John Henry Blair. It is always presumptuous to put words in mouths. The play is not biography and does not intend to be.

In the play, time is not linear. The hearings actually took place after the Dreiser Committee arrived in Kentucky. In the structure of this piece, they are a counterpoint to earlier parts of the story.

about staging

A set for the hearings should be onstage all the time. It is simple. There is a table and chairs for the committee and benches for the community and the people who testify. Other scenes must not take much set at all or else it is a piece about changing scenes.

about the number of characters and casting

The play can be played by an ensemble, most of whom play multiple roles. The stage should be populated. If it is not populated by people, (or if it is, for that matter) a designer can include cutouts, scarecrows, skeletons, and other variations on human images, especially in the hearings.

The truth of the history is that there were some blacks among the miners, but not many. The author encourages casting outside the history in the matter of race.

A couple of musicians cast as characters (Hoit Bessman and Cecil Powers, for instance) are of great service with scene changes, mood, and the like. Music from the place and time is great stuff.

And one more note: Every character in this play sees himself or herself as a good person in a bad situation trying to do the right thing. Playing any character as a straight bad guy is too easy; the story is tougher than that.

the characters

The Committee

THEODORE DREISER: the novelist, crusader. He is 61.

JOHN DOS PASSOS: novelist, among the American intelligentsia who flirted with communism during the Depression. He is 35 or so.

MARIE: a young, pretty, action-hungry woman. She is a secretary at the hearings; she keeps the testimony.

ANNA ROLLINS: a shaker and mover, Communist Party member, in her 30's.

And Related

HELEN: Dreiser's mistress of many years. She is about 40.

THE NEW SECRETARY: one of a series of Mr. Dreiser's secretaries.

ADAM KARP: a young hot-shot Associated Press reporter on assignment in Kentucky.

REPORTER: *(in New York)* he's aggressive.

Kentucky Residents

HERSHEL LILLY: owner and editor of a newspaper that is not sympathetic to the miners. About 40.

JOHN HENRY BLAIR: the infamous sheriff of Harlan County. He keeps lists of names of people who testify at the hearings.

HENRY FOLLETTE: a traitor, but traitor to whom depends on which side you are on.

PREACHER: concerned for Mr. Dreiser's soul.

And Related

GEORGE AND PAUL: Blair's deputies, have paying jobs in a

place where paying jobs are short. Blair's deputies were often imported, some had criminal records other places. They were hired by mining companies as guards and deputized so they could carry guns.

MILITIA MAN: he's lame.

From the Hearings

MOLLY JACKSON: a NMU organizer, nurse, midwife and radical woman, about 50.

THE TWO GIRLS WHO SING: sisters, 12 and 14 or so.

HOIT BESSMAN: Coal Operators Association member, opposed to any union, especially a communist union. He keeps lists of names of people who testify at the hearings.

JIMMY CALDWELL: a National Miners Union organizer who is murdered.

JEFF CALDWELL: Jimmy's brother, testifies at the hearings.

A MAN, A WOMAN: and others who testify but who will not say their names, are miners, or the wives of miners.

CECIL POWERS: gives testimony at the hearings.

HALLOWAY COBBS: testifies at the hearings.

ELIZABETH WILSON: testifies at the hearings.

THESE NOTES MUST BE INCLUDED IN ANY PROGRAM

The song *Which Side Are You On* was written by Florence Reece and/or her daughters, depending on which source you use.

The song *Kentucky Miner's Wife's Hungry Ragged Blues* was written by Molly Jackson.

I found the words and music for both songs in *Hard Hitting Songs For Hard-Hit People*, compiled by Alan Lomax, published by Beekman Publications.

Theodore Dreiser and the Committee published transcripts of the hearings the committee held in Kentucky (and a series of essays) in a book called *Harlan Miners Speak, Report on Terrorism in the Kentucky Coal Fields,* published first by Harcourt, Brace and Company, 1932. I found the Da Capo Press reprint (1970) from the Civil Liberties in American History series. Some of the hearings material in this play is adapted from that book.

(Optional) Late in his life, it is said of Theodore Dreiser that he joined the Communist Party and took communion in the same week.

.

act 1

FROM THE HEARINGS

Two Girls, twelve and fourteen, sisters, enter. They are nervous, they giggle. They are dressed in clean, threadbare dresses, neither of which fit very well.

THE FOURTEEN-YEAR-OLD. We made up this song.
THE TWELVE-YEAR-OLD. Our mama helped
THE FOURTEEN-YEAR-OLD. We made it up. And our mama thinks we should sing it for ya'. You start.
THE TWELVE-YEAR-OLD. No. You.
THE FOURTEEN-YEAR-OLD. *(Starts to sing)*
THE TWELVE-YEAR-OLD. *(Joins her)*

> Come all of you good workers, good news to you I'll tell
> of how the good old union has come in here to dwell.
> Which side are you on, which side are you on?

THE GIRLS.

> We've started our good battle, we know we're sure to win
> because we've got the gun thugs lookin' pretty thin.

> Which side are you on, which side are you on?

(Other voices join the singing)
> With pistols and with rifles they take away your bread
> and if you miners hinted it, they'd sock you in the head.

> Which side are you on, which side are you on?

> If you go to Harlan County there is no neutral there,
> you'll either be a union man or a thug for J.H. Blair.

A MAN'S VOICE. Which union is it this week?
THE GIRLS. Which side are you on, which side are you on?
Which side are you on, which side are you on? *(The song fades)*

THEODORE DREISER'S APARTMENT IN NEW YORK CITY

There is a rocking chair with a broad arm that serves as a place to write. It is a custom made item. Theodore Dreiser is at work. He sits in the chair. Helen enters. She has a blanket thrown over her arm and a picnic basket in her hand.

HELEN. Well, look who's working. *(Helen puts the things down, hugs and kisses Dreiser who is not pleased by the interruption)* Time for lunch. I have done something very special and we are going to have a picnic. *(She spreads the blanket on the floor)* Somebody has to take care of you and it looks like I'm elected. I'm not here for the afternoon. The minute you eat enough to keep you from dying of malnutrition before tomorrow, I'll pack it all up and go away and I won't even come back tonight unless you call me and say you want me to.

DREISER. Helen . . .

HELEN. But you call then. I know how to fix you up just like you like. *(She pulls at him playfully, gently)* You could be my teddy bear right now if you wanted. There's room at the picnic.

DREISER. I cannot be interrupted at your whim.

HELEN. This is not my whim, this is lunch. Or are we breaking in a new secretary this afternoon? What time does she get here?

DREISER. Helen. I am working.

HELEN. What are you working on?

DREISER. A piece about telephones; the telephone company is charging much too much money and someone has to speak up.

HELEN. Theo, nobody's going to quit using them. *(Helen sets fried chicken out of the basket and begins eating a piece)* Umm, good, if I say so myself.

DREISER. I look at the words I write, all these words, I have so many words, and they don't mean what they used to; they don't even mean what I wanted them to when I wrote them down. Evidently, they don't mean much to anybody else either.

HELEN. You never used to care who liked what you wrote.

DREISER. I never used to have trouble selling it. People begged me for work; now they tell me not to send any more of it.

HELEN. My yoga teacher thinks that forgetting about writing—forgetting about work—just for awhile might be what you need. A vacation. Miami Beach. Or a month in the mountains. You might learn to ski.

DREISER. My work—or lack of it—is not a subject for your public conversation.

HELEN. Don't be silly. I only mentioned that a friend of mine. . .

DREISER. I know you, you mentioned your lover and you mentioned my name.

HELEN. I did not. I said Theodore Dreiser who used to be my lover and used to be a novelist is having trouble and isn't either anymore.

DREISER. Dammit!

HELEN. Theo, you have to learn to take things as they come. Like pieces of fried chicken. Here. Eat something. *(Dreiser takes a piece of chicken)*

DREISER. When I wrote Clyde Griffiths, I knew him, I knew what he had to do before the first word of that novel was written. I knew the same of Carrie and Hurstwood. There is no character who speaks to me now, no voices in my dreams. I cannot see with Carrie's eyes, I cannot walk full of Carrie's shame and hope, and I could once. Now, I am full of shame and hope, but it is my own. It means I can only want what I want and while I can tell you exactly what that is, I haven't the vaguest notion how to get it.

HELEN. Yoga would help you if you'd do it.

DREISER. I want another novel, Helen, not some position to sit in. I already have a position. I sit in my chair, I flex these muscles *(The fingers he writes with)* and I spend hours at it. You would envy my state of mind.

HELEN. You have to clear your mind to do yoga.

DREISER. I'm telling you, I may not like it but you would envy it.

HELEN. You might learn something, you ox.

DREISER. Please.

HELEN. Please, yourself. I'm trying to be good to you and all I get is insults. Someday it's going to be one too many. We didn't open the wine yet, Teddy, I brought wine. I found a year you like . . . look.

DREISER. Leave it.

HELEN. Leave it?

DREISER. Leave the chicken too.

HELEN. Theo! You're being impossible, now stop it. I brought this to share with you and I won't be run off. I came to eat lunch. I'll go when I finish. Now, shall I open the wine?

DREISER. Open it. *(Helen opens the wine)*

HELEN. Do you want a glass? *(Helen gets a crystal glass from the picnic basket)*

DREISER. Yes. I want a glass.

HELEN. I love you, Theo. I know you don't like for me to say . . . *(Helen gives Dreiser a glass of wine and pours herself one)*

DREISER. Then help me. Somebody has to help me. I'm afraid. I don't know what to do. *(Helen holds him)* I hardly know who I am. *(Theodore Dreiser stays in focus during this change)*

FROM THE HEARINGS

DREISER. Ladies and gentlemen, the hearings will now come to order. My name is Theodore Dreiser and I am a novelist, a writer and editor and I am the chair of this committee.

ANNA ROLLINS. My name is Anna Rollins. I organized this Committee for the Defense of Political Prisoners and I am honored to be here again. Hopefully, we can be of service to you.

JOHN DOS PASSOS. My name is John Dos Passos and I am here with the committee in the interest of social justice.

DREISER. We have come to Kentucky to test free speech and the rights to assembly, rights guaranteed by the Constitution of this nation, rights which, according to reports, have been ignored in Harlan County . . .

MOLLY JACKSON. If I may say so, Mr. Dreiser, you are here to listen to the stories of these starving people and carry them out with you so the rest of the world will know we're dying here.

DREISER. You have a way with words yourself. I couldn't have said it better. Now, the Governor of Kentucky has promised there will be no reprisals for anything that is said at these hearings.

A VOICE. The governor don't live here.

DREISER. You don't really want him, do you?

A VOICE. Mr. Dreiser, the governor's got interests in coal.

DREISER. Then the governor should have some interest in your well-being. I promise you, he will hear from us. We have a representative of the militia to guarantee our safety.

A VOICE. Who's gonna' be here when you're gone?

DREISER. It is true, we leave. We go away and you stay. But your stories will be public knowledge. We will make them public, we are your witnesses, and that should be some protection for you. Now. We ask that you be as straightforward as possible in your answers to our questions, and in that interest we will ask that you state your name and swear by it that what you say is the truth.

A VOICE. Mr. Dreiser, a man saying his name here is the same thing as writing it on a blacklist.

DREISER. We are not asking for what we don't need. We are prepared to hear testimony. We have a stenographer to keep accurate notes. *(A gesture to Marie)* And you know best how urgent it is that we begin. Who will say their name and be first? *(Nobody)*

MOLLY JACKSON. People, we wanted this chance. We asked for it. So somebody's got to stand up here and start. *(Nobody. Henry Follette stands in the hearings scene and moves into the next scene in focus)*

THE EDITOR'S OFFICE AT THE MOUNTAIN SUN NEWSPAPER

Hershel Lilly is at his desk. Henry Follette enters. He is shy, nervous.

HENRY FOLLETTE. Mr. Lilly?

LILLY. I'm Hershel Lilly.

HENRY FOLLETTE. I know ya'.

LILLY. Well, what can I do for you?

HENRY FOLLETTE. I want to leave here. I'm goin' to Detroit. I hear work's better in Detroit.

LILLY. I hear work's no better anywhere.

HENRY FOLLETTE. I need to leave here. A man can do his damnedest here and still be doing the wrong thing and I'm sick of it.

LILLY. You want this in the local news? Society section?

HENRY FOLLETTE. No, Mr. Lilly, I got another piece of news.

LILLY. OK. Spit it out.

HENRY FOLLETTE. I'm aimin' to sell it.

LILLY. I'm not in the habit of buying news.

HENRY FOLLETTE. You've done it before, I know who you paid.

LILLY. In that case, we are negotiating a price.

HENRY FOLLETTE. Twenty dollars.

LILLY. That's a blessed fortune. Two dollars.

HENRY FOLLETTE. Twenty. It's worth it. It's about a new union . . . a different kind 'a union.

LILLY. United Mine Workers of America.

HENRY FOLLETTE. I told you, new. UMWA ain't supportin' this strike no more. New.

LILLY. Tell me more.

HENRY FOLLETTE. Not without money. *(Lilly pulls out his billfold and gives Follette a five)* Twenty. I said twenty. This is just a five. *(Lilly pulls out another five and holds it up)*

LILLY. Ten's top.

HENRY FOLLETTE. I can't leave here for 10 dollars.

LILLY. Friend, if it is big news, there's no telling what it is worth and no telling what else you might get. But it is 10 dollars in cash.

HENRY FOLLETTE. It's a communist union come out of Chicago.

LILLY. Communist?

HENRY FOLLETTE. People are a-signin' up. Costs a quarter a week, first month's free. They're runnin' soup kitchens now and promisin' clothes. Clovertown's got a soup kitchen. Lots of people are out there. Organizers are . . .

LILLY. Who? *(Henry Follette points to the other five. Not yet)*

HENRY FOLLETTE. Organizers are goin' to be coming out of Chicago this week.

LILLY. A name.

HENRY FOLLETTE. I don't know no names.

LILLY. You need to think of one.

HENRY FOLLETTE. Might be Jimmy Caldwell organizing. Hard to tell, you know. *(Hershel Lilly hands Henry Follette the second bill)*

LILLY. Who told you all this? *(Henry Follette pulls a card from his pocket to show to Lilly. Lilly takes it)* National Miners Union.

HENRY FOLLETTE. They don't come right out and say it's communist first thing but you find out later. I ain't no communist.

LILLY. But you are Henry Follette. You joined, did you? *(Henry Follette would like to take the card back)* Oh, no. I paid for this.

HENRY FOLLETTE. I ain't a communist. The preacher's been talking about communists and I ain't one of 'em. You give me today and tonight. Print it up tomorrow mornin'.

LILLY. This doesn't seem to me to be printing news, Mr. Follette. Seems more like the sort of news Sheriff Blair needs to hear.

HENRY FOLLETTE. That ain't necessary, sir, it'll be enough if it comes out in the newspaper. It ain't necessary to call no names either. It'll scare 'em when they find out you'ns know it. Just print it up.

LILLY. Mr. Follette, you have your money, I have my news. *(Henry Follette exits. Hershel Lilly holds focus in the change)*

FROM THE HEARINGS

DREISER. Mr. Lilly, your occupation?

LILLY. I am a newspaper man and a printer. I also work for the Associated Press Wire Service.

DREISER. Are you opposed to the National Miners Union?

LILLY. I am opposed to communism. I am opposed to the philosophy and its manifestations in every form.

MOLLY JACKSON. Mr. Lilly, I am opposed to people bein' hungry and dyin' of it.

ANNA ROLLINS. Do you know the communist philosophy, Mr. Lilly?

LILLY. Can I quote Karl Marx? No. Do I read the newspapers? Yes. And the truth is I am more than just opposed, I am frightened by communism. Any man who values his freedom better be frightened.

DREISER. Are you opposed to any union?

LILLY. No, but I think it is the right of the employer as to whether he will hire a man who belongs to a union. And I have expressed the opinion—in print—that during this period of depression, I am not in sympathy with the strike. I think it behooves each of us to work all the harder and we must share and share alike.

MOLLY JACKSON. You know how much these people make and you say that? Lord keep me from spittin' on you. They ain't got nothin' to share.

LILLY. If they keep working they can sign up at the Red Cross, Molly, and you know it.

A VOICE. I'm in line at your Red Cross, Hershel Lilly. It ain't enough to eat and they don't even bother for salt!

LILLY. Friend, it is more than this committee is offering you.

DREISER. Mr. Lilly, do you make a hundred dollars a week?

LILLY. My salary is not public business.

DREISER. Seventy-five? Sixty?

LILLY. But in the interest of truth, I don't mind. Sixty.

DREISER. That's two-hundred and forty a month plus.

MOLLY JACKSON. It don't cost you nothing to hate communists, does it? You got food in your belly and money in your pockets. Makes it easier, don't it?

THE SHERIFF'S OFFICE

Sheriff John Henry Blair and two deputies, George and Paul, are here. Adam Karp enters.

JOHN HENRY BLAIR. Come on in. It's not often we have the pleasure of volunteer company. Boys. *(The deputies nod their greetings)*

KARP. I am Adam Karp. I write for The Associated Press Wire Service.

BLAIR. Mr. Karp, yea. Like the fish?

KARP. With a K.

BLAIR. Our newspaper editor, Mr. Lilly—like the flower—writes for the Associated Press. He does just fine. We ain't seen much of what you wrote yet.

KARP. They decided they ought to send someone in full time. I drew the assignment.

BLAIR. Well, you tell the truth and we'll do everything we can to make it easy.

KARP. Thank you, I'll try. You mind if I ask you some questions?

BLAIR. Shoot.

KARP. There are rumors outside of here that a move toward

communism has begun in Harlan County. Do you have any comments?

BLAIR. Yes. Over my dead body.

KARP. How do you see your job, Sheriff Blair?

BLAIR. I am elected to protect the lives and the property of the people who live in Harlan County.

KARP. The lives of everyone?

BLAIR. Except lawbreakers. And the property.

KARP. Is being a communist against the law in Harlan County?

BLAIR. It is.

KARP. How do you justify that with the rest of the country? It's not against the law in New York.

BLAIR. In Harlan County, it is advocating the overthrow of the government. It is criminal syndicalism or treason depending on how hard you need to hit a man. Courts are more likely to convict for criminal syndicalism.

KARP. Is it against the law to join a union in Harlan County?

BLAIR. Not exactly, it's just against the law to do most of the things a union does.

KARP. Like what?

BLAIR. Like picket and keep men that want to work from going in.

KARP. According to the same government you are protecting from treasoners and criminal syndicalists, picketing is not against the law.

BLAIR. Picketing is an activity that doesn't allow people to do what they want to do with their own property. Owners have got rights too.

KARP. Are you or any of your staff paid by any of these owners?

BLAIR. People that pay taxes pay me. But they just pay the deputies a quarter for an arrest, so if the boys want to pick up a little extra on the side, guarding or something, I don't tell 'em not to.

KARP. Guarding mines?

BLAIR. They ain't guarding sheep.

KARP. I hear guarding mines can pay two dollars a day. That's a lot of money here.

BLAIR. It's dangerous work. A company pays the man to stand hitched if there's trouble.

KARP. How many deputies do you have?

BLAIR. I don't know exactly, it's in the courthouse records.

KARP. Some say you have more than six hundred deputies, Sheriff. How can a man keep up with that many deputies?

BLAIR. I wouldn't say it was that many. I don't think I know six hundred people.

KARP. How many? Ball park guess.

BLAIR. I told you I don't care to answer that question.

KARP. But I can find out at the courthouse?

BLAIR. Let me save you the trouble. George, Paul, why don't you give this gentleman an introductory tour of the sights.

KARP. Thank you, but I can find my own way.

BLAIR. Not like they'll show you. Show him Pine Mountain, boys, show him Black Mountain. *(George and Paul escort Karp from the office. Blair looks after them)* Take him all the way to the top.

FROM THE HEARINGS

A WOMAN. I will tell the committee what I know but I cannot tell my name.

MOLLY JACKSON. You need to say your name.

WOMAN. My husband didn't want me coming down here, but I wanted to come and I promised him I'd not say my name. I will tell you we have had one dollar in the last four days to live on, my husband, myself, and three children.

DREISER. How do you distribute that money?

WOMAN. We live on beans mostly, and we don't get no dinner.

DREISER. What do you call dinner, noon or night?

WOMAN. We used to have dinner at noon. Now, I have breakfast and I put up a little lunch for him to take to work. I'll tell you what I had to put in his bucket this mornin'. There was a little cooked pumpkin without no sugar and fat white bacon. And what we had for breakfast was water gravy and black coffee.

DREISER. What is water gravy?

WOMAN. Water and grease and a little flour.

DREISER. What did you give the children?

WOMAN. They don't get nothin' different and they don't get no dinner either.

DREISER. But supper, you eat supper?

WOMAN. If you call dried beans with no flavorin' a meal.

MOLLY JACKSON. Mr. Dreiser, she eats. There are those that don't eat but what they beg. They beg from her. Her husband ain't been blacklisted. It's why she can't say her name.

CECIL POWERS. Her husband is a scab.

WOMAN. He is not.

CECIL POWERS. He signed a yellow dog contract and stuck by it.

WOMAN. That ain't scabbin' and you know it. He ain't that low, he's just trying to get by.

MOLLY JACKSON. *(To Cecil Powers)* You can say your name. You ain't got nothing to lose by it. *(A freeze almost, for everyone except the committee, and a moment of considerable indecision for Cecil Powers. Helen enters, hands Anna and John glasses and Dreiser a glass and a bottle. The party moves downstage)*

THE BALCONY OF THEODORE DREISER'S APARTMENT IN NEW YORK CITY

HELEN. Shall we go out to the balcony? I love to look out at night, all the lights.

DOS PASSOS. Artichokes, oysters, lamb chops. I'm stuffed, and you want me to move. Helen, that was a meal fit for a king.

HELEN. I cook for a tyrant. You know, Scheherazade. 1001 recipes.

DOS PASSOS. Well, I thank you, and I will until I weigh myself the next time.

HELEN. My pleasure.

DREISER. Comrade Rollins? *(He offers to pour brandy for her)*

ANNA ROLLINS. My new title. *(She holds out her glass)* Ten years of work and I've earned Party membership. I should have gotten a Ph. D. It wouldn't have taken near so long and I'd have something to show off, you know, letters after my name. *(Dreiser offers to pour for John who holds out his glass)*

DOS PASSOS. Theo, where do you come by this? French brandy.

DREISER. Helen has her sources. And her secrets.

HELEN. I have my bootlegger. Shall I get you a bottle next time I see him?

DOS PASSOS. You hear this, the offer of a bottle, not an address.

HELEN. It's my only secret; it's why he keeps me.

DOS PASSOS. Yes, I want one. Please.

HELEN. Done.

ANNA ROLLINS. I promise, when the revolution gets here, prohibition will be the first thing to go. Communists are not puritans. Unlike Republicans.

DREISER. Helen?

HELEN. Please. *(Dreiser fills Helen's glass and his own)*

ANNA ROLLINS. And our esteemed Mr. Dreiser. What a view you have up here, Theo. I don't often get this far off the ground.

DREISER. Yes, adds a certain perspective, doesn't it? Bottoms up, my friends, dinner should be topped off.

ANNA ROLLINS. *(A toast)* To our business.

DREISER. Anna, this is all very mysterious. . . . I suspect the three of you are in cahoots.

DOS PASSOS. I wouldn't call it cahoots. We're not nearly so well organized.

DREISER. Helen, you talked me into this. I'm holding you responsible.

HELEN. All I did was the dinner.

ANNA ROLLINS. Well, shall I pop it? I feel like I'm proposing! Theo, we hope to talk you into going to the Kentucky coal fields . . .

DREISER. Kentucky? Who the hell goes to Kentucky? What about Miami Beach? Helen thinks I need a vacation.

HELEN. It would be like your trip to Pittsburgh, Theo, during the coal strike there.

DREISER. So you are part of this.

HELEN. I want to go this time, I'm tired of missing everything. I'll be John's secretary.

ANNA ROLLINS. The difference is we'd organize it for you. You have to know about Kentucky. John L. Lewis . . .

DREISER. John L. Lewis is in bed with big business making big money again? Comrade Anna! How dare you say it?

ANNA ROLLINS. The news is we are "in" in Kentucky and growing fast. It could be the beginning of the revolution we've been working for—I hardly dare hope.

DREISER. We?

ANNA ROLLINS. Oh, don't tip-toe, Theo, you're too big. The UMWA does not support the current strike . . .

DREISER. The bottom's fallen out of coal because there is no war right now to pay for it, and the UMWA does not have the money to support the current strike . . .

ANNA ROLLINS. Whatever, Theo. My point is that a second union is organizing very succesfully. And the National Miners Union is an arm of the Communist Party in America.

DREISER. Oh, yes! Send me to Kentucky. Draw a large red target over my heart that says communist union supporter and see how long it takes before I get shot.

DOS PASSOS. It'd be through the International Labor Defense Fund, Theo. We were thinking of a committee of politicians and journalists that would accompany you.

DREISER. And what does the International Labor Defense Fund get for all this?

DOS PASSOS. Nothing. It's a mission of mercy.

ANNA ROLLINS. I've been there, Theo. People are starving.

DREISER. And the Labor Defense Fund could use some mercy credit. Not much stock in defending rabble rousers all the time. Just lots of bad press.

ANNA ROLLINS. Theo. The coal industry is committing murder and everybody's looking the other way.

DREISER. Everybody always looks the other way.

ANNA ROLLINS. We hope to call attention to the situation. You know, bring some pressure to bear for these people, raise some money. We need you.

DREISER. Send John.

ANNA ROLLINS. We're thinking of that already, thanks.

DREISER. And you'll go?

DOS PASSOS. I intend to, Theo, I don't see how I could say no. Not if I can help.

DREISER. And the Labor Defense Fund distributes any money you raise?

ANNA ROLLINS. Yes.

DREISER. Through the Party.

ANNA ROLLINS. In part, yes.

DREISER. And, no doubt, with a great deal of publicity. You have my blessings.

DOS PASSOS. It needs your name, Theo.

ANNA ROLLINS: We need to be able to organize it in your name.

DREISER. John is getting more published that I am.

HELEN. But you are known for this sort of thing. You went to Pittsburgh for that strike, I thought you'd want to do it.

DREISER. So it is a little conspiracy here. Let me tell you about Pittsburgh. It was a working week for death and I am not so young that I could not feel him right behind me. Theo, he said, I need your name.

ANNA ROLLINS. Kentucky is a great story, Theo, the biggest story in a decade of big stories.

DREISER. You and your Party won't have me, but you are certainly willing to use me, aren't you?

ANNA ROLLINS. You don't hold the Party line and you know it. The truth is you take a great deal of pride in not holding any line.

DREISER. If I went to Kentucky, I would go out of compassion.

ANNA ROLLINS. Do we lack your compassion? Maybe we can improve our attitude.

DREISER. Compassion means you share the fear, you share the pain, you do not seek to share the publicity.

ANNA ROLLINS. Theo, if I lack your brand of compassion, perhaps it is because I am realistic about how to change the situation and that includes carefully designed publicity and lots of it. I suspect it's your difficulty with the Party in a nutshell. Romantics never make any plans and they don't ever think of publicity until after they write their autobiographies.

DREISER. Who else would you invite?

DOS PASSOS. Senators, governors, church people, newspaper people. Of course, they have to choose to go, but it would be hard to say no to you.

DREISER. I can see that.

DOS PASSOS. You'll do it?

DREISER. I will hold hearings.

ANNA ROLLINS. A tour of Harlan and Bell Counties was what we had in mind. You know, soup kitchens, jails and union halls.

DREISER. I want a week of hearings, and I won't do it unless we hold hearings. I want to hear stories. I want people sworn to tell the truth. I want testimony.

ANNA ROLLINS. You would do better to trust your eyes.

DREISER. I can use stories. I write stories. And for that matter, I can hold hearings in Kentucky without the International Labor Defense Fund.

DOS PASSOS. Anna, I like the idea of hearings.

ANNA ROLLINS. What makes you think people would risk testimony?

DOS PASSOS. They risked joining the union. And real testimony is stronger than anything a reporter can write. Testimony can go to Congress if we have to take it that far.

ANNA ROLLINS. We can try.

DOS PASSOS. I bet people would jump at the chance.

ANNA ROLLINS. A toast then, to hearings, a week of hearings. Chaired by the finest and most socially relevant novelist of our time, Mr. Theodore Dreiser. *(They toast and freeze. Helen collects the glasses, exits, and the committee returns to the hearings table)*

FROM THE HEARINGS

The action resumes from the previous moment.

MOLLY JACKSON. You can say your name. You're already on the blacklist.

CECIL POWERS. My name is Cecil Powers.

DREISER. Mr. Cecil Powers. What does it mean to sign a yellow dog contract?

CECIL POWERS. It means you won't join no union while you work for that company.

DREISER. Have you ever signed one?

CECIL POWERS. I've had to sign 'em, yea. To work. But I didn't stick by it.

DREISER. Someone spoke of a blacklist . . .

CECIL POWERS. It's one of the things happens when you join a union. I seen 'em run to the books and look when a man asked about work. They come back and they say "you can't get no work." They done it to me.

DREISER. Do you know why?

CECIL POWERS. Cause I joined a union.

HOIT BESSMAN. Which union, Mr. Powers?

CECIL POWERS. UMWA.

HOIT BESSMAN. He joined the NMU, the National Miners Union.

CECIL POWERS. I joined the UMWA, but they said this strike was a wildcat strike and they wasn't going to support it. And the National Miners Union come in, and they put up soup kitchens and they give us tents. I joined 'em.

DREISER. Tents?

CECIL POWERS. I ain't got a house no more. We was evicted. The NMU give us a tent.

DREISER. You're planning on living the winter in a tent?

CECIL POWERS. I reckon. There ain't much place to walk to with a woman and four children.

HOIT BESSMAN. You traded a company house for a union tent. I bet it's a little crowded with all those children.

CECIL POWERS. My young'uns ain't the problem, Mr. Bessman.

HOIT BESSMAN. *(To Dreiser)* The house Mr. Powers lived in belongs to the owner of the mine he was working at when he broke his contract and joined the union. *(To Powers)* And you struck, if I remember . . .

CECIL POWERS. We did. We had to. I like to feed them young'uns. They don't cry so much when they ain't hungry.

HOIT BESSMAN. The owner of the mine will give the house to a man who will work.

CECIL POWERS. A scab.

HOIT BESSMAN. A mine is under no obligation to hire a union man, Mr. Powers. It is policy determined by the Coal Operators Association. I know what's gone into making that policy, and it is an attempt to be fair whether you like it or not. *(To Dreiser)* I am president of the Coal Operators Association. Everybody in this room knows which mines will tolerate a union and which won't. It is public policy.

CECIL POWERS. Mr. Bessman, did you know your Coal Operators Association is killin' people?

HOIT BESSMAN. Mr. Powers, did you know your NMU is a communist organization and one of the basic tenets of communism is the seizing of private property?

CECIL POWERS. As a matter of fact, I do know that.

HOIT BESSMAN. And you joined them.

CECIL POWERS. At first, I joined for the food. But there comes a time when an animal'll turn around an' fight you if you pester it long enough. Listen to yourself, carrying on about which mines "will tolerate a union." Well, a man gets mad enough, he'll fight too and I'm ready to fight and it'll be the communists I'm fightin' for, and when we win, there's gonna be a bunch of owners and operators that'll wish they'd figured out some way to "tolerate a union" back when they had the chance. *(Sheriff Blair stands up)*

HOIT BESSMAN. Those are dangerous words.

CECIL POWERS. A dangerous man said 'em. *(Sheriff Blair remains standing)*

THE TOP OF PINE MOUNTAIN/ADAM KARP'S SCENIC TOUR

Adam Karp, George and Paul approach the top of Pine Mountain.

ADAM KARP. Is this the ten, the fifteen, or the twenty mile boy scout hike?

GEORGE. Just keep walking. My job is to show you everything the Sheriff wants you to see and I'm doing it. And he thought you ought to see this. This here is the top of Pine Mountain. Pretty, ain't it?

KARP. Pretty, yes, very pretty.

GEORGE. High, too, ain't it.

KARP. Yes. High.

GEORGE. You got good taste in scenery, son. I'll tell the sheriff. All right. Let's march. *(George and Paul escort Karp off)*

FROM THE HEARINGS

Sheriff Blair remains standing.

HENRY FOLLETTE. My name is Henry Follette. I am thirty-one years of age and I was born and reared in Harlan County, Kentucky. I commence workin' in the coals mines when I was 16 years of age and on September 14, I joined the National Miners Union at the invitation and the two-bits of the organizer, Jimmy Caldwell. *(Jimmy Caldwell stands up)*

MOLLY JACKSON. Henry Follette, what are you doing? Is this the kiss of Judas?

HENRY FOLLETTE. I did not know at the time that it was the communists and I was supposed to get other people to join and I did that, and I was workin' in good faith, but now I find out I was only a tool of the communist party 'cause the National Miners Union was gonna' be turned over to 'em. *(Jimmy Caldwell exits. Jeff Caldwell follows)* The communists teach that there is no god, that a colored man is equal to a white man and that a colored man has the right to marry a white woman. They teach that Christ is a myth and there ain't nothin' to the resurrection and that the government of the United States should be destroyed and the Russian government set up here. They teach that. They say every church in the United States should be thrown in the lake 'cause it's churches that's holdin' us back. They say they're gonna' overthrow the government in eight months. I was misled in joinin' this organization and I want to tell all my friends that it is un-American and absolutely for the purpose of destroyin' the teachins of Jesus Christ.

DREISER. Is that all you have to say?

HENRY FOLLETTE. It is.

ANNA ROLLINS. Who told you that about communism? You are a whole garden of misconceptions.

HENRY FOLLETTE. Everybody goes to church knows it. Ain't that right, Sheriff?

MOLLY JACKSON. *(Notices Blair standing)* Is the sheriff holdin' your hand or your balls, Henry? *(Henry Follette exits)*

THEODORE DREISER'S APARTMENT/JIMMY CALDWELL'S MURDER

Theodore Dreiser and The New Secretary are in the apartment. Dreiser is trying to seduce her. Over the course of the scene, he takes her blouse off so that by the time she lets John Dos Passos in, she is in her slip. It cannot be a rape scene.

THE NEW SECRETARY. Could we just talk for a minute?

DREISER. You smell so good.

THE NEW SECRETARY. Please!

DREISER. Please what, darling?

THE NEW SECRETARY. Stop it. Mr. Dreiser . . .

DREISER. Call me Theo.

On a different part of the stage, Jimmy and Jeff Caldwell are sitting together, they are nervous and watchful.

JEFF CALDWELL. Jimmy, I don't see you got any choice. He named you as an organizer. He said . . .

JIMMY CALDWELL. I heard what he said.

JEFF CLADWELL. Look, just leave here for a while. You could go up to the saltpeter cave. Eating might be better up there than it is down here. We used to get lots of squirrels up there.

JIMMY CALDWELL. I've spent too many too many nights at too many barns waiting for some man who's scared and hungry to get there and then waiting some more while he decides whether or not to sign his name. I misjudged Henry Follette but that don't mean I can quit. What would it look like if I ran? The bottom would fall out.

JEFF CALDWELL. It's stronger than that. Just leave for awhile. Two weeks won't kill this union.

JIMMY CALDWELL. Two weeks in that cave might kill me. Somebody has to stand up sometime.

JEFF CALDWELL. I want a brother, not a martyr.

JIMMY CALDWELL. Don't worry, I'm not interested in dying.

THEODORE DREISER'S APARTMENT

THE NEW SECRETARY. Mr. Dreiser, this job is to be your secretary. Dictation! Stenography! Typing! And you spent all morning talking a lot about editors you want to do things to. Do you want me to type that? I can do it, I can remember, it was about college boys who have never written anything . . .

DREISER. Don't be silly. I always carry on about editors.

THE NEW SECRETARY. Please. You're famous and all that and I'd like to work for you but I already have somebody I love!

DREISER. This isn't about love. We hardly know each other yet. This is about the things you've been told are wrong by people who are frightened of their own shadow. They are not wrong. They are natural. Have you read my book *Sister Carrie?*

THE NEW SECRETARY. I did.

DREISER. You know what they say about it, don't you? That it is a terrible, blasphemous book because it is in sympathy with a fallen woman. Carrie is not a fallen woman. There is no such thing. Carrie had the strength and freedom to live with her heart, and people are frightened of her, that's all. I love Carrie. And I want the freedom and the strength to live like Carrie. And you must have it too. Can you see that?

THE NEW SECRETARY. I'm here to apply for a job.

DREISER. Just relax. I'm not going to hurt you. We won't do anything you don't want to do.

THE NEW SECRETARY. We're already doing things I don't want to do.

DREISER. Relax, my sweet Ginger, there isn't a woman in the world that doesn't like this when she gives herself permission. Ginger. What a sweet name. Spicy. Ginger, in the mornings we work. Sometimes, you will take dictation, sometimes you will be typing. Sometimes, it will be your job to listen patiently while I rave about the ignorance of editors and others.

Molly Jackson enters where Jimmy and Jeff are sitting. She carries two bowls of soup, she gives them to the two men.

MOLLY JACKSON. National Miners Union Soup, Jimmy. You should be proud even if you can't come around front and eat it.

JIMMY CALDWELL. I am. Looks pretty good, too.

MOLLY JACKSON. It is good.

JEFF CALDWELL. Will you tell this dummy to leave town for awhile.

MOLLY JACKSON. *(To Jimmy)* Leave town like your brother tells you. Sounds to me like good advice.

JIMMY CALDWELL. Can't.

MOLLY JACKSON. They'll put you in jail.

JIMMY CALDWELL. If they do, I reckon it'll hold me.

JEFF CALDWELL. I ain't worried about jail.

JIMMY CALDWELL. I know, me neither.

MOLLY JACKSON. Don't say it out loud, or you can call it to you. Your brother's right. You should leave town.

JIMMY CALDWELL. I just don't see I can do that.

MOLLY JACKSON. *(To Jeff)* He don't listen to me no better than he does to you. *(Molly Jackson exits, Jeff and Jimmy eat)*

Theodore Dreiser's Apartment.

DREISER. Sometimes in the afternoon, we have the opportunity for a little recreation. It could become your greatest pleasure, I'm very good at it. *(There is a knock on the door. Dreiser puts his finger against her lips)* Let's not be home. *(Another knock)*

THE NEW SECRETARY. *(To whoever it is)* He's coming! *(To Dreiser)* You have to get it. *(She opens the door. John Dos Passos is there) (To Dos Passos)* Please come in. *(To Dreiser)* My name is not Ginger. *(She exits)*

DOS PASSOS. A new secretary? Not Ginger. Do we have any other guesses? Gloria? Virginia? *(Dreiser straightens himself. He does not answer)*

On the other part of the stage, George and Paul enter with rifles in their hands.

PAUL. We're looking for Comrade Jimmy Caldwell.

JEFF CALDWELL. He ain't here.

PAUL. That's funny, this sure does look like him.

JEFF CALDWELL. I'm Jimmy.

PAUL. You ain't.

GEORGE. *(To Jeff)* Sit here and shut up. For all you know, we're joinin' the union. *(Jimmy Caldwell runs, George and Paul run after)*

JEFF CALDWELL. Molly! Cal! Somebody! *(They don't hear, don't come. Jeff follows after Jimmy and the Deputies)*

Theodore Dreiser's Apartment.

DOS PASSOS. Well. Why don't you invite me in? I promise I won't try to kiss you. *(Dos Passos carries an assortment of opened envelopes)*

DREISER. You picked a bad time. Come in.

DOS PASSOS. Here. *(He gives the envelopes to Dreiser)*

DREISER. What's this?

DOS PASSOS. Rejections. All of them.

DREISER. Rejections from what?

DOS PASSOS. The invitations we sent to go with you to Kentucky.

DREISER. So Comrade Anna has no committee after all. The senator?

DOS PASSOS. Prior commitments.

DREISER. He has to go. I will write to him.

DOS PASSOS. He requests a copy of any report the committee makes. His large congressional rear end is covered.

DREISER. What are these?

DOS PASSOS. Read. *(As Dreiser opens a couple of the envelopes)* "My health does not permit," "proposed committee cannot achieve desired result," "proposed committee is a stinking idea," "keep your nose out of other people's business" . . .

DREISER. Is duty out of fashion?

DOS PASSOS. Evidently.

DREISER. I am going to Kentucky, by myself or not.

DOS PASSOS. No one expects that, Theo.

DREISER. I have to go. It will make me again, John. It will be my next book.

DOS PASSSOS. Well, that's good news. Helen can stop beating the bushes for novels. She never was sure what one looked like and I never knew what to tell her.

DREISER. I've been working wrong for so long I'd almost forgotten how I work. Newspapers, magazines are not my medium. They are too short and too little. My stories are bigger than they are. And Kentucky is such a story that this nation will weep.

DOS PASSOS. You might be right, you have a nose for stories.

DREISER. Of course I'm right. And I'll tell you something else. Magazines hire college boys for editors, young men whose fathers paid for their fancy clothes, young men who've never lived anything, or wanted for anything, or imagined anything beyond what's under an occasional skirt.

DOS PASSOS. Seems to be a literary pursuit. And if I remember, the college boys have never written anything either.

DREISER. God knows, they have never written anything and they have been instructed by their publishers to demand extensive rewrites of anything that crosses their desks. I have my twenty-second rejection slip this month. Don't they know who I am?

DOS PASSOS. What are you writing?

DREISER. I am rejected for being too big! Well, they won't get the chance to reject Kentucky, and for those who speak into their afternoon cocktails about how Theodore, poor Theodore, has lost his art, let them read this book. It is a story that is my size, a whole people who are used and thrown away.

DOS PASSOS. The woman who isn't Ginger might say something similar of you.

DREISER. I pay her, she is my secretary. You stumble over pebbles, John.

DOS PASSOS. Are the gratuities part of the job? Does she always work in her slip?

DREISER. All I do is volunteer my services.

DOS PASSOS. That young woman just didn't volunteer to receive them.

DREISER. What happens in the privacy of my apartment has no bearing beyond the limits of it. If I publish my adventures, you can write the review.

DOS PASSOS. Theo, there are those who will say, who have already said *(A gesture to the envelopes)* that what happens in Kentucky has no bearing beyond the borders of that state. I am in your camp. I disagree. But I am a bleeding heart and I bleed at perceptions of abuses like others' noses bleed in rarefied air. Perhaps it is my curse to see the small injustices and waste myself before I even get to the big ones. Perhaps you see the big ones but you miss the small.

DREISER. What can be said of you is that you speak of another man's affairs.

DOS PASSOS. What can be said of me is that I am trying. *(He came to deliver this news)* Theo, I have spoken with Anna about Kentucky. And she and I will go. With you. As The Committee for the Defense of Political Prisoners.

DREISER. Just us?

DOS PASSOS. Without the participants from the Senate, we'll ask the governor for military protection. And we will hold hearings, a week of sworn hearings as you suggest.

DREISER. It might be better, you know, the company of friends instead of strangers. We'd know what we could expect from each other.

DOS PASSOS. Theo, it is not our intent to escort you on a research jaunt, but if it furthers your literary career, fine, and if your greatest work is about Kentucky, I will personally stand on 5th Avenue and cheer.

DREISER. John, this is actually good news. We will go. Care for a nip to celebrate? A toast of Helen's secret.

DOS PASSOS. No. My best to Helen. *(Dos Passos is on his way out)* You should marry Helen. She loves you. *(Dos Passos exits)*

THE TOP OF BLACK MOUNTIAN/ADAM KARP'S SCENIC TOUR

George, Paul, and Adam Karp enter.

PAUL. This here is the top of Black Mountain. *(Adam Karp sits down, he's exhausted)*

PAUL. I said this here is the top of Black Mountain.

KARP. It's lovely. I'm ready to go back to my hotel now.

PAUL. Not just yet. This ain't all we like to show tourists. Get up. *(He hauls Karp up)*

GEORGE. It's cold as old polar bear shit up here.

PAUL. Since when you know so much about polar bears? *(They exit)*

FROM THE HEARINGS/JIMMY CALDWELL'S FUNERAL

A WOMAN. Scrip is what a miner gets instead of money. We ain't seen real money out of that hole in two year. Scrip. Little pieces of metal that's supposed to do like money except you have to spend it at the company store. They don't like you spending it nowhere else. Which is just as well, I guess, cause you can't hardly find nowhere else to spend it. But prices at the company store is bad, a pound of bacon that costs fifteen cents at Howard's costs twenty at the company store. And you can tell when there's gonna' be a pay cut 'cause they cut the prices a little then they cut the pay a lot.

During the woman's speech, on a separate part of the stage, the lights come up on Jimmy Caldwell's funeral. There are not many people. They cross the stage carrying a poor man's pine box coffin. They also carry hand-lettered signs: JIMMY CALDWELL

DIED FOR YOU AND THE NMU, JIMMY CALDWELL WAS MURDERED BY CAPITALIST LAW. The mourners move slowly.

The Hearings Continue.

MOLLY JACKSON. Tell your name.
THE WOMAN. My husband's a-workin', Molly. I don't want to live in no tent.

Behind the mourners at the funeral, unknown and trying to stay unknown, is Henry Follette. He also mourns this death. He weeps.

A MAN. You don't see no money. They've took out two dollar for a doctor, one for buryin' insurance, six for rent on a house that's got cracks in it big enough to poke your fist through, and two for 'lectrics. I don't burn no 'lectric lights 'cause I can't afford no light bulbs but they still take out 'cause I'm hooked up for 'lectrics. And then you have to buy your carbide and your tools and then, there's what's gone for food and mighty little of it. I dig coal and we quit a'buyin' it. My children goes out to the railroad track to pick up what we burn for heat. Ever'time I get in the pay line, they tell me I owe them.
HALLOWAY COBBS. You're a-workin', you scab! All of you still working are scabs!
THE MAN. I have to, they say there ain't no more tents to give out.
HALLOWAY COBBS. I'm telling you, all of you, we stand together or we fall apart.

Jeff Caldwell in the funeral procession notices Henry Follette. Jeff is a pallbearer, the coffin must be set down. Jeff Caldwell crosses to Henry Follette.

JEFF CALDWELL. You traitor, you god-damned dog.
HENRY FOLLETTE. I didn't know . . .
JEFF CALDWELL. See if you ain't the next one needs a pine box. See if it ain't me that puts you in it.
HENRY FOLLETTE. I didn't know. *(Jeff Caldwell returns to his position at his brother's coffin and the funeral procession exits)*

MARIE/THE TRAIN

A light and into it walk Marie and Dreiser. Marie is escorted by him. She carries a small traveling case and wears, among other things, a red tam.

MARIE. I'm so excited. I've never been out of New York before. I went to Chicago when I was a baby but that doesn't count because I don't remember a thing about it. Do I look all right? I thought the red might cheer us up. Is it cold in Kentucky? I have this coat, of course, I mean I'm wearing it. I hope I don't need more. I'll bet I should have brought some boots. Oh, well. Too late now. Surely they'll have that sort of thing when we get there. I mean, we're not just going out somewhere. Harlan is a town, right? *(To Dreiser)* I'm so glad you chose me to go. It's like I get to be part of history and when you write your book I'll be in it, right? I know I will. I'll take my notes in shorthand and then I'll have to be around to read them to you. I'll read myself in. *(Dreiser steps away)* I am a little frightened, did you know that? I mean, people have died in Kentucky and what if people are so cold they try to take your clothes or so hungry that you can't eat in a restaurant without them looking at you? It might be really awful, I mean what if somebody died right there? I don't know what I'd do. Cry, probably. You know what I did do? This is really silly but I thought it might be nice. I bought some peppermints. A lot of peppermints, really. And I thought maybe if we wanted to, we could give them out. I mean, I thought I would. I know it isn't very much, just a gesture, but it seemed like a peppermint might be something a little special. Well, anyway, I have them. They are the only thing in my little case. How long does it take to get to Harlan? *(John Dos Passos joins Theodore Dreiser)*

DOS PASSOS. Who is she?

DREISER. You mean Marie? She's my new secretary. She's very good.

DOS PASSOS. In bed?

DREISER. Efficient.

DOS PASSOS. In bed?

DREISER. Secretaries do have functions, John. They type, take notes, do research. Marie is a stenographer. I thought it might be helpful to have her along.

DOS PASSOS. All this from flat on her back?

DREISER. I'm paying her fare. It's not costing you or the committee.

DOS PASSOS. We are not out for a weekend in the Catskills.

DREISER. It is not your concern if Marie finds me attractive.

DOS PASSOS. Look, I don't care what you do in New York, I don't care if a new secretary a week "finds you attractive." It does not bother me that the couch in your studio smells of spent semen. But this is different. We felt obliged to ask for military protection to come here and the governor felt obliged to promise it. And then, I find our party includes this woman whose job it is to keep you warm at night and she wants to know if it is all right to hand out peppermints.

DREISER. It is the gesture of an innocent heart. We should all have peppermints. Since you don't have peppermints, I will thank you to hold your tongue. You spend more time on my affairs than on your own. I guarantee that should anything happen between Marie and myself, it will be done with the utmost care and discretion.

DOS PASSOS. Jesus!

DREISER. I suspect you will find Marie very valuable. It is she who will make our notes.

DOS PASSOS. Your notes. I will make my own notes.

DREISER. Have it your way. My notes. It will be my book.

A CONDUCTOR'S VOICE. *(Offstage)* Harlan, Kentucky.

The committee arrives in Kentucky. The Lame Militia Man marches on, snaps to attention. Molly Jackson enters. Other Kentucky People, including Jeff Caldwell, come onstage, but they hang back.

MILITIA MAN. *(To Molly)* You're not armed, are you?

MOLLY JACKSON. No.

MILITIA MAN. I'd have to disarm you if you was armed. You here for them New Yorkers?

MOLLY JACKSON. I'm here for the committee, yes.

MILITIA MAN. Well, see you don't make no aggressive moves, ok?

(The Committee, Dos Passos, Dreiser, Anna Rollins, and Marie enter)

ANNA ROLLINS. Molly!

MOLLY JACKSON. Well, there you are. Welcome back. I've got a greeting party here somewhere. *(Kentucky People come forward)* You all remember Anna.

DREISER. I'm Theodore Dreiser, this is John Dos Passos; with Anna, we are the Committee for the Defense of Political Prisoners.

DOS PASSOS. I can't tell you how honored I am to be here. I hope we are of service.

A VOICE. We're glad to lay eyes on you, too. *(The Militia Man hands Dreiser a note)*

DREISER. Where is the rest of our escort?

MILITIA MAN. I'm it, friend.

DREISER. The governor promised us a military escort.

MILITIA MAN. What you see is what you get.

DREISER. What's this? *(The note)*

MILITIA MAN. I don't know. Somebody give it to me to give to you. I ain't usually the mail service.

DREISER. *(Reads)* Do not hold hearings on Wallins Creek.

MILITIA MAN. I wouldn't worry about that right now. What'd you say we get us somethin' to eat. I'm hungry. You hungry?

DREISER. I beg your pardon?

MILITIA MAN. I said I want to eat. If I can find a place around here that's clean enough. *(The Militia Man exits)*

MOLLY JACKSON. Welcome to Kentucky. Not everybody gets a left over from the Civil War for an escort. We can show you to the hotel.

GEORGE. *(Off)* Come on, son.

Molly Jackson, The Committee, and The Kentucky People except for Jeff Caldwell exit. Jeff heard George. Jeff hides. George, Paul, and Adam Karp enter.

GEORGE. This here is the last of our little tour. This is the rail-road station.

KARP. I can see that.

PAUL. And this is where you get on the train. You want a one-way ticket.

KARP. I'm ready to go back to my hotel.

PAUL. He don't get it yet.

KARP. My clothes are at the hotel.

GEORGE. Somebody here can use 'em. You are goin' to get on the train.

KARP. I refuse.

GEORGE. You're gonna' get lost real bad if we do more of the scenic tour.

KARP. You are threatening me!

PAUL. Jew-boy ain't as dumb as he looks.

KARP. I'll come back.

PAUL. Get on the train.

KARP. I will be back.

Karp leaves the stage in the direction of the train. George and Paul watch. Jeff Caldwell pulls his hat low on his face, turns away from George and Paul and follows Adam Karp.

act 2

MOLLY JACKSON/THE HEARINGS

MOLLY JACKSON. *(She is intense, electric, this is a performance)* I'm gonna sing you a song. It come to me back when my husband was working coal and I sung it in New York and Chicago when we were trying to raise some money for these starving people, and I am honored to sing it here at these hearings held by Mr. Dreiser and this committee.

I'm sad and I'm weary, I got the hungry ragged blues,
I'm sad and I'm weary, I got the hungry ragged blues.
Not a penny in my pocket to buy the thing I need to use.

You could hear some of the worst stories you ever heard, I can tell 'em 'cause I seen 'em and I lived 'em and I helped bury the children I pulled into this world as a granny woman. Bury 'em out in the back yard. Four on a good week, seven on a bad. A grave a day. It's just a little hole though, it's babies we're a-burying.

When my husband works in a coal mine, he loads a car
    on ever' trip,
When my husband works in a coal mine, he loads a car
    on ever' trip.
Then he goes to the office that evenin' and gets denied
    of scrip.

I am a communist. I belong to the National Miners Union. I am a communist because I love America, but I do not love the thing the capitalist loves. I do not love money. I love my comrades, my brothers and sisters and their children and the capitalists is killing 'em in Kentucky. I'd be ashamed to be a capitalist. Hoit Bessman should be ashamed of the Coal Operators Association. Hershel Lilly should be ashamed of the *Mountain Sun*. I'd be ashamed to be either one of 'em. I'd be ashamed to be workin' in coal right now. But it ain't no shame to be poor and it ain't no shame to be hungry.

All the women in the coal camps are sittin' with bowed
    down heads,
All the women in the coal camps are sittin' with bowed
    down heads.
Ragged and barefoot, the children are a-cryin' for bread.

Don't go under the mountain again. Don't nobody go under the mountain again till the money stops jingling in the operators' pockets, till there ain't no fat on them like there ain't no fat on us, till they ain't got no clothes to keep warm and no shoes. Do you have shoes? Don't go under the mountain again till you get a decent place to live and fair credit for what you load, and if that don't never come, then don't never go under the mountain again!

Some coal operators will tell you the hungry blues are
    not so bad,
Some coal operators will tell you the hungry blues are

not so bad.
They are the worst blues this poor woman ever had.

Dreiser joins her in a private conversation.

DREISER. How can you say what you do? They don't mark down
your name.

MOLLY JACKSON. They already know me.

DREISER. They don't harrass you.

MOLLY JACKSON. Yes, they do. My family's everyone somewhere
else already or dead. The time will come for me. I might
end up your neighbor in New York City, Mr. Dreiser.

DREISER. I can't imagine such a displaced person.

MOLLY JACKSON. I can. What do you figure you'd think of me
then?

DREISER. They don't shoot you, they don't put you in jail.

MOLLY JACKSON. They can't afford to. See, I do the things they
don't want to do. I catch babies and I tend the dying. There
ain't one among them wants that job. And because I do it,
I get to talk out loud.

DREISER. I don't know how you find the courage.

MOLLY JACKSON. It's easy. I got a natural flapping tongue and
I've come onto faith.

DREISER. Faith? Faith in what?

MOLLY JACKSON. In myself, in these people, in God.

DREISER. The coal operators run God too. Billy Sunday was paid
to say God doesn't like communism.

MOLLY JACKSON. My faith is not in Billy Sunday's god.

DREISER. My mother's faith was not in my father's god. I envy
you. I swear, I wish I had your strength. I wish what I do
made as much difference as what you do.

MOLLY JACKSON. You don't want to do what I do.

DREISER. I might.

MOLLY JACKSON. Then catch babies, Mr. Dreiser. Feed the living
what you can, and tend the dying. That's all there is to it.
(The scene returns to the hearings)

DREISER. I didn't get your name.

MOLLY JACKSON. I am Molly Jackson, called Aunt Molly Jackson
by folks I've borned or their parents. Mark it down, Hershel

Lilly. Write it on your list, Hoit Bessman. I want everybody to get it straight who I am and which side I'm on.

THE MOUNTAIN SUN OFFICE

Lilly is there, Karp enters.

LILLY. Mr. Karp! You got my message. Thank you very much for coming by. You are the new AP correspondent, right? My name is Hershel Lilly.

KARP. A pleasure to meet you, Mr. Lilly.

LILLY. I'm the owner, editor and chief bottle washer at this little rag and I have written occasionally for the folks at Associated Press.

KARP. They said there was a man who contributed occasionally.

LILLY. I thought I might be civilized about it and offer you the resources of an office . . .

KARP. That's generous of you.

LILLY. Well, what do you think of God's country? Beautiful, huh?

KARP. Yes. I had the pleasure of seeing some of it. And I came back anyway.

LILLY. Yes, I read about your unfortunate introduction to the mountains. There are isolated incidents that prove rather embarrassing but we are not all cut in the mold of Genghis Khan. I hope to provide you with a more gracious aspect. If it is just those isolated incidents that wind up in the news, it presents a rather distorted picture.

KARP. My tour was arranged by the sheriff of this county. I felt that made it newsworthy.

LILLY. As a man with access to the wires, I'm sure you wrestle with the questions of what's appropriate on a daily basis.

KARP. Yes, I do. And I remember your article, the one in response to the Dreiser committee, about your Society for the Protection of Defenseless Children on the Streets of New York City. I'm sure you wrestle with the obligations of the news sometimes too.

LILLY. Good. I'm glad you saw it. That's precisely the point I want to make. If Hoit Bessman and Henry Blair and I cart off in search of horrors in New York, I'm sure we can find

them. The Puritans found witches, the Inquisition found
heretics, the Crusaders found infidels . . .

KARP. And wire correspondents find isolated incidents. Mr. Lilly,
it is a whole class of people here who are held in virtual
slavery. That's news.

LILLY. They are free to leave anytime they want to, free to go
anywhere they want to go.

KARP. How do they leave and where do they go to from here?

LILLY. Mr. Karp. These are the worst economic times this country has ever been through. People here are trying to do what
everybody else is doing right now: they're trying to keep
from losing anymore than they've already lost. None of it is
pretty anywhere. And here, so much is lost, I hardly know
how to begin to talk about it.

KARP. Then let me. Some people lost a lot of money like coal
operators and owners. Some people lost a little money, yourself, for instance. Some people went from three meals a day
to three meals a week. And some people get shot. Jimmy
Caldwell was shot. Are you ever going to do anything for
this paper or AP or anybody on Jimmy Caldwell or is he just
an isolated incident?

LILLY. Mr. Caldwell was part of an unfortunate group here who
got their bellies full of communism and are making trouble.

KARP. Jimmy Caldwell was getting his belly full of soup. At the
National Miners Union soup kitchen at Clovertown.

LILLY. He was an organizer, Mr. Karp. We have proof of that.

KARP. It wasn't the troublemaking communists who shot him,
Mr. Lilly. There was a witness. It was troublemaking somebody else. Part of the same group that arranged my tour.

LILLY. That witness is not reliable.

KARP. The witness is the dead man's brother.

LILLY. The witness is a communist union supporter.

KARP. And that makes him blind?

LILLY. It makes him prejudiced and subject to outside coercion.

KARP. And you are not prejudiced?

LILLY. Oh, no, I am prejudiced. Make no mistake. I am a prejudiced man. But I am not subject to outside coercion.

KARP. I see.

LILLY. You and this Dreiser committee—you are one of them,

right?—you are treating these people like saints with old crazy Molly Jackson over there leading the hallelujah chorus. They are not saints. They are trouble, real trouble, and it would serve the citizens, the private, property owning, tax paying citizens who live here and love this part of the country better if you would keep them out of the news.

KARP. I am a news correspondent, Mr. Lilly. I'm on an assignment. I'm reporting on the Dreiser committee same as you. *(Karp exits)*

FROM THE HEARINGS

ELIZABETH WILSON. Molly Jackson helped me bury my littlest youngun and I had to beg the box to put her in. We'd been askin' for a doctor for a month. It was a company doctor, we was supposed to have done paid for him. When he finally did come, all he did was look at her from where he was a-standin' and tell me to feed her milk. She had the flux.

MOLLY JACKSON. It was a bloody flux. That means she was a-starving.

ELIZABETH WILSON. Well, I ain't got no milk, no money to get any. Molly Jackson got me some but it wasn't enough. Or it was too late. When that doctor come back, he said, "That youngun finally die?"

MOLLY JACKSON. Your name?

ELIZABETH WILSON. I don't want to say my name, I'll say my youngun's name. It was Marie. *(Marie is caught, touched)*

MOLLY JACKSON. Your name.

ELIZABETH WILSON. Aunt Molly . . .

MOLLY JACKSON. Say it, honey, you need to say it.

ELIZABETH WILSON. My name is Elizabeth Wilson. *(Elizabeth Wilson starts off. Marie follows)*

MARIE. Mrs. Wilson!

ELIZABETH WILSON. No!

MARIE. Wait up a minute, will you?

ELIZABETH WILSON. I said too much already.

MARIE. I was glad you said your name. I'd be so scared.

ELIZABETH WILSON. What do you want with me?

MARIE. I want to give you something. I've been in the hearings . . . This seems silly now but I brought some stuff from New York to give away and I thought maybe if I gave you the whole thing, you could trade it or sell it or something . . . *(Marie gives the traveling case with the peppermints in it to Elizabeth Wilson)*

ELIZABETH WILSON. I ain't got nothin' to put in somethin' like this.

MARIE. No, look inside. *(Marie opens the case)* It's not much but maybe you could trade it.

ELIZABETH WILSON. This is candy.

MARIE. Peppermints. I feel pretty stupid.

ELIZABETH WILSON. You a-givin' me candy?

MARIE. If you don't want it, I'm sorry, I thought maybe you could trade it.

ELIZABETH WILSON. You're a-givin' me this candy?

MARIE. I didn't understand when I bought it, I had no idea. . . . Here, wait. *(Marie finds some money in her pocketbook. She puts that in the case too. Elizabeth Wilson is astounded, uncomfortable, and she just looks at Marie. More silence. Marie pulls off her red tam and adds it to Elizabeth Wilson's load)*

ELIZABETH WILSON. No . . .

MARIE. I want to give it to you. Please. Take them. I'm sorry about the candy. *(Marie begins to cry)*

ELIZABETH WILSON. No, child. I'm a-thankin' you for the candy. I ain't had no sugar for two year. *(Elizabeth Wilson shifts her load and hands the tam and the money back to Marie)* You put that back in your purse. And you put this back on.

MARIE. You keep it, keep it all. And the hat, wear it when you want to brighten things up a little. *(Marie puts the red hat on Elizabeth Wilson)*

ELIZABETH WILSON. I'm much obliged. *(Elizabeth Wilson exits. Marie returns to the hearings)*

FROM THE HEARINGS

HALLOWAY COBBS. My name is Halloway Cobbs and I don't live in no company house. I live in a house belonged to my daddy before he died. He died in a mine. That's the way a poor man dies around here. And my wife keeps a garden durin' the summer and puts things by so we ain't starvin'. I'm better off than most, I know that. But my house has been searched four times. There's thugs that come in with guns when you ain't got one—they took all ours already— and they split open mattresses and chairs.

DREISER. What are they looking for?

HALLOWAY COBBS. Papers. They ain't got no warrant, there ain't no bother with a warrant no more, and they stand the children up against the wall and try to get 'em to tell on their daddy.

DREISER. What papers?

HALLOWAY COBBS. To prove I'm workin' for a union, or liter'ture to prove I'm communist.

DREISER. Did they find them?

HALLOWAY COBBS. I ain't in jail, am I? Four times I been searched, and then my house was shot up. Six of 'em come drivin' by in three cars, one of 'em with a machine gun and they shot up my house. My wife and children was at church on Sunday morning. And me, first shot come and I run out back and up the hill, and I seen 'em sittin' out there in front of my house workin' that machine gun, and I know who done it. (*Sheriff John Henry Blair stands up, a threat to Halloway Cobbs. Cobbs was going to say who did it*)

HALLOWAY COBBS. Write that down, anybody that wants to. My name is Halloway Cobbs and I know who shot up my house.

JEFF CALDWELL. I'm Jeff Caldwell. Jimmy Caldwell was my brother. They shot him dead back of the NMU soup kitchen at Clovertown. Henry Follette was the rat. And the Harlan County justice held what they said was a trial the same day we held the buryin' for my brother, but they didn't tell nobody they was holdin' it and they didn't call no witnesses. They let them two bastards . . .

VOICES. Name them, say their names!

JEFF CALDWELL. They let Deputy George Sweet and Deputy Paul Foot go for sayin' it was self defense. It wasn't. It was murder. I was there. So I'm witnessin' right now. I'm witnessin' in front of God and this committee. If justice don't happen in a court of law, then justice is gonna' happen outside of it.

JOHN HENRY BLAIR. Caldwell, you're threatening lives of officers of the law.

DREISER. Sheriff Blair, we are testing free speech in these hearings, a right guaranteed in this country by our constitution and Mr. Caldwell merely spoke his mind.

JOHN HENRY BLAIR. Mr. Dreiser, it don't matter to me what you're testing. I arrest people who threaten officers.

DREISER. Arrest him and the story will be in every newspaper in this country.

BLAIR. Tell you what I'll do, Mr. Dreiser, I'll wait till the day after you've gone to arrest him. How's that? Then it won't bother you so much. *(Blair leaves the hearings and stays in focus for the change)*

JOHN HENRY BLAIR'S OFFICE

Blair is swearing in a new deputy. We see the deputy's back.

BLAIR. Now is the part where you raise your right hand. *(The new deputy raises his right hand)* I'm going to ask you to swear to uphold the law and you're going to swear to do that. You know the law, son?

THE NEW DEPUTY. Some.

BLAIR. I am the law right now in Harlan County and you got to swear to do what I say. You think you can swear to that?

THE NEW DEPUTY. I'm tired of swearing stuff. I thought I might not swear no more for a while.

BLAIR. Look. Something's bound to happen to you. We both know that.

THE NEW DEPUTY. Jimmy Caldwell wasn't out to hurt nobody. He didn't have to die.

BLAIR. Jimmy Caldwell was a rattlesnake. And a dead rattlesnake is still poison and I've heard they can still bite.

THE NEW DEPUTY. I seen snakes curl dead, I ain't never seen nothing bite dead.

BLAIR. Every communist in two counties is looking for you.

THE NEW DEPUTY. You're a pointing right at where I am! Lookie here, lookie which side he's on now.

BLAIR. So I get one thing, you get something else. People don't murder my deputies, son, deputies have names around here.

THE NEW DEPUTY. People don't like your deputies either.

BLAIR. You're not running for elected office. You can swear to uphold the law and walk out of here with a license to carry a gun or you can walk out of here just like you are.

THE NEW DEPUTY. I ain't got no gun.

BLAIR. I do.

THE NEW DEPUTY. I guess I swear, then.

BLAIR. Swear it to God.

THE NEW DEPUTY. I believe in God.

BLAIR. I like God-fearing deputies. Swear it to God.

THE NEW DEPUTY. I swear to God.

BLAIR. *(Blair gives the new deputy a gun)* Didn't hurt a bit, did it? *(The new deputy turns around. He is Henry Follette)*

THE NEW DEPUTY. It gets easier.

BLAIR. All right, deputy, I got a job needs you to do it. I want you to keep your eye open for anything that ain't right with Mr. Dreiser and that committee. See, I think they're communist and I know they don't know the law like you do. You think you see anything, you come and get me before you do anything about it.

THE NEW DEPUTY. I can do that.

BLAIR. I thought you might not mind.

FROM THE HEARINGS

LILLY. Mr. Dreiser, do you mind if I ask you a few questions?

DREISER. Not at all.

LILLY. You are a very famous novelist and have written several books. Would you tell what your royalties amount to?

DREISER. I do not mind. About two hundred thousand. Probably more.

LILLY. Being banned in Boston is profitable, isn't it? Do you contribute to charity?

DREISER. No, I do not.

LILLY. Thank you, Mr. Dreiser.

DREISER. Is that all?

LILLY. It is all anybody here needs to know. You see, Hoit Bessman there contributes. I happen to know, I'm treasurer of the charity he contributes to. I contribute. Hoit and I organized the food line at the Red Cross to feed "these starving people".

DREISER. Would you like to know why I do not contribute to charity?

LILLY. Not particulary. I'll bet Molly Jackson's not real interested either. I bet Mr. Dos Passos and Miss Rollins don't care why you don't give money either but I'll bet they care that you don't. Do you give to any organization at all?

DREISER. I give to the Civil Liberties Union, old age insurance. Sometimes I've given to Children's Home.

LILLY. I see. Boundless generosity.

DREISER. You do not see! I am from a large family, a poor family, and when they saw that I had made money, they called on me to support them. I've kept several of my near relatives.

LILLY. What do you give that way?

DREISER. I've given a few thousand.

LILLY. A year?

DREISER. No.

LILLY. I give five dollars a week and I'll bet give a higher percentage of my income to charity than you do to keep your family.

DREISER. I don't make two hundred thousand a year; that's the total of my royalties.

LILLY. What do you get a year?

DREISER. About thirty-five thousand.

LILLY. Mr. Dreiser, I'll bet I give a higher dollar to support these people than you give to anything, even your family. And I am not in New York holding hearings. Though perhaps I should hold hearings for your family. Are you generous or do they have to beg?

DREISER. What I give is not the question here.

LILLY. It is now. You've pretended your charity to come here.

DREISER. Let me tell you what I give. I give a damn about the lives and dignity of these people and you don't. It serves you very well when they are poor and need jobs. You have to buy mules when they die but you can always just hire another man. I am interested in equality. I am searching for what is good and decent and I'm not afraid of the truth and you are. I employ secretaries and I do not pay them any small amount in salaries. They work continuously on facts. Facts. And me, I am not dancing at the Waldorf. I am here at my own expense because I want to be able to speak the truth about Kentucky.

LILLY. Mr. Dreiser, do you disagree with the principle of private ownership?

DREISER. I am not a communist if that's what you're asking. They will not have me because I am more interested in truth than I am in the party line.

LILLY. Admirable. Do you believe in the Soviet Government from Russia?

DREISER. I have visited Russia. And I believe their form of government can be more equal than ours. Capitalism doesn't work like they want you to believe. Oh, it works for a few. A few who are a little more equal than anybody else. Look around this room and tell me where you see equality.

LILLY. I see as only a person who lives here can see.

DREISER. You see like a man with interests to protect!

LILLY. You see like a man with two faces, Mr. Dreiser. You should pick one and be consistent.

A VOICE. He needs a new face now. We've seen both the old ones.

DREISER. I was poor. I know what it is to be poor! My mother sent her children begging! I know what a meal from the Red Cross tastes like, Mr. Lilly. And I'll bet you don't. I am sixty-one years old and I have worked like an ox for what I have. Keep this in mind: I will write about you and I will write about Kentucky. My pen is the plow I drag behind me and if I turn up hatred or greed, it is because it lay like worms in the path of the furrow. I did not veer left or right to unearth some small town newspaper editor who has lost his perspective on truth!

LILLY. It is a long row between New York and Kentucky, Mr. Dreiser, a very long row even for such a literary ox.

DREISER. Is that all you have to ask me?

A VOICE. Ask him to put his money where his mouth is.

LILLY. You heard the man.

DREISER. What I give is not the issue!

DOS PASSOS. *(Interrupting)* Gentlemen! We're here to take testimony from these people, not to listen to your arguments. We'll adjourn the hearings for this afternoon. Thank you all for your participation; it has been a very full day. We will resume tomorrow morning.

A VOICE. Tomorrow morning, you'll hear the wind. *(Hoit Bessman, Henry Blair join Hershel Lilly as they exit)*

BESSMAN. Congratulations, Hershel. You nailed the son of a bitch.

LILLY. My pleasure. •

ANNA ROLLINS. *(Speaks to Dreiser on her way out)* You could have exaggerated your charitable contributions, Theo, you exaggerate everything else. *(All exit except Dreiser. Marie holds back a moment. She almost goes to Dreiser, but she doesn't. A Preacher approaches Dreiser)*

PREACHER. The Lord said the Infidel would come. He said the Infidel would stand among us and the weak in heart would follow him because they was weak. And the Lord said it is the biggest rut in the road to hell.

DREISER. The Lord said no such thing. The interests in coal may have said it, but the Lord didn't.

PREACHER. And the Lord told me I was to stand up to the face of the Infidel so that he might know the error of his ways.

DREISER. So I am the infidel, am I? Communist or plain?

PREACHER. You have come here where you ain't got no business. . . .

DREISER. An outside infidel.

PREACHER. You get people stirred up to where they're acting contrary to the way of the Lord.

DREISER. I have done nothing contrary to your Lord. And I know your Lord. My father died in his search for your elusive Lord.

PREACHER. Your father heard the higher callin'.

DREISER. My father heard his bottle calling. My father prayed when we cried for food. My mother begged food and fed us.

PREACHER. The Lord didn't make no promises but trials about the Vale of Tears. The Promised Land is after.

DREISER. I have found your promised land. You hear me? I have found it. You could open your eyes and look at it right here.

PREACHER. This is heresy.

DREISER. But I cannot find how we are equal in it and I keep running into people I don't like very much.

PREACHER. Me, right?

DREISER. I was thinking of Hershel Lilly but you can be included.

PREACHER. Be careful, sinner. On the Day of Judgement there's gonna be a harlot that rides the beast and it's those people who made light of the way of the Lord that's the harlot and the damnation of the harlot is unspeakable . . .

DREISER. I am the beast himself, you ass. Ask anyone who knows me. And you could make yourself useful and find a harlot who'd like to ride.

PREACHER. This is heresy and blasphemy, you are damned.

DREISER. Probably.

NIGHT AT THE CUMBERLAND HOTEL

The scene changes around Dreiser. There are two rooms and a corridor in the hotel. The rooms belong to Dreiser and Dos Passos. Henry Follette hangs out in the hall. Henry Follette is drilling a hole in the wall with his pocket knife so he can look into Dos Passos' room. Anna Rollins comes to the door of Dos Passos' room. Henry Follette must cover his activity. Anna Rollins knocks on the door. Dos Passos opens it.

ANNA ROLLINS. I'd like to talk with you and Theo.

DOS PASSOS. Certainly. *(Anna and Dos Passos cross to Dreiser's room and knock. Dreiser opens the door. Henry Follette tries to listen)*

ANNA ROLLINS. May we come in? *(They enter Dreiser's room)* I'm asking that we confer a moment with an eye towards the events of the afternoon. It had to be a rather embarrassing moment for you, Theo. I'd like to think we might avoid that sort of incident again.

DREISER. By all means. But Mr. Lilly has had his day. He'll not have the opportunity again.

ANNA ROLLINS. Mr. Lilly is free to ask questions; I don't see that you can keep him from it. I don't see that we want to.

DREISER. Anna, I don't think he'll be so anxious to speak up again. I did promise to write about him.

ANNA ROLLINS. I don't agree at all. Write about him? He's probably sitting over in that newspaper office right now writing about you and the story will be on the AP wires first thing in the morning. Theo, I'm sorry but I'm recommending that John chair the hearings for the rest of the week.

DOS PASSOS. Anna!

DREISER. You're what?

ANNA ROLLINS. Not that I think you are inadequate but I do think you lost credibility in that exchange with Mr. Lilly and there are the rest of the hearings to consider.

DREISER. I'll be damned.

ANNA ROLLINS. It is critical that people continue to participate and if you made the gesture . . .

DREISER. I'm not here to be betrayed!

ANNA ROLLINS. I beg your pardon?

DREISER. Isn't it enough that we stand among enemies, we eat, we are preparing to sleep among enemies without tearing at friends? Don't women ever know the difference between enemies and friends?

ANNA ROLLINS. Theo, we all have shortcomings, yours are no worse than anyone else's, yours just happen to be in the spotlight at the moment.

DREISER. Solidarity, Comrade. Or have you forgotten your party's philosophy? Or have you forgotten your party? You certainly didn't remember it this afternoon. I'm not the communist, you are!

ANNA ROLLINS. Mr. Lilly's questions were not addressed to me. And the issue was not communism, it was good capitalist Christian charity! For your information, communism doesn't need charity to work. And I was as interested in your answers as he was. There's not much to you but talk, is there?

DREISER. I will not step down. You can make your own committee and I will be my own if you choose to do that, but I will not step down. Get out of my room.

ANNA ROLLINS. Right here is the reason you will never be in the Party. I'll see to it. *(Dreiser shows Anna Rollins the door. Dos Passos follows, with a gesture to Dreiser to stay put. Deputy Follette is obliged to try to fade into the wallpaper)*

DOS PASSOS. Diplomacy isn't your strong point, is it?

ANNA ROLLINS. The literary ox left a big steamy pile in the middle of the hearings and we're supposed to just ignore it? People's lives are at stake here, they've trusted us, they're testifying! *(Dos Passos and Anna Rollins can't help but notice Henry Follette. Dos Passos opens his door and lets her in, a measure for privacy, and closes the door)* When I believe in something, I act on it. I organized this trip and I will disorganize it before I see it fail for his inconsistencies.

DOS PASSOS. I just wish you'd told me what you were thinking before you started the conversation.

ANNA ROLLINS. So you could try to talk me out of saying anything? Why should he be protected? You're not. I'm not. Or do you think, by virtue of who he is, he is not responsible for what he does? *(Dreiser comes from his room to Dos Passos's door and knocks)*

DREISER. John? Can I come in?

ANNA ROLLINS. If he doesn't know I'm mad, you can tell him.

DOS PASSOS. *(To Dreiser)* A moment, please. Anna and I are talking.

DREISER. I need to speak with you.

DOS PASSOS. *(To Anna)* Pardon me. *(Dos Passos steps from his room into the corridor)*

DREISER. Do you have anything to drink?

DOS PASSOS. No.

DREISER. I thought you carried the bottle Helen got for you . . .

DOS PASSOS. I didn't. Goodnight, Theo. *(Dos Passos starts for his room again. Dreiser stops him)*

DREISER. I'm afraid I reacted a bit strongly to Anna's suggestion.

DOS PASSOS. I'd say that's an understatement.

DREISER. I'm trying to apologize for any discomfort I caused you.

DOS PASSOS. Apologize to Anna.

DREISER. I will not. It was an inappropriate suggestion.

DOS PASSOS. A startling suggestion, a surprising suggestion, maybe a rude suggestion but it was not an inappropriate suggestion. And you threw a temper tantrum. Most people outgrow them by five or six years old.

DREISER. It was a power play, John.

DOS PASSOS. It was a salvage operation.

DREISER. God, you are an innocent. She got mad when I said I wasn't a communist and this is her revenge.

DOS PASSOS. Theo, she is trying to preserve the integrity of the committee after this afternoon. It is a problem in my mind too. *(Henry Follette is listening again. Dos Passos guides Dreiser back to Dreiser's room. They go in and shut the door)*

DREISER. Look. I can stand bad press. Which is all this afternoon will amount to. I do not need to be loved.

DOS PASSOS. You've come to the right place.

DREISER. But it is my committee, John.

DOS PASSOS. And mine and the International Labor Defense Fund's. And Anna organized it. It's hers if it is anybody's.

DREISER. The hearings were my idea.

DOS PASSOS. My, my, my.

DREISER. I do not need to be loved by you either. But I have to keep the chair. You tell me what it would look like to be "relieved of the duty." I can hear the press now. "Poor Teddy has lost his grip." I'm such a favorite already.

DOS PASSOS. You just said you didn't need to be loved.

DREISER. I will not stand more ridicule. What have I written lately that hasn't been picked to pieces by those crows? Please, John. I'm asking for your support. She'd throw me out. *(Anna looks out Dos Passos' door to see what came of him; she sees Henry Follette trying to listen at Dreiser's door. She makes a noise. Henry Follette jumps. She closes Dos Passos' door again. Follette goes back to Dreiser's door)*

DOS PASSOS. Theo, you are public because you make yourself public, the hearings are public because you demanded public hearings. No one questions your courage in it. We admire your courage. But ridicule is the risk you run. And in this case, you set yourself up for it.

DREISER. I am a public figure and I came here to wage a war.

DOS PASSOS. You came here to hold hearings.

DREISER. I did not anticipate having to fight skirmishes within the committee.

DOS PASSOS. Theo, this is not a public moment.

DREISER. It can turn public in the next issue of *The Nation*. You're a writer. I know what's good on paper.

DOS PASSOS. Go apologize to Anna. Ask Molly Jackson what she thinks should happen. See where that gets us.

DREISER. If you say the word, I will back down and you can assume the chair. I'll leave here tomorrow morning on the train. I will plead ill health.

DOS PASSOS. Now there is a public gesture, turn tail and run.

DREISER. By tomorrow it will be true, I will be ill.

DOS PASSOS. Theo, I don't like theatrics and I won't be manipulated.

DREISER. Tell me I have your support or I will leave. I will announce it tonight.

DOS PASSOS. Good God, just talk to Anna.

DREISER. I will not. And on my way out of town, I will announce that she is a member of the communist party, and no doubt, Mr. Lilly and Mr. Blair will have some questions for her!

DOS PASSOS. Don't be stupid!

DREISER. I mean it. Or, you can tell me I have your support.

DOS PASSOS. Stop this!

DREISER. Now, John, or I'm going downstairs. *(Dreiser almost gets out his door into the hall. Dos Passos stops him)*

DOS PASSOS. Ok, you have it! Just don't say anything else. Not tonight. Not tomorrow. And go to bed. By yourself.

DREISER. I am by myself in ways you will never understand, your heart is not big enough. *(Dos Passos leaves Dreiser's room, collects himself for a moment and finds himself standing next to Henry Follette)*

HENRY FOLLETTE. Helps if they rattle before they bite, don't it?

DOS PASSOS. What?

HENRY FOLLETTE. Snakes. If they rattle, you know they're snakes. *(Dos Passos goes into his room and shuts the door. Henry Follette cuts two slivers of wood from a door frame and stands them up against Dos Passos' door—Anna is still in the room—and retreats a little way)*

DOS PASSOS. The old man.

ANNA ROLLINS. Did he come to apologize or was it a social call?

DOS PASSOS. He will not stay here without the chair. He will back down if we say so, leave the committee with a few vindictive parting shots and go back to New York. You were right about him. Shall we hang or drown?

ANNA ROLLINS. I hear drowning is rather pleasant once you get over the initial panic.

DOS PASSOS. Anna, I told him he had my support to keep the chair.

ANNA ROLLINS. You tell me I'm right and you support him. Are you confused, John, is it past your bedtime? Which side are you on?

DOS PASSOS. It's true. I'm not a soldier of a particular political ideology, but I'm not fumbling around Kentucky looking for my next novel either. My failing is plain vanilla good intentions and I am the voice of reason by default. He said he was leaving if I didn't support him.

ANNA ROLLINS. Let him. Good riddance.

DOS PASSOS. And on his way out, he threatened to announce your party membership.

ANNA ROLLINS. I am not ashamed. I can take questions from Hershel Lilly or anyone else. I know why I believe what I do. And in the meantime, I do give to charity.

DOS PASSOS. Anna! Communists get shot here; the lucky ones just go to jail! You'd be smart not to say the word out loud. The walls have ears. They were standing out in the hall when I came in.

ANNA ROLLINS. Yes, I've met them.

DOS PASSOS. Look. He could plead ill health till he is blue in the face and then go home, but you and I both know the story, with all the quotes, is already on the wires. Anyway, if he left tomorrow it would just make it worse. I figured we sit still and take our medicine. Send him home day after if we still want him to go.

ANNA ROLLINS. I don't know how I can show my face. He'll behave as though nothing happened. "We ask that you swear by your name that what you say is the truth."

DOS PASSOS. I don't see much other choice.

ANNA ROLLINS. I hate this. I'd rather kick him out and take my chances.

DOS PASSOS. Sleep on it. If you feel the same in the morning, we'll talk to him again. I'll talk to him.

ANNA ROLLINS. What if no one comes to the hearings tomorrow?

They may not come. I wouldn't. It might be easier if no one comes.

DOS PASSOS. I know. Would you like to go early to breakfast?

ANNA ROLLINS. Without him.

DOS PASSOS. We can decide then. We'll miss watching Marie feed him bits of egg first thing.

ANNA ROLLINS. I'll feed you bits of egg; we can confuse our spy. *(Anna Rollins leaves Dos Passos's room. The slivers of wood fall over. Dos Passos' room goes to black. Henry Follette is in the hall)*

ANNA ROLLINS. *(To Henry Follette)* Communist, c o m m u n i s t.

HENRY FOLLETTE. Sssssssss . . . *(Like a snake. Anna Rollins turns the corner to go to her room, offstage. Henry Follette follows her. Marie comes down the corridor and knocks on Dreiser's door. He opens it. Follette comes back to the corner in time to see without being seen)*

MARIE. I've been thinking about this afternoon, it had to be awful for you and I just want to say how sorry I am. People are so stupid; it shouldn't matter . . .

DREISER. I need you. God help me, I need you. *(Dreiser takes Marie into his room and shuts the door. The lights go to black in Dreiser's room. Henry Follette recovers the toothpicks that had fallen from in front of Dos Passos' door, or cuts new ones, and places them against Dreiser's door and sits to wait. The light fade on the hotel)*

ON THE EMPTY HEARINGS SET

Molly Jackson enters.

MOLLY JACKSON. Mr. Dreiser's been askin' for stories, let me tell you a story, something out of my mama, a saying almost. "Nothing shows up more often than a preacher with a horse to ride." It was from before they started mining coal, before the coal companies hired the preachers to tell you who to obey. And they had circuit preachers cause no place could afford a preacher by itself. Folks was poor then too, they just owned the stuff to be poor with. Well, when the man come to a place on his circuit, it was somebody's job to take him in, give him a spot in a bed and feed him. Well, food to feed a extra man was hard and you'd kill a chicken you couldn't afford to kill just yet or something like it to have enough to go around. You didn't say nothing. It was a point of honor with my mother that the man didn't know what a chicken meant to her. Now, he was there with good intentions, the saving of souls, but the truth was he made it harder on the day by day. Well, say he got him a horse to ride. He could do his cricuit that much faster, get to your place that much more often, keep a better check on your eternal soul. And then, you had to feed his horse as well. There was folks that bled their cows almost to dying and drank the blood to keep from starving themselves. I know what you are thinking: they had cows and we don't. Well, we got preachers with horses to ride, a whole bunch of 'em, and all of them setting down to eat hardy with the best intentions.

MORNING AT THE CUMBERLAND HOTEL

It is early morning. Henry Follette is asleep. The toothpicks are still standing on Dreiser's door. Dos Passos comes from his room, sees Follette asleep and ties his shoelaces together. Dos Passos sees the toothpicks but he doesn't think much of them. He finishes his job with the shoelaces and goes up the hall to get Anna. We hear him knock.

DOS PASSOS. *(Off)* Anna! Coffee! Biscuits! Are you up yet? *(Henry Follette wakes, finds his shoelaces tied when he tries to get up, pulls the shoes off and checks on the toothpicks)*

HENRY FOLLETTE. Now, here's something the sheriff might like. *(Henry Follette exits to get Blair. Dos Passos returns, notices Follette gone, the shoes, the toothpicks still standing. Anna Rollins is close behind. Dos Passos picks up the toothpicks and shows them to Anna)*

ANNA ROLLINS. Toothpicks, so what? *(Dos Passos knocks on Dreiser's door)*

DOS PASSOS. Theo!

ANNA ROLLINS. I thought this was breakfast without him.

DOS PASSOS. I'm afraid our spy set a trap.

ANNA ROLLINS. How? *(Dos Passos bangs on Dreiser's door)*

DOS PASSOS. Marie! Are you in there?

ANNA ROLLINS. Is she?

DOS PASSOS. I hope not.

MARIE. *(From inside)* Who is it?

DOS PASSOS. Oh, Christ! Open the door! *(Dreiser opens the door. He has on a night shirt)*

DREISER. What the hell are you trying to do, wake the dead?

DOS PASSOS. They set a trap.

DREISER. Don't be foolish. Nobody saw anything.

DOS PASSOS. Theo, don't argue, just move! Get out of this room. *(Dos Passos pulls Dreiser into the hall)* Marie!

MARIE. I'm not dressed yet. *(Dos Passos takes off his jacket and gives it to Marie. When she steps into the door, she has on her slip, shoes, and the jacket. Dos Passos pulls her into the hall too)*

ANNA ROLLINS. Spent the night, did you? *(Dos Passos closes Dreiser's door and sets the toothpicks back up against it)*

MARIE. My clothes . . .

DOS PASSOS. Wear mine.

DREISER. What do you propose we do?

DOS PASSOS. Leave. Run.

HENRY FOLLETTE. *(Off)* This way, sheriff.

ANNA ROLLINS. Hide.

Anna Rollins pushes Dreiser and Marie into Dos Passos' room and behind the door. The door is not closed. Deputy Follette, Adam Karp, John Henry Blair, and Hershel Lilly enter. Blair looks into Dos Passos' room on his way by. He does not see Dreiser and Marie. Dos Passos knocks at Dreiser's door as if he were just trying it.

ANNA ROLLINS. *(To the four men)* Look who's here. What brings you out so early? Care to join us for breakfast?

JOHN HENRY BLAIR. Stand aside please. *(Deputy Follette points to the slivers of wood Dos Passos replaced against the door)*

JOHN HENRY BLAIR. Gentlemen of the news, Deputy Follette's evidence is still standing. Theodore Dreiser, famous author of books and other things, I have a warrent here for your arrest in Harlan County. It's gonna look pretty in the news. You better come on out peaceful. *(No one comes out. Blair throws open the door and goes in. No one is there)* You're fired, Follette. *(Blair takes back Follette's gun)*

FOLLETTE. I did exactly what you said to do; I came to get you first. They were here when I left. What am I supposed to do now?

BLAIR. Chew your fingernails. Jerk off. I don't care. *(To Anna and Dos Passos)* Where are they?

ANNA ROLLINS. Damned if I know. Maybe they've run to the state line to get married.

FOLLETTE. Sheriff, I'd be glad to go after 'em, except I ain't got a car and if . . .

BLAIR. Go sit somewhere and wait for your goddamned ship to come in. *(Blair exits. Follette goes into Dreiser's room. Lilly goes into Dreiser's room, then sticks his head in Dos Passos' room on his way out but he does not see Drieser and Marie behind the door. Karp walks into Dos Passos' room. He sees Dreiser and Marie. Karp walks back out. Lilly and Blair are gone)*

KARP. He's a little big to hide behind a door.

DOS PASSOS. What are you going to do?

KARP. Find them a ride to the Tennessee line and print the story. *(Henry Follette stays in focus in the change)*

JEFF CALDWELL'S REVENGE

Jeff Caldwell attacks Henry Follette, pulls a knife, and holds it to his throat.

JEFF CALDWELL. I promised you this, you rat. I'm gonna lay you flat on your back in your own pine box and you can say all the names you want to all the way to glory. *(Jeff Caldwell is going to do it, except Henry Follette doesn't fight. Henry Follette lifts his head for better access to his neck. Henry Follette feels this is justice. Jeff Caldwell has a change of heart. He chooses not to murder Henry Follette. Jeff Caldwell runs. Henry Follette watches him go. Henry Follette stays in focus in the change)*

FROM THE HEARINGS

Henry Follette steps into Dreiser's place.

VOICES. Look who's here! You shit! Get him out of here!

HENRY FOLLETTE. My name is Theodore Dreiser . . .

VOICE. Hang him! *(Henry Follette has to avoid these people, he climbs onto the hearings table)*

HENRY FOLLETTE. My name is Theodore Dreiser and I write stuff and I am here to listen to these starvin' people and put them in books and people has got to swear to tell the truth or I ain't going to listen to them.

MOLLY JACKSON. *(She holds people back)* Henry, you are not welcome here.

HENRY FOLLETTE. And when I am tired of that, I go over to the hotel and have me a big dinner of pork chops and green beans. Not dried beans, I like green beans out of cans. I asked 'em special for green beans.

VOICE. Damn green beans!

VOICE. He's a traitor, Molly!

HENRY FOLLETTE. You'uns with all these stories should come with me. If you had you some pork chops and green beans, there might not be all these terrible stories and we could sit over there at the hotel where there is a white table cloth and I could tell you about being a rich writer in New York City.

MOLLY JACKSON. You gone crazy, Henry?

HENRY FOLLETTE. Yes, mam. I ain't made nothing but enemies so far, I thought I might make me some more.

MOLLY JACKSON. Go home.

HENRY FOLLETTE. I ain't got no home, Molly, ain't got no tent either. I got everything to want, and not a goddamned thing to lose, and I got a piece of news and I'm trying to give it to you free if you'uns will just hush-up and take it.

MOLLY JACKSON. Why don't you just say it instead of trying to play act like Mr. Dreiser.

HENRY FOLLETTE. Cause I ain't to that part yet. First, you got to understand how much warmer and sweeter it is in the bed if there is a pretty little girl who thinks you are the cat's whiskers while other folks think you are a mule's hind end.

MOLLY JACKSON. You're a fool.

HENRY FOLLETTE. Yes, mam, I'm that too. But there ain't nobody else to sit in this chair and listen anymore.

MOLLY JACKSON. These are the hearings. They're not going to be what they ought to be this morning, but they are going to commence again because there are things that haven't been said yet.

HENRY FOLLETTE. Mr. Dreiser has gone.

MOLLY JACKSON. Gone?

VOICE. Gone to give away some money.

VOICE. Gone to my house for a poor man's breakfast.

HENRY FOLLETTE. Gone somewhere. Disappeared into the air. Poof. He had to. John Henry wrote out a warrant against him.

VOICE. Since when does John Henry Blair write out warrants?

MOLLY JACKSON. What for?

HENRY FOLLETTE. For having that girl in his room all night.

MOLLY JACKSON. What girl?

HENRY FOLLETTE. The one that wrote names and stories down for him. She's gone too.

MOLLY JACKSON. How do you know?

HENRY FOLLETTE. Cause I saw 'em gone. Cause before I knew which side I was on, I'm the one went and told John Henry she was there. (*Henry Follette runs. Kentucky People begin to leave. John Dos Passos and Anna Rollins and the Militia Man enter and take their places for the hearings to continue*)

DOS PASSOS. My name is John Dos Passos.

ANNA ROLLINS. My name is Anna Rollins.

DOS PASSOS. We are here to investigate reports of social injustice in Eastern Kentucky and we are present this morning on Wallins Creeks—we were warned not to come to Wallins Creek—to take testimony. Let me assure you that whatever our failings are, and they are many, we are still capable witnesses. We are here as witnesses, called to you by conscience, I suppose, because your need is so great, and, while we can promise nothing else, we can and do promise to bear witness. (*Kentucky People are gone*)

MOLLY JACKSON. (*To the audience*) You must say your names with or without him. You must tell your stories to those who will listen and those who will not. And you must speak your names out loud. You cannot whisper your names or you have no names. And here, you will rot inside some mountain if you have no name. So stand up, stand in the face of them everyone, and tell your stories and say your names out loud.

THE LAST STOP ON THE SCENIC TOUR

A car pulls to a stop offstage. The headlights shine across the stage. The lights turn off. Two doors open and shut. A third door opens.

LILLY. Get out. *(A third car door shuts)* Turn the lights back on. *(The car's headlights shine across the stage. Hershel Lilly, John Henry Blair, and Adam Karp enter. Lilly and Blair have Karp prisoner. They push Karp into the light from the headlights)* Right here's good. Mr. Karp and I are going to talk. I been reading what you write.

KARP. I write what I see. News, Mr. Editor. Different from your mountain rhapsodies, Jello salad recipes, society sections, and coal company advertisements.

LILLY. Cracker Jack, you could end up writing a story about what you see in a jail cell. You are an accessory in Mr. Dreiser's escape.

KARP. Did the Associated Press fire you yet?

LILLY. Yes, thanks to you, they did.

KARP. More news.

LILLY. Listen to me. You drop yourself back in New York where you came from and you forget us. You don't know what is going on here, it's not your story, you are not trying to live it. Take that as a little friendly advice and go home.

KARP. Friendly Advice. That's a good name for this story.

LILLY. You god-damned pig-headed communist. *(Lilly hits Karp)* One word of this hits print and I'll shoot you.

KARP. If I live to write it, it will hit print. If I don't, it will hit print anyway. It is more news, Mr. Lilly, news, like Kentucky is news. It is just not news you like. *(Lilly does shoot Karp in the thigh with a .22. It is as much a surprise to Lilly as it is to Karp)*

KARP. You shot me!

BLAIR. That boy try to hurt you, Mr. Lilly? But he shot himself by accident. *(Lilly gives the gun to Blair, he wants rid of it)*

LILLY. *(To Karp)* Now, you walk. Tennessee is that way. *(He points away from the car)*

BLAIR. You better take it easy on that leg. That's some real friendly advice.

LILLY. Take it or leave it. Just go. Before you get your mouth blown off. *(Lilly and Blair leave stage and drive away. Karp exits toward Tennessee)*

A TRAIN STATION IN NEW YORK

VOICE. New York City, Grand Central Station. *(A Reporter is waiting. Dreiser and Marie, both wearing Dos Passos' clothes, enter)*

REPORTER. Mr. Dreiser! *Press,* sir, *Times.* I understand you left Harlan County early.

DREISER. I did.

REPORTER. Why?

DREISER. It has no bearings on the findings of The Committee for the Defense of Political Prisoners. Would you like to hear those stories? They are the only thing I am willing to comment on.

REPORTER. Mr. Dreiser, there is a warrant for your arrest in Harlan County for sexual misconduct. Do you have any remarks?

DREISER. Nothing happened in Kentucky.

REPORTER. One of the women traveling with the committee spent the night in your room.

DREISER. How do you know that?

REPORTER. It's on the wires, sir. Toothpicks. Somebody stood toothpicks in front of your door and they hadn't fallen down in the morning.

DREISER. Toothpicks?

REPORTER. The new AP man said he saw you, said you were hiding in another room and the Sheriff didn't look in that one. Is it true?

DREISER. I will tell you this. Nothing happened in Kentucky. Nothing. The woman was my secretary. She accompanied me on business.

REPORTER. Did she spend the night in your room?

DREISER. What the hell is it to you?

REPORTER. News.

DREISER. She did but I am impotent.

REPORTER. Sir?

DREISER. You heard me. Nothing happened in Kentucky but literary discussions. We were both unable to sleep. Literary discussions.

REPORTER. You stated that you are impotent?

DREISER. I did.

REPORTER. Thank you, that is all.

DREISER. Aren't you interested in what we found in Kentucky?

REPORTER. The AP man is writing books on that already. Same old story.

DREISER. If you print—and you will—that I am impotent, then you must print that this country is impotent too.

REPORTER. Sir?

DREISER. I said write down that this country doesn't give a damn. Write it. Can't afford to give a damn about anything but money . . .

MARIE. Theo . . .

DREISER. Write that people die so you and I can sit safe in our houses, lie warm in our beds and search under the covers for the American Dream. Write it! Write it, you little seeker of news! Write it until your name is as unspeakable as mine!

REPORTER. Mr. Dreiser . . .

DREISER. The news is that I slept with a woman? Is it really such a piece of news that a man might want to sleep with a woman?

REPORTER. My editor seems to think so.

DREISER. Go file your story. *(The Reporter exits)* Marie, I am impaled on toothpicks.

MARIE. And, for my part in history, I am the other body in your bed. I did one thing, Theo, one good thing. I gave away those peppermints.

DREISER. Oh, God, I hope that doesn't make the news.

MARIE. And I did more than you did by doing it.

DREISER. Bullshit. I can still write my book.

MARIE. I don't have your notes. *(This news is a blow)*

DREISER. Maybe John can bring them.

MARIE. Maybe John can write your book.

DREISER. I'm afraid I don't have money on me for a cab. I can call Helen.

MARIE. I can walk. *(Marie exits. The voices of the two girls are heard)*

THE GIRLS.

>With pistols and with rifles they'll take away your bread
>And if you miners hinted it, they'd knock you in the head.

DREISER. Catch babies, feed the living, tend the dying. Find faith.

THE GIRLS. Which side are you on, which side are you on?

Helen enters.

HELEN. Well, you're back.

THE END

which side are you on?

Come all of you good work - ers; Good news to you I'll
tell, Of how the good old un - ion has come in here to dwell.

Chorus:

Which side are you on? Which side are you on?

kentucky miner's wife's hungry, ragged blues

Best sung unaccompanied

I'm sad and I'm wea-ry, I got those hun - gry, rag - ged blues. I'm
sad and I'm war - ry, I got those hun - gry, rag - ged blues. Not a
penney in my pock - et to buy one thing I need to use.

research for the play

About Aunt Molly Jackson, from a biography in progress by Carol Murphy

About Theodore Dreiser: W.A. Swanburg's biography, *Dreiser;* Vera Dreiser's apology for her uncle, *My Uncle Theodore*

Bruce Crawford Collection, Clinch Valley College Archives

Dreiser Collection, Special Collections of the Van Pelt Library, University of Pennsylvania

Harlan Miners Speak, Report on Terrorism in the Coal Fields, published by Harcourt, Brace and Company, the Dreiser committee's report and transcripts of the hearings

Herndon Evans Collection, University of Kentucky Libraries, Appalachian Collection

Interviews with people who were miners, or married to miners, or children of miners in the 30s, in Harlan and Bell Counties of Kentucky, who joined the NMU or participated in the strikes, including Florence Reece and Tillman Cadle

John Dos Passos, the following works: *USA Trilogy* and *Adventures of a Young Man*

Theodore Dreiser, nonfiction: from Dreiser's autobiography, *Dawn, Newspaper Days;* other, *Tragic America* and *Letters*

Theodore Dreiser, the following novels: *The Genius, An American Tragedy, Sister Carrie, Jenny Gerhart, The Bulwark*

Transcripts of the Robert La Follett Hearings on Civil Rights Violations in Congress, 1937

Newspapers from the time and place:

Crawford's Weekly, Harlan Town Enterprise, and the *Pineville Sun*

Periodicals from the era:

American Mercury, February, 1932, "War in the Kentucky Mountains"

Dissent, Spring, 1972, Theodore Draper, "Communists and Miners"

Fortune, February, 1932, "Harlan County Faces"

Literary Digest, 111:9. N.28, 1931, "Dreiser's Feud With Kentucky"

Nation, February, 1932, Oakley Johnson, "Starvation and Reds in Kentucky"

Nation, June 1, 1932, Arthur Garfield Hays, "The Right to Get Shot"

Nation, June 5, 1932, J.C. Byars, "Harlan County: Act of God?"

New Republic, 69:32-39, N.25, 1931m, "Toothpicks"

New Republic, October, 1931, Boris Israel, "I Get Shot"

New Republic, December 2, 1931, John Dos Passos, "Working Under the Gun"

New Republic, March 2, 1932, Malcolm Cowley, "Kentucky Coal Town"

Histories and related:

John F. Day, *Bloody Ground*

Anthony Dunbar, *Against the Grain*

John D. Diggins, *Up from Communism*

Jim Garland, *Welcome the Traveler Home*

John W. Hevener, *Which Side Are You On?*

George Titler, *Hell in Harlan*

Edmund Wilson, *The Thirties*

Howard Zinn, *People's History of the United States*

Film:

Seeing Red

about the authors

INTRODUCTORY ESSAYS

John Egerton is a journalist and author living in Nashville, Tennessee. For two decades he has written about areas of great interest to the South: race relations, education, politics, and food. His essays have appeared in *The Washington Post, Saturday Review, New York Times Magazine, Southern Living, American Heritage, Southern Exposure,* and other periodicals. Author of seven books, including *The Americanization of Dixie and Generations,* his most recent book, *Shades of Gray: Dispatches from the Modern South,* was published in 1991 by Louisiana State University Press.

Betty Jean Jones is an Associate Professor and Director of Graduate Studies in the theatre division of the Department of Communication and Theatre at the University of North Carolina at Greensboro. Her area of specialization is American Theatre and Drama with an auxiliary interest in American Film Studies. She is a stage director and dramaturg whose scholarly writings have been published in books and journals in America and abroad. She maintains a continuing emphasis in performance studies treating the reconciliation/synthesis of history and theory with the production/performance modes in theatre.

Ruby Lerner is currently the Executive Director of the Association of Independent Video and Filmmakers, a five-thousand-member national organization representing and serving independent media producers. She was the Executive Director of Alternate ROOTS from 1981–1986.

BLIND DESIRE

The ensemble that created *Blind Desire* included Margaret Baker, John Fitzpatrick, Emily Green, Kelly R. Hill, Jr., Christine Murdock, and Eugene Wolf under the direction of Robert H. Leonard. Leonard studied theatre at Catholic University and began exploring improvisation in 1982. Since

335

founding The Road Company in 1975, he has directed the development of eighteen new works through ensemble and/or collaborative efforts.

RED FOX/SECOND HANGIN'

Don Henderson Baker is a freelance writer, director, and performer. He grew up in Wise County, that part of Virginia west of West Virginia. He is married, has two sons and lives in Atlanta, Georgia. A 1968 graduate of Washington and Lee University, he worked as an educational counselor for the Royal Thai Embassy and then as an arts and drama rehabilitation therapist for the Psychiatric Institute of Washington before returning to his hometown in 1971. He became the founding director of Roadside Theater, a part of Appalshop, Inc. in Whitesburg, Kentucky in 1974 and continued to direct the project until 1980 when he began researching and scriptwriting for Appalshop's Appalachian Film History Project.

In 1983 he co-founded Lime Kiln Arts, Inc. in Lexington, Virginia and served as its producing and artistic director until February 1993. He has written and directed for stage, film, and video and performed in all three. The focus of his work has been the life, history, and culture indigenous to the southern Appalachian Mountains. As a performer, he has toured throughout the country, and his plays have toured internationally. His writing credits include *Pretty Polly, Stonewall Country, Ear Rings, Backlife, Three Drops of Blood,* and others.

Dudley Cocke is the Director of Roadside Theater, the professional ensemble company that for seventeen years has been creating original plays about central Appalachia. Roadside Theater is a part of the pioneering arts and education collective, Appalshop, founded in 1969 in Whitesburg, Kentucky. Mr. Cocke's recent cultural essays are collected in *Voices from the Front: Achieving Cultural Equity* (1993) and he recently coedited *From the Ground Up: Grass Roots Theater in Historical and Contemporary Perspective* (1993).

YOU CAN'T JUDGE A BOOK BY LOOKING AT THE COVER:
SAYINGS FROM THE LIFE AND WRITINGS OF JUNEBUG JABBO
JONES, VOLUME II

John O'Neal was Producing Director of the Free Southern Theater of New Orleans, and for the past twenty years has been an advocate of a direct relationship between art and politics. He is a playwright and performer of international reputation, a recipient of a Rockefeller Playwriting Fellowship, a Louisiana Artists Fellowship in Theater and other awards from the Ford Foundation and the Rockefeller Foundation. Among his plays are the Junebug Jabbo Jones trilogy, *Sayings from the Life and Writings of Junebug Jabbo Jones*, performed by the author all over the United States and abroad; *Don't Start Me Talking or I'll Tell Everything I Know* (with Ron Castine and Glenda Lindsay); *You Can't Judge a Book by Looking at the Cover* (with Nayo Barbara Watkins); and *Ain't No Use in Goin' Home, Jodie's Got Your Gal and Gone* (with Nayo Barbara Watkins and Q.R. Hand). John's other plays include *Hurricane Season, Where is the Blood of Your Fathers, When the Opportunity Scratches, Itch It,* and *If I Live to See Next Fall.* John was born in Mound City, Illinois, attended Southern Illinois University, and was active in the Student Non Violent Coordinating Committee of the Civil Rights movement. He recently served for three years as Visiting Professor at Cornell University.

MR. UNIVERSE

Jim Grimsley is a playwright and novelist who lives and works in Atlanta, Georgia. Jim has written ten full-length and four one-act plays, including *The Lizard of Tarsus, White People,* and *The Existentialists.* He has been playwright-in-residence at 7Stages Theatre since 1986. In 1988 he was awarded the George Oppenheimer Award for Best New American Playwright for his play *Mr. Universe.* Jim's first novel, *Winter Birds,* will be published by Algonquin Books in 1994 and has already been published in Germany and France (selections from the novel have appeared in U.S. quarterly magazines). His second novel, *Comfort and Joy,* was published in Germany in 1993. He is a member of the Southeast Playwrights Project and Alternate ROOTS. He was recently awarded the first-ever Bryan Prize for Drama, given by the Fellowship of Southern Writers for distinguished achievement in the field of playwriting.

DARK COWGIRLS AND PRAIRIE QUEENS

Linda Parris-Bailey is the executive and artistic director of the Carpetbag Theatre. In addition to *Dark Cowgirls and Prairie Queens,* she has written *Circus Maxim* with David Fuller, *Ce Nitram Sacul,* a praise poem to African American 'wild women', and *Cric? Crac!,* a play for children. She has conducted workshops for parents and children as a Wolf Trap Institute artist and summer youth workshop project director at the Highlander Research and Education Center. She is a graduate of Howard University and has served as an associate professor at the University of Tennessee.

Her creative life is supported by her family, husband Emanuel, son Atiba and daughter Samiyyah, parents Reynard and Betsy, brothers Reggie and Barry and sister Rasheeda and an extended family that includes the many close friends that she has been blessed with. Her inheritance includes love from grandfather Chester, service from grandfather Sinclair, women's mysteries from grandmother Delcina and storytelling from both the Jones and Parris clans.

BLOOD ON BLOOD

Rebecca Ranson is Artistic Director of Southeastern Arts, Media and Education Project (SAME), a gay and lesbian arts organization in Atlanta. She has written more than forty plays, many of which explore or respond to a particular social justice issue. Her plays have been produced in New Orleans, Philadelphia, Honolulu, San Francisco, Los Angeles, New York City, Rochester, Phoenix, London, and other cities.

A PREACHER WITH A HORSE TO RIDE

Jo Carson is a writer and performer from Johnson City, Tennessee.

Daytrips, a play, won the Kesselring Award for 1989 and has been produced widely, including Los Angeles Theater Center, Women's Project, and Hartford Stage Company, and is published in an anthology by Heineman, *New American Plays, Volume 2* and also in an acting version by Dramatists Play Service.

The Bear Facts has considerable workshop history, including The Mark Taper Forum, Women's Project, Oregon Shakespeare Festival, and The Road Company. A first production is planned for 1993 by Darkhorse Theatre in Nashville, Tennessee. *Bear Facts* won Jo a playwright's fellowship from NEA for 1993–94.

A series of monologues and dialogues called *Stories I Ain't Told Nobody Yet* (from Orchard Books) made Editor's Choice on Booklist and American Library Association's recommended list, in 1990. Theatre Communications Group brought out a paperback edition in 1991. This work has served as performance material for Jo for several years, in a variety of venues, in this country and abroad.

Pulling My Leg and *You Hold Me and I'll Hold You,* picture books for children, are published by Orchard Books. *You Hold Me and I'll Hold You* made the ALA's recommended list in 1992. An account of the New Madrid Earthquakes of 1811 and 1812 called *The Great Shaking,* also for children, is forthcoming from Orchard, late in 1993.

A short story collection called *The Last of the Waltz Across Texas and Other Stories* was published by Gnomon Press of Frankfort, KY, in 1993.

Aside from writing, Jo is a companion to an old Labrador retriever and a source of apples for a great trail horse. She is poetry editor for a small magazine called *Now and Then,* from the Center for Appalachian Studies and Services of East Tennessee State University. She spends some time in local schools. "It may be the most important thing I do, to stand in front of the third or fourth grade with a book that has my name on it and to say, 'I am from here and I made this story.'"

340

(Continuation of the copyright page)

Library of Congress Cataloging-in-Publication Data
Alternate roots: plays from the Southern theater / edited by Valetta
Anderson and Kathie deNobriga.
     p.   cm.
   Contents: Blind desire / members of the Road Company Ensemble—
Red fox; Second hangin' / Don Baker and Dudley Cocke—You can't
judge a book by looking at the cover / John O'Neal—Mr. Universe /
Jim Grimsley—Dark cowgirls and prairie queens / Linda Parris
-Bailey—Blood on blood / Rebecca Ranson—A preacher with a
horse to ride / Jo Carson.
   ISBN 0-435-08632-4 (TBD : acid-free paper)
   1. American drama—Southern States. 2. Southern States—Drama.
I. Anderson, Valetta. II. deNobriga, Kathie.
PS551.A48 1994
812.008'0975—dc20   93-20879
                                                                  CIP